Chicken Soup
for the Soul.

The Magic of Dogs

Chicken Soup for the Soul: The Magic of Dogs
101 Tales of Family, Friendship & Fun
Amy Newmark

Published by Chicken Soup for the Soul, LLC www.chickensoup.com
Copyright ©2020 by Chicken Soup for the Soul, LLC. All Rights Reserved.

The publisher gratefully acknowledges the many publishers and individuals who granted Chicken Soup for the Soul permission to reprint the cited material.

Front cover photo courtesy of gettyimages.com/EyeEm (©EyeEm)
Back cover and Interior photos: white dog reaching courtesy of iStockphoto.com/GlobalP (©GlobalP), Boston Terrier courtesy of iStockphoto.com/vauvau (©vauvau), puppy with ball courtesy of iStockphoto.com/GlobalP (©GlobalP), dog holding leash courtesy of iStockphoto.com/PK-Photos (©PK-Photos)
Photo of Amy Newmark courtesy of Susan Morrow at SwickPix

Cover and Interior by Daniel Zaccari

Distributed to the booktrade by Simon & Schuster. SAN: 200-2442

Publisher's Cataloging-In-Publication Data
(Prepared by The Donohue Group, Inc.)

Names: Newmark, Amy, compiler.
Title: Chicken soup for the soul : the magic of dogs : 101 tales of
    family, friendship & fun / [compiled by] Amy Newmark.
Other Titles: Magic of dogs : 101 tales of family, friendship & fun
Description: [Cos Cob, Connecticut] : Chicken Soup for the Soul, LLC,
    [2020]
Identifiers: ISBN 9781611590678 | ISBN 9781611593020 (ebook)
Subjects: LCSH: Dogs--Literary collections. | Dogs--Anecdotes. | Human-
    animal relationships--Literary collections. | Human-animal
    relationships--Anecdotes. | Dog owners--Literary collections. | Dog
    owners--Anecdotes. | LCGFT: Anecdotes.
Classification: LCC SF426.2 .C455 2020 (print) | SF426.2 (ebook) | DDC
    636.7/088/7/02--dc23

Library of Congress Control Number: 2020933855

PRINTED IN THE UNITED STATES OF AMERICA
on acid∞free paper

25 24 23 22 21 20   01 02 03 04 05 06 07 08 09 10 11

Chicken Soup for the Soul.

The Magic of Dogs

101 Tales of Family, Friendship & Fun

Amy Newmark

Chicken Soup for the Soul, LLC
Cos Cob, CT

Changing the world one story at a time®
www.chickensoup.com

Table of Contents

❶
~Magical Miraculous Dogs~

❷
~Natural Therapist~

❸

~Meant to Be~

❹

~What a Character!~

❺

~A Dog's Purpose~

6

~What I Learned from the Dog~

7

~Melting Hearts~

8

~Who Rescued Who?~

9

~Living in the Moment~

10

~Best Friends~

Magical Miraculous Dogs

Hope in Red

*The bond with a true dog is as lasting as the ties
of this earth will ever be.*
~Konrad Lorenz

We were newlyweds and cash was tight, so Genie and I moved into our first — and what would turn out to be our only — house under a rent-to-own arrangement. Of course, if we decided not to buy the house, we'd be required to move out, leaving it in the same condition as when we'd moved in. Problem was, no one told Ruby that was the deal.

Ruby was a red-and-white Border Collie, which is rare; most Border Collies are black-and-white. When I say red, I really mean chestnut. That's important because Genie also had striking, chestnut-colored hair. Genie's hair was long and glorious, and it really flamed red when the sun hit it.

Maybe their shared color was why Genie picked Ruby from a litter of eight.

Ruby was only six weeks old and not much larger than a guinea pig when she first stepped into the house. She seemed far too young and way too small to be making decorating decisions. Yet she started assessing the house. The only thing she lacked was a clipboard.

Now assessing and acting are two different things, so we didn't worry about it initially. But Ruby started making changes without consulting us. Maybe she knew we'd object, and Border Collies don't like being told they're wrong. Ruby lived up to the notion that Border Collies are the smartest dog breed. She had no problem outfoxing us.

Even before the candles on her "Welcome Home" cake had burned out, Ruby had taken down wallpaper and removed copious amounts of wood trim. She started in unused rooms that were out of our flight path. We simply didn't see what she was doing.

She slept under a certain bed in a spare room. She removed the carpet under that bed, but only when Genie and I were out of the house. We never figured out why. Was the carpet too soft… or did it make her sneeze?

Neither Genie nor I loved the house. It wasn't a style we would have bought, but because of Ruby's "changes," we did buy it. We had to. It would have cost too much to fix all that she had, uh, changed. Did we discipline her? No. We merely acquiesced, and we wound up staying in that house for the rest of our marriage, some twenty years. We made it *our* house, with even more of Ruby's "decorating" assistance. Looking back on it, I see it was one of the smartest things we ever did.

Ruby had other peculiar traits, such as chasing flying geese. Not cats, dogs or geese milling around on the ground. Nope. It had to be flying geese, those already in the air. It started in our unfenced back yard one day when a skein of geese flew overhead. They squawked, which caught Ruby's attention. In a flash of red, she took off and kept running, even with us calling and chasing her. She ran as fast as the wind. We lost sight of her as she ran through the woods behind our house.

She always came back after her fruitless goose chases. And she never gave up, even when she got older and arthritis moved into her joints.

One day, Genie asked, "Doesn't she realize she's not going to catch them? Why does she keep running so hard? It's got to hurt."

I thought a minute. "I don't think it's about catching them. I think they're a guide."

"For what?"

"Maybe it's about getting to the other side of the horizon," I said. "Maybe if we can get there, we can leave this world behind and know peace."

"What? Like heaven? If only," Genie said.

A few years later, Genie was diagnosed with breast cancer. After having a mastectomy and enduring chemotherapy, she was declared cancer-free. We kept our fingers crossed.

A year later, Ruby died, with no indication that anything was wrong. She simply dropped dead. In fact, the day before she'd run after the geese that flew by.

Genie and I had seen other dogs get sick and die. We knew how ugly things could get, protracted and painful. But like with everything else involving Ruby, she did it her way. There was no lingering or suffering. She just blew past all that.

Occasionally, Genie and I talked about Ruby's life and death. Genie would say, "Maybe Ruby wanted to make sure she knew the route to take. You know, to get to heaven." Genie had never been a big believer in religion, but having cancer changed things.

A few years later, Genie's cancer came back. It was now an aggressive killer. All the treatments failed.

On the afternoon she started hospice, I found Genie standing at the window. She always had to see nature.

Without turning, she said, "I haven't seen any flying geese in a long time."

She was right. We'd been having a brutally hot summer, and the geese that were still around were hunkered down at the river, trying to stay cool.

She said, "If Ruby were here, she'd find the geese, and she'd make them fly. Then I'd know which way to go."

The next morning, with Genie in a wheelchair, we went for a walk. It was early, around 6:30. Though there's light in the sky then, there are many more shadows, and maybe a hint of surprise.

I walked Genie through the garden and stopped at the edge of a large, wide lawn. I situated the wheelchair so Genie would have a view of the distant horizon as it changed colors from dark indigo blue to a softer daytime hue.

Taking a seat next to her, I took her hand and stared at the horizon.

I was wishing, hoping, and praying.

Then it came. A noise from behind. Far at first, then closer. A rhythmic whooshing sound. Geese flew so close over our heads that we could have reached up and touched their goose-down bellies.

Softly, Genie said, "Ruby."

The geese flew into the most peaceful of early morning blues.

Behind, in the eastern sky, the direction from which the geese had come, the sun had burst into the sky. It came in with startling color. Oranges, yellows, and reds. But would anyone argue if I said I saw some chestnut sprinkled in?

— David Weiskircher —

Love at First Sight

Dogs have a way of finding the people who need them,
filling an emptiness we don't even know we have.
~Thom Jones

I grew up in the city, so moving to the country with my fiancé, Dillon, was a challenge. He was working away from home two weeks at a time.

I had a cat I loved, but I wanted the companionship of a dog. However, I still worked in the city and was gone from home at least ten hours a day. It would be irresponsible to get a dog.

So, I did what many people do when they are a bit lonely and can't have a dog: I started volunteering at the local Humane Society. I wanted to interact with the dogs, but with my work schedule and experience, the volunteer coordinator decided that I was better suited to work at the front desk. Every Tuesday, I filed, answered phones, greeted visitors, and helped families begin the adoption process.

I got to know some of the adoption counselors. Many of them had adopted from the shelter. They would say the same thing: "You love all the animals that come through, but sometimes one will grab your heart, and you realize you have no choice but to adopt it."

I had been volunteering for more than a year when a couple walked in with a sad, scared, and sick one-year-old Boxer/Collie mix. Her name was Bella, and one look at her ripped my heart wide open. The couple who were surrendering her had tried to take care of her after their neighbors moved away and left her behind.

After a few weeks, Bella was healthy enough to be put out on the adoption floor. My heart sank. Bella had scored incredibly well on her behavior test; she was good with cats, kids and other dogs. She was the trifecta of adoptability.

After I promised to bring her a coffee the following week, the adoption supervisor let me in to visit Bella after the building closed. I stayed with her for fifteen minutes, trying to convince myself that it still wasn't a great time to get a dog. Anyway, Dillon had just left for two weeks, so he couldn't meet her. The Humane Society had a rule that potential adopters had to spend time with the dog at the shelter before they could be approved.

I couldn't ask for special treatment just because I volunteered there. And it really wasn't the right time to adopt a dog. But when I returned the following Tuesday with the promised coffee, I ran to see if Bella was still there. She was. I had another visit with her and said goodbye, knowing deep down that it was for good.

For months, all I talked about was Bella — how she had been my first case of love at first sight and how I wondered if I would ever feel that way about another dog.

That spring, Dillon took a job where he no longer had to work away from home. One Saturday in June, we were grocery shopping in the city when we saw that a local rescue was putting on a dog adoption fair. We walked over and met a few dogs, but none of them was a fit for us. We decided to drive over to the Humane Society. I looked at the adoptable dogs on their website as we were driving and saw a dog named Penelope who reminded me of Bella. We arrived and asked to meet her.

An adoption counselor I had never met before took us into a shared office and started reading us Penelope's file. Halfway in, I turned to an adoption counselor I knew, who was working at the desk beside us, and said, "This sounds like Bella's file from back in December." He nodded and said, "Yeah. It is Bella; they just changed her name."

I started to cry. This was my love-at-first-sight dog. I didn't understand why she had been given up for a third time, and I didn't care. We knew we were taking her home with us before Dillon even met her. I cried the entire way home with Bella in the back seat happily hanging her head out the window. And I cried again when we called our families to tell them we were doggy parents.

Now, two and a half years later, she is sitting beside me on the couch, trying to lick my face because she doesn't understand that the tears on my face are happy tears. We should have stopped and bought a lottery ticket the day of her adoption, because it was the luckiest day of our lives.

—AJ (Cross) Nunes—

Chicken Soup for the Soul

Dogged Determination

He is your friend, your partner, your defender,
your dog. You are his life, his love, his leader.
He will be yours, faithful and true,
to the last beat of his heart.
~Author Unknown

My grandmother Nina greeted me at the door when I returned from school. Wrapping her arms around me, she explained, "Your daddy is very sick. While you were at school today, an ambulance came and took him to the hospital."

While I cried in her arms, our Boxer, Buddy, sat beside us waiting to be of service. Eventually, I slipped to the floor and buried my face in his warm fur. His dark eyes looked sad, too. Buddy was more than just a pet. He was a family member, and he was missing Daddy, too.

As I walked home from school the next day, I knew my father would still be in the hospital. Mama would have to go to work every day, but in the evenings she would keep watch at Daddy's side. I prayed for good news. Maybe he would be coming home soon. In the meantime, Nina, Buddy, and I would wait together.

Turning the knob of the big oak door, I called out, "Nina, Buddy, I'm home!"

Silence greeted me.

I'd expected the thunderous sound of Buddy galloping to the door. There should have been a deep yelp of excitement, too, as he ran toward me, ready to shower me with after-school kisses and drool.

Only my grandmother crept quietly into the room, though, with tears in her eyes.

"Is Daddy okay? Where's Buddy?" I asked, my voice cracking with fear at the sight of Nina crying.

"Your daddy is still in the hospital, but I'm sure he's getting better," she said. "Buddy, though…"

"Is he outside?" I asked, running through the house to look out the back door.

Buddy's world was limited to the house and a large, fenced-in back yard. He was a giant of a dog, much too big for me to walk. Mama and Daddy worked so much that they didn't have time to take him on walks. I couldn't ever remember Buddy riding in the car either. If he wasn't in the house, he had to be in the back yard. There was simply no other place he could be.

"He's not here," my grandmother said softly. "We don't know where he is."

"Buddy!" I shrieked, and then dissolved into tears.

That evening was cold and lonely. Buddy was absent from his usual corner in the kitchen while Nina and I ate dinner. I played with my food as I stared at Buddy's empty corner. Later, I stretched out on the floor to watch television before bedtime. Normally, Buddy would be stretched alongside me, keeping me warm in the winter and making me hot in the summer. Buddy had simply been there my whole life. Now, my best friend in the world and lifelong companion was gone.

The next day, I walked home from school slowly. It was hard to be excited about coming in from the cold when my daddy was in the hospital and my dog was nowhere to be found. As I turned the corner onto our street, I saw Mama's car in the driveway. She wasn't supposed to be home until visiting hours at the hospital were over, which was after my bedtime. Filled with uncertainty, I ran the rest of the way home and up the steps to the front door.

"Mama!" I called out as I burst inside.

In response, I heard a thudding of paws pounding on the hardwood floors, followed by the excited yelp I knew so well. Buddy ran to me. My face was soon drenched as I cried tears of happiness, while Buddy showered me with kisses.

"I'm not sure who missed who the most," Mama said as she came into the room.

"Did Buddy find his way home all by himself?" I asked.

"Not exactly," Mama said. "Wash your hands and face. I'll tell you about it over a snack at the table. You're going to need to sit down to hear this."

I ran through the house, with Buddy once again in his natural place as my oversized shadow. Returning to the kitchen in record time, I sat in a chair, with Buddy leaning against me. His normal spot in the corner of the kitchen was simply too far away for either of us at the moment.

"This afternoon, your grandmother received a call saying that someone had found Buddy," Mama said. "She phoned me at work, and I left right away to pick him up."

"That's great!" I exclaimed. "It's a good thing we had our phone number on his tags. Was he far away?"

"I suppose that depends on your point of view," Mama said.

"I don't understand."

Nina and Mama were sitting on either side of me at the table, smiling. Buddy had slid down to the floor and was sleeping beneath my chair. He was obviously exhausted from his outing.

"You know Daddy is at the Veterans Hospital," Mama began.

"I know. He went there in an ambulance the other day while I was at school," I replied, confused by the turn our conversation was taking.

Mama nodded at the massive lump of fur and jowls beneath my chair. "That's where Buddy was found. He was sitting outside the hospital door, apparently hoping someone would let him in."

"Buddy went all the way to the hospital? To see Daddy? How?"

"I have no idea how he tracked your father there, but he did," Mama mused, bending down to scratch Buddy's favorite spot just behind his ears. "We'll never know the details of his little adventure."

"It simply baffles me," Nina said. "Not only is it quite a distance, but your father rode to the hospital in an ambulance! There couldn't possibly be a scent to track."

Mama replied, "Buddy may not have had much of a scent to follow, but he didn't need it. He had other guiding forces, like sheer determination and love."

— Linda Kinnamon —

My Two Grand-dogs

This is not a goodbye, my darling, this is a thank you.
~Nicholas Sparks

Heidi came flying out of a thick stand of mountain laurel and pounced—scaring me to death and almost knocking me over. Smokey followed, charging me before turning and pushing away her sister. Standing on their hind legs, their front legs pawing my shoulders and each other, they danced circles around me, vying for my attention as we inched toward my neighbor's house where they lived.

As many times as I'd watched the pair, I should have been ready for their welcoming antics. However, my brilliant "grand-dogs" loved to hide in the woods and never would attack from the same place twice.

Why were they my "grand-dogs?" Our mutt, Honus, had fathered the dogs with a purebred, short-haired German Shepherd. While Heidi looked like her mom, Smokey had shaggy brown-and-black hair and larger ears. Our family adored them and got to spend a lot of time taking care of them over the years. We loved them as much as our own dogs.

Along with their traditional welcome attack, my grand-dogs had a farewell custom. Heidi would sit, kiss me goodbye, and then watch her sister walk me home down the long gravel driveway. "Come on, girl, come with us," I'd say, but Heidi always refused.

Smokey would stay by my side until her invisible-fence collar beeped. Then she'd sit, kiss me goodbye, and watch me walk the rest of the way. Once I turned left, out of sight, she'd let out a mournful howl.

When Smokey lost her battle with cancer years later, her death devastated Heidi, who was now alone during the long hours our neighbors were away at work. When the neighbor told me they couldn't do anything to make Heidi happy and they wanted to put her to sleep, my heart skipped a beat. I'd already lost one grand-dog. I couldn't imagine losing another.

Since I was home, I promised to visit Heidi several times throughout the day. We played. I spoiled her with treats and gave her a lot of love. Heidi and I grew closer than ever, and she seemed much better.

Every time I left Heidi, I had high hopes that she'd take Smokey's place and walk home with me. I always pleaded, but to no avail.

Months later, my neighbors had to leave town unexpectedly for an extended period. There wasn't time to board Heidi, and they couldn't take her with them. For months, I'd visited throughout the day, so it wasn't a big deal for me to care for her in the evenings.

For several weeks, I watched Heidi day and night. She seemed sassier than ever, but she still wouldn't walk me home.

On the night my neighbors were due back, I did my usual routine with Heidi. For the first time since Smokey's death, I did not ask her to walk me home. I'd decided that it wasn't fair of me to expect her to take Smokey's place.

I gave her my usual love and kisses; Heidi kissed me back, and I turned to leave.

This time, Heidi stood and walked by my side, in the same touching way that Smokey had always done. I should have jumped for joy, but I had the feeling something wasn't right. Heidi looked chipper, but when I searched her eyes, I knew in my heart that Heidi was saying goodbye.

Although this made no sense, I'd had enough otherworldly experiences with animals to trust the feeling in my gut.

When her collar beeped, we sat on the gravel and held each other tight. Heidi licked the tears that streamed down my face. I thanked her for being such a loving dog, told her I'd miss her, and asked her to give Smokey my love. Still, I hoped I was wrong. We snuggled together until I could get up the courage to leave. When I turned the corner, out of sight, Heidi let out a mournful "Smokey howl" that sent chills down my spine.

The following day, our hearts broke all over again when our neighbors drove Heidi to the pet hospital. Later, they phoned to tell us that Heidi had passed away from the same cancer that took her sister.

I was devastated, but I also found great comfort in knowing that Heidi and Smokey were together again. Most of all, I felt grateful that Heidi had walked me home for the first and last time so we could say our goodbyes.

—Jill Burns—

Angels Don't Always Have Wings

*Angels appear in many different forms to hold your
hand through the difficult times.*
~Doreen Virtue

I n 1972, I was spending the summer in Passau, Germany,
studying at the Goethe-Institut. Passau is a lovely little city
that sits on the border between Germany and Austria right at
the confluence of the Inn, the Ilz, and the Danube rivers in
a hilly part of southern Bavaria. From the tops of the cliffs above
the rivers, one can see three bands of color floating downstream for
several miles. The flower-filled garden of the institute sits on one of
those hills, and the views from there are breathtaking.

One particular evening, though, I wasn't thinking about the view.
I'd stayed late that night for one of the cultural activities the institute
puts on for its students. Feeling warmed by conversation and a couple
of the excellent local brews, I was ready to walk the two miles home.
Normally, walking around a city in Germany, even today, is safe for
single women regardless of the time of night because lots of locals are
out, and there's an active police presence on foot, even in the quieter
parts of town. People stop and talk to each other. So, I thought nothing
of setting off on my own through the mild summer night to get back
to the house I shared with several other students.

I set off at a brisk pace, enjoying the night sounds and scents. My path took me through one of the more tired parts of town, with lots of cheap restaurants and *Kneipen* (pubs) that serve food and lots of beer. Normally, I just walked through, nodding to people on the street, and would make my way home without a problem. But this night, as I walked past one of the *Kneipen*, four young men noticed me wobbling past in my short skirt and platform shoes. They called out a few rude things, but I ignored them and kept walking. Instead of ducking back into the *Kneipe*, they came out and started to follow me. I walked faster, but so did they. I turned up and down a few streets, hoping to lose them, but they followed me like Bloodhounds.

After the fourth or fifth turn, I knew I was in trouble and started praying more fervently than I had in a long time. The young men were catcalling and jogging to catch up with me as I was almost at a run now. Suddenly, from one of the darkened yards along the residential street, a huge German Shepherd came bounding out. He was barking excitedly, wagging his tail, and circling me like he'd been waiting for me to come home. I slowed down to pet the dog, who licked my hands repeatedly. Then I started walking again — but this time, the dog fell in beside me. If I sped up, so did he; if I slowed down, he did, too.

Now, I'd never been a huge dog lover (big dogs especially tended to scare me), but at that point I could have hugged that dog. What was even more unusual was that dogs were not allowed to run free in German cities. Where had he come from? And why did he act as if I were a long-lost friend?

The young men spotted the dog, slowed to a walk, and then turned down the street at the next corner. I was relieved and expected the dog to get tired of my company and go home, but he didn't. In fact, he walked beside me, close enough so I could rest my hand on his massive head, up and down those hills and along all the winding streets until I got to my door. He walked with me for at least half an hour.

As we approached my door, I slowed down to pull my key out of my purse. The dog kept his pace and walked right past my house without even looking at me. I watched him vanish into the darkness as if he'd never existed.

Coincidence? Or divine intervention? I know what I think.

—Deborah Kellogg—

Always with Me, Still

*If you have a dog, you will most likely outlive it; to
get a dog is to open yourself to profound joy and,
prospectively, to equally profound sadness.*
~Marjorie Garber

Everyone saw it — the way he looked at me, followed me everywhere, hung on my every word. Strangers looked at us and said things like, "You only get one like that," or "He's a keeper," or "Look at the way he looks at you! His eyes never leave your face." Even my husband Matty reminded me regularly that I would "only get one Jack."

Jack was a rescue dog with a propensity for digging up moles in our back yard. He always looked like he was smiling and he wagged his tail whether he was excited, happy, or impatient.

We unexpectedly lost Jack a year ago. Two days before, he had been out walking as usual with me and our Beagle, Sadie. But then, after two emergency trips to the vet for his sudden illness, Jack made a nest for himself under our shed. I texted our primary vet, filled her in on the latest details, and asked for her honest, professional opinion.

"I think it's time," her text read.

Crying, I put my arm around Jack. He stood beside me, squinting in the sun, wagging his tail the way he always did no matter how he felt.

Less than an hour later, Jack was lying on a cold table draped in a blue blanket, with the hairs of other dogs stuck in the fibers. He trembled. I squatted, my face level with his front paws, my hands on his shoulders. I talked to him. I sang to him. I told him not to be scared. I lifted my face to look into his eyes. He held my gaze until his eyes glazed over, and he gently lowered his head. I rested my forehead on the edge of the table. After a moment, I stood, pressed my face into the fur on the back of his neck and inhaled deeply. I would miss his warmth, his softness, his smell.

Three days later, I went for a run. Jack and I had taken a walk every single morning, no matter what. He, Sadie, and I would eat breakfast, and then Jack and I would head out. Sadie would join us if it wasn't too dark, too early, or too cold, by her standards.

Without Jack, my morning routine felt disjointed. I was awake. I had eaten. But Jack wasn't there to walk. So, I laced up my shoes and stepped out into the cerulean morning. Alone.

Half a mile into my run, a black sock on the shoulder of the road stopped me in my tracks. The sense that Jack was with me was overwhelming. First thing every morning Jack had stood patiently in front of my dresser, waiting for me to give him a pair of socks. He'd run around the house, the socks in his mouth, until his breakfast was ready. Every afternoon when I got home from work, Jack rooted around in my gym bag to find a sock to parade around the back yard. Matty and I were forever finding our missing socks out there.

In this moment, in the quiet predawn when I would have been out walking Jack, he was with me.

The next day, Matty, Sadie, and our friends traveled to the Northern Neck. It was the first weekend we would be there without Jack. As I walked Sadie with my friend Ashley and her dogs, I looked down. There, on the sidewalk, was a single green sock.

Two days later, Ashley and I took our dogs to Pony Pasture. It was the first time Sadie and I would walk those trails without Jack. Eleven days before, he had walked them with us. We were almost there when something caught my eye on a tree: a white sign with pink-and-red hearts. It said "Be Kind" in bold black letters — and I had seen the same sign at the emergency vet.

About a week later, I was at the Richmond SPCA, where Jack and I had completed several agility classes. As I sat in the lobby with Sadie and Matty, I looked up. There, above the reception desk, was the same sign I had seen at the vet and Pony Pasture: "Be Kind." Jack was with me.

Another week went by, and I met my family at a local diner for brunch. Outside the entrance, I saw a stone with a dog painted on it — a dog that looked like Jack. When I walked inside, the floor mat bore the same canine likeness. I glanced around the restaurant. Over the bar hung the sign: "Be Kind."

After we ate and paid, my family walked me to my car. As I got in and closed the door, I looked up to see the back of my dad's T-shirt. "You Should Know Jack," the lettering said. And I did. Jack and I shared an understanding that transcended words.

A vet Jack had seen several years before had commented on how in-tune Jack and I were. Strangers approached me to comment on the way Jack watched me. Matty always said, "I have known people with dogs and had dogs all my life, and I have never seen anything like what you and Jack have." If any dog could find a way to communicate with me, Jack would be that dog.

Recently, out for a run, I came across some neighbors walking their dogs. I crouched down to pet the dogs. As I talked, I heard myself say, "When Matty and I walked Jack and Sadie earlier…" I stopped. "Well, Sadie." The conversation waned, and one of the dogs wandered off to sniff something in the grass alongside the road. I stood to see what it was. A sock. I started running again and knew Jack was there, too.

— Amanda Sue Creasey —

Pandemic Puppy

I am joy in a wooly coat, come to dance into your life,
to make you laugh!
~Julie Church

I stared at the photograph my daughter had e-mailed me and shook my head. Had my daughter lost her mind? "What a stupid time to adopt a dog!" I shouted to the rest of my family.

With all the chaos that COVID-19 had caused, my daughter was already overwhelmed with troubles. School had let out for the year, leaving her with a nine-year-old at home and no babysitter. Her job position fell under the heading of "essential employee," which meant she still had to frequent the office and expose herself to co-workers who refused to take suggested precautions. What made it even worse was that she and my grandson had serious health issues, which made them more vulnerable should they come down with the virus.

To top it all off, Amy already owned two dogs: Murphy, a fourteen-year-old Golden Retriever, and Koda, a rambunctious two-year-old Siberian Husky. Amy had sworn she wouldn't adopt more dogs, but instead of voicing my disapproval, I decided to bite my tongue and try to sound positive.

I e-mailed her back: "Cute puppy. What's the story?"

Amy phoned me right away. "Well, it all started with our cruise," she said.

"Cruise?"

"I was looking forward to taking my first cruise at the end of April to Cozumel, Mexico. Well, thanks to the pandemic, they've canceled it."

"So, you decided to get a puppy since you couldn't go on your cruise?" I teased.

"No, but I thought it might be fun to look… you know, take our minds off our troubles. We had no intention of bringing home a dog."

"Right," I said, wondering what had gone through her mind. Even I knew that once you looked, you're usually hooked.

Amy proceeded to bring me up to date on her elderly dog, Murphy. Instead of acting like his usual laidback self, he had suddenly turned into a crotchety, old dog.

Murphy and Koda had always been buddies, but that had changed. Now, the old dog wanted nothing to do with Koda. Koda had spent his puppy years glued to Murphy. Losing Murphy's friendship had depressed Koda so much that he had started moping around the house.

Of course, I wondered if the wise and elderly Murphy could sense his human family's anxiety during the pandemic. After all, dogs are sensitive creatures and extremely in touch with their humans' emotional state. Perhaps Murphy was suffering, too.

After explaining the details, my daughter assured me that since adopting the puppy, Murphy no longer had to worry about Koda annoying him. Koda's depression had vanished since he had a new playmate. And, of course, getting a new puppy thrilled my grandson.

The longer I listened to Amy chatter on about her newest family member, the more I realized that something remarkable had taken place. The strain and stress in my daughter's voice had disappeared.

Her bouncy tone sent me reeling back to a darker time in my life when my three young children and I had found ourselves living in a strange town, penniless, hungry, and not knowing a soul. Even though it made no sense at all, I adopted an adorable black-and-white puppy whom the children named Oreo. Despite our troubles, this little bundle of love brought us hope and a lot of joy during an impossible downhill time.

I could hear Amy singing the same song I had sung so many years ago. There was joy in her voice as she described the puppy's hilarious antics. Amy described his adorable eyes, floppy ears, puppy breath, and soft, fat belly. Even I reaped the benefits when my daughter's newfound happiness sent my spirits soaring!

Without even trying, this lovable pandemic puppy had already spread more magic and bliss around than any cruise ever could, filling Amy's family with nothing but love and sunshine during an uncertain and frightening time. Obviously, I'd made a big mistake. My daughter could not have picked a more perfect time to bring home a puppy!

—Jill Burns—

8

The Commission

Dogs are not our whole life,
but they make our lives whole.
~Roger Caras

When I lost my canine running companion Joan (a gorgeous Lab/Great Dane mix), I was heartbroken. Joan and I ran the greenbelt trails of Houston for twelve years before lymphoma first slowed her down and then claimed her life.

Joan's story didn't end when she slipped from this world to the next. Two months after her death, in the middle of a rainstorm, she sent two underfed strays to the door of the office where I work — a young and bouncy Boxer and an old Lab with gray around her muzzle and on her paws. They were both underfed, but the Lab was far more malnourished than the Boxer. "They are a bonded pair," a co-worker said. He'd seen them running loose through the neighborhood for a while now.

Looking at their age disparity — and the Boxer's energy level — it occurred to me that, in order for them to stay together, either the Lab was really pushing herself or the Boxer was slowing down from time to time so the Lab could catch up. It was touching either way.

"People have tried to catch them," the co-worker remarked, "but they never could."

That day, they were ready to be caught.

As I leaned down from my place at the office door to look closer at the two in front of me, the Lab looked up at me with soft brown eyes shining from her beat-up, old body — and I felt it. The commission.

As I gazed into her eyes, I knew that Joan had sent them. It came over me in a flash. I knew I would look hard for the owners but not find them. I knew the dogs would not have microchips. And I knew that I would keep them.

Even though my heart was still hurting from the loss of Joan, I knew she wanted me to take them in and care for them. And so, I accepted the commission.

I will care for the old Labby and do right by her, I told myself. *The funny, bouncy Boxer will be my reward.* Turns out, I got that part wrong.

As we fed and loved Lilly the Lab, she loved us back so much. She lay at my side in the study when I wrote. She slept by my bed at night. She accompanied my husband outside for his early morning coffee and slipped away from my bedside late at night to sit with my son while he watched Netflix.

When I took Lilly to the veterinarian to check for a microchip and get a physical exam, the vet said Lilly had had many litters of puppies and a "rough life." She was also in chronic renal failure. We shouldn't expect much, he cautioned kindly. But Lilly the Lab got better and better anyway. She got so much better that she was able to accompany me on the greenbelt, running through puddles and sniffing trees. I could hardly keep up with her! A year flew by, and that year was so wonderful that I forgot all about her former rough life and the chronic renal failure. Lilly forgot all about it, too.

So, I was taken aback when the chronic renal failure took a sudden, nasty, fatal turn. I was stunned to discover that my heart could break again over a love I had known for only a year.

And that's when I came to understand that the funny, bouncy Boxer was not my reward for caring for Lilly. *Lilly* was my reward for taking care of Lilly.

I loved that dog, and she loved me. She became a joy in my life. When the dogs showed up on our office doorstep, I thought I was being given a commission to take care of Lilly — and I was — but I was also given a gift.

— Kelly Frances Hanes —

Lazarus, Come Forth

Miracles happen every day. Not just in remote
country villages or at holy sites halfway across
the globe, but here, in our own lives.
~Deepak Chopra

L ate one evening, I noticed that Lazarus, my beloved German Shepherd, was not acting like himself. He began pacing and whining, and just couldn't settle down to get comfortable. When he started to vomit, my husband and I knew a trip to the emergency vet was in order.

I arrived at the emergency clinic with Lazarus at 11:30 p.m. Vitals were taken, and he appeared to be stable. However, my boy continued to show signs of abdominal discomfort. So, we decided that X-rays were needed. The results were inconclusive and sent off to a radiologist for analysis. The doctor felt that Lazarus might need surgery and recommended he be kept overnight in case the radiologist confirmed her suspicions. I agreed to leave him at the clinic in hopes his discomfort would pass by morning without the need for any further treatment. The doctor assured me that she would call regardless of the time if there was any change or Lazarus needed to go into surgery.

All I could do was go home and wait. It was one of the longest drives home I had ever experienced. I began to pray as I lay on my bed. Lazarus is a huge part of our family. He is loyal, protective, and has an extreme ability to solve problems. He sired a litter of puppies, and some are now serving as search-and-rescue dogs.

"God, I absolutely love this dog. He is very special to me and my whole family. My children will be devastated if anything happens to him. Please, please help him pull through," I pleaded.

Next thing I knew, my phone rang. It was the doctor at the clinic. My heart sank, and I found myself kneeling on the floor with the news about Lazarus's condition. The doctor told me that she had started his abdominal surgery and discovered that Lazarus had mesenteric torsion (twisting of the intestines). This diagnosis has nearly a 100% mortality rate, and his chances of survival were not very good. She had done her best to revive his large intestine for nearly an hour, but it was not regaining its color, meaning it wasn't getting proper blood flow. She advised that we euthanize him while he was still under anesthesia since his colon was still very compromised.

Shock took over as I found myself giving verbal permission to put down my dog. My voice trembled when I spoke, knowing the next time I would see him, he would be in a wooden box that would be buried under our fruit tree in the back yard.

There was nothing I could do about it… or was there? Remembering the story of Lazarus in the Book of John, I began to pray.

"Lazarus, come forth," I whispered. "I speak life back into your body, and I say, 'Come forth.'"

Within moments of uttering those words, my phone rang again. Once again, it was the doctor. This time, she was calling to say that while she was prepping to close his incision and move forward with euthanasia, his colon had somehow regained enough color that he might have a slim chance to pull through. My husband and I discussed whether it was possible for Lazarus to recover and live a quality life. We decided that he deserved the opportunity to come home and try.

The next twenty-four hours would be crucial for Lazarus. Most dogs that have mesenteric torsion develop peritonitis rather quickly. If that happened, there was absolutely no chance to save him. We watched the clock and prayed continuously for healing and restoration for our Lazarus.

Minutes turned into hours, and then we got the news. Lazarus stood up! He was able to get to his feet and walk with assistance. No one, especially the doctor, expected him to make such an improvement after his traumatic surgery less than twelve hours earlier.

Each day, Lazarus continued to make great strides. The entire staff at the animal hospital started calling him a "walking miracle." He is one of only a handful of dogs across the country to have survived a true mesenteric torsion.

Lazarus was at the clinic for four days. And then, instead of coming home in a wooden box, he walked through our front door and is still with us today. He has even been certified as a Canine Good Citizen (CGC) and is now awaiting training as a therapy dog.

— Marisa Hanna —

Quarantine Tank

Saving one dog will not change the world, but surely
for that one dog, the world will change forever.
~Karen Davison

I live in a luxury apartment complex that caters to people with dogs. I would estimate that eighty-five percent of the people who live here have a dog or two! Within the course of one afternoon walk around the complex, I can guarantee you're going to see at least six or seven dogs. And within my building alone, I know at least five of the dogs by name.

So, I was rather struck about a month ago when my dog Poe and I were headed down to my car and came upon a girl and a dog in the stairwell — neither of whom I had ever seen before.

As Poe and I approached, I could hear the girl speaking softly. I would have sworn it was a mother consoling her child, but when we turned the corner, I could see her petting a furry blackish-brown dog that was turned away from the descending stairs in front of him.

"Sorry," she said. "We just rescued him. He's afraid of everything — even going down the stairs."

When she finally got him to turn and face us, I could see that he wasn't a very attractive dog either. He appeared to be some type of Shepherd mix but very dark with a sharp, pointed muzzle. The girl went on to tell me that she was a graduate nursing student at the local university and had moved into her apartment two weeks earlier. She told me that her name was Katie, and she and her boyfriend had decided that "now was a good time to rescue a dog." They had picked him up from a farm the previous night.

"He was happy and running everywhere, but the minute we put the leash on him, he shut down," she added.

"Must have had a bad experience, huh?" I asked. "What's his name?"

"Tank," she said.

"Tank?" I asked. I hit the "T" hard when I pronounced it.

"Yep, that was his name… Tank."

I tried to hide what I was thinking: *Too bad that ugly dog also has such an ugly name.* Instead, I asked, "Do you know how old he is?"

"Two," Katie responded.

I tried to be positive. Since many of us had been quarantined due to the COVID-19 pandemic, it really was a great time to get a dog. Being home, there was plenty of time to train it. Katie also impressed me by rescuing an adult dog of mixed origin instead of paying hundreds of dollars for a purebred puppy. We kept a good distance between us during that first day's chat because our conversation occurred at the onset of the "Stay at Home" order that took place the third week of March 2020. The idea of "social distancing" was new, but Katie and I understood the importance of separation.

Now I'm writing this four weeks after I first met Katie on the stairs. Since we're both home now — and because I was intrigued by how Tank might shape up — Katie and I have an unspoken meeting time at four o'clock every day in a grassy area next to the complex. Somehow, we've both ended up there at least fifteen times since we've been at home. It's easy to keep a safe distance apart while we watch our dogs at play.

It has been amazing to watch Tank blossom into a friendly, confident animal. He responds well to commands with a speck of good mischief mixed in. Tank is a smart dog who just needed a little time to get adjusted. Like anybody stepping into a brand-new situation, he felt nervous and unsure. But I can picture him yesterday carrying his knot toy over to Poe and laying it in front of him. When Poe didn't respond, Tank nudged the toy toward Poe with his nose until Poe got the message: "Let's play tug of war!"

Being able to spend a lot of time with Tank has enabled Katie to bring out his truly charming personality. Tank is so aware and alive now. Katie's even got a cute, lovey-dovey "dog mom voice" she uses when she's talking to him. They're a great match.

There are certainly a lot of problems with living through a pandemic situation. Not being able to interact with many people is the pits, and there are some days when I am completely alone. But when I look back on this time, I'm going to have a positive memory at the top of my list: During the COVID-19 quarantine, I got to know a lovely young nurse named Katie who lived in my building. And I also got to know her really cool dog, Tank.

— Rebecca Edmisten —

11

Golden Mystics

You may be gone from my sight,
but you are never gone from my heart.
~Author Unknown

Sheba was my son's red-headed sister. At least, that was the family joke. As an only child, eleven-year-old Justin took his relationship with his Golden Retriever seriously, and she was *his* dog through and through. They were best buddies. She was his rock during an emotionally challenging time. When Justin was having a particularly rough day, Sheba was always there to lift him up, working her magic on him.

Anyone who has ever met a Golden Retriever knows they are magical. When Sheba panted, a huge smile graced her face. She always looked like she was in on a private joke. And she sort of shimmered when she ran — her reddish-blond fur bouncing with every step, glistening in the sun. And she would gaze at us with a depth of knowledge we didn't understand until later.

In the late spring of 1999, four-year-old Sheba began having difficulty walking. We took her to the family vet and learned she had lupus — rare in dogs but not unheard of. Over the next couple of months of treatment, her condition only worsened, and my son's mood along with it. Although not yet diagnosed, my son was bipolar. Although that knowledge was still two years away, the signs were all there; we just missed them.

The specialists began an aggressive course of treatment for Sheba's lupus. By now, Sheba could barely make it to her feet. Lugging an eighty-pound dog in and out of the house became our norm as we fought to save her from an autoimmune disease that was rapidly stealing her vitality.

One morning in June, Sheba was unable to rise. Even if we helped her up, she couldn't stand on her own. We rushed her to the specialist for in-patient treatment. They asked us to come the next day for a visit. Knowing it might be the last time, we encouraged Justin to spend time with her. We all sat in the kennel with her, stroking her luscious fur and telling her how much we loved her.

It would be the last time.

Driving home the following day, I got the call I'd been dreading. Oddly enough, I knew it about ten minutes before the phone rang. At that time in my life, I'd been studying medical intuition and had become quite good at it, even across long distances. With my hands tight on the steering wheel, I talked to Sheba, telling her in my mind that it was okay if she had to go. She had always been such a good girl and never took action without permission. I began to feel the beginnings of an intuitive "hit," and then I felt her leaving. When I saw her running, the phone rang. She was gone.

To say it was devastating doesn't even begin to explain the crush of losing her. Although my husband and I agreed not to get another dog for a while, Justin and I couldn't help ourselves. We wanted another puppy. An overpowering urge drove me to seek out the breeder where we'd found Sheba — a provider for a Seeing Eye dog organization that always got first pick. The breeder would sell the rest of the puppies for a normal, family upbringing.

It turned out the breeder had a litter that would be ready soon. We picked out the lightest blond pup because Sheba had been reddish, and we wanted fewer reminders, fewer comparisons.

Within a month, our new bundle of love joined us. From the start, there was something remarkable about this puppy — a feeling that I already knew her. I also felt Sheba's presence so clearly that there were times when I swear I saw her playing with the new pup — a big dog romping with the thirteen-pounder.

We had all agreed to avoid a name starting with "S," thinking it would be too hard on us to be reminded constantly of Sheba. While trying to come up with a name, the song "Sara" by Starship began playing while I was on hold on a telephone call. It hit me as soon as I heard the line about there never being a good time for a goodbye. Our little bundle of joy's name became Sarah.

One morning a few days after Sarah joined our family, I told her, "Go wake up Justin." She got really excited, raced to his room and jumped on the bed, proceeding to lick his face, her fluffy tail wagging in delight. For our household, this wasn't unusual; Sheba had done this every day for four years. We'd taught her to do it because it was cute and funny, and it helped Justin get up in a good mood. The thing is, we hadn't taught eight-week-old Sarah. She just knew.

What followed that first "How did she know how to do this?" episode was a string of others we couldn't explain. She simply knew how to do all kinds of things we never taught her. It was unlikely the breeder could have taught her these things because they were specific to our household and routines.

I began puzzling about this phenomenon, seeking answers during my daily meditations. One day, I had the chance to visit with a psychic in town for a class I was taking. I'd been to a couple of psychics before and they'd been ridiculous, only providing information about things they picked up from what I said. This one was different. Christine told me things she couldn't possibly have known. Without mentioning the strange connection my new puppy seemed to have with her predecessor, I asked her if she could tell me anything about Sheba. I didn't even tell her that Sheba was a dog.

What Christine said had a profound impact on me. She told me that Sheba hated to leave Justin so she stayed around for the first month we had Sarah to teach her how to be a member of our family. That strong urge to find a new puppy was Sheba pushing me. The new puppy who seemed to have an uncanny knowledge of how our household worked had been under her loving tutelage.

Sarah lived to be almost fourteen — quite old for a Golden Retriever. Although she was tired and partially deaf, and had the white mask of old age, she was still ready for a head pat and she lit up when her humans came home. Her entire life, she was an old soul and a dedicated member of our family — always protective of Justin. And always magical.

Once you've had a Golden Retriever own you, they never truly leave. Every once in a while, when cleaning out a long-unused cabinet or hidden corner, a stray bit of golden fluff will float up, reminding me of the furry mystic who came into our lives at a time we needed her to help us heal.

— Jeanne Felfe —

Chapter

2

Natural Therapist

12

When Peter Met Annie

When an eighty-five-pound mammal licks your tears away,
then tries to sit on your lap, it's hard to feel sad.
~Kristan Higgins

It was June in Indiana — tornado season — with countless watches and warnings that, in the end, would most likely amount to nothing. My co-workers and I had become pretty adept at ignoring weather forecasts, so we didn't pay this one any particular attention. It was just one more storm on its way through. But then the city's weather siren began to blare, and it got us worrying.

I was working as an office nurse at a family practice near downtown Indianapolis in an area of the city well past its prime. Our medical building had been erected on a vacant lot three years before and looked out of place, with its large, modern picture windows forming two sides of the waiting room.

The schedule was full that day. But Barry, one of the doctors, noted the siren and said we'd better get the patients out of the way of potential flying glass and into the interior of the building. We pulled chairs from the exam rooms and lined them up along the walls in the back hallway to provide seating for everyone. Then the other two nurses and I went to shepherd the patients out of harm's way. They were a compliant group, all Hoosier natives who understood that it wasn't a bad idea to take a tornado siren seriously. They picked up their belongings and filed through the door from the waiting room to the exam room area beyond it — all except one.

Peter, an eight-year-old kid with autism, was in for one of his regular checkups. He handled these visits well as long as they followed an exact, prescribed pattern: the same waiting-room chair, the same exam room, the same nurse to admit him, the same scale to weigh him. The noisy alarm and shuffling of people from front office to back pushed him quickly out of his comfort zone, and he showed it. He began to scream and thrash around as his mother nudged him gently toward the door. The other patients tried to ignore the commotion and gave him wide berth as they filed past him to safety. He wouldn't budge.

I turned to Rita, who was acting as traffic warden. "I'm just going to take Annie down to the basement, and I'll be right back to help," I said. Annie was my Rhodesian Ridgeback hound, an eighty-pound two-year-old who I had been bringing to the office with me since she was a pup. The doctors in the practice were both animal lovers. They had gotten into the habit of occasionally bringing in their own pets, Hershey the dog and Raja the cat. The animals made themselves at home in the doctors' private offices, and nobody thought a thing of it. It's likely no one even knew they were there.

Annie waited for me in her large crate in the practice manager's office, the room next to the waiting room. In order to get her to the basement, we had to walk through an open area.

As I headed her quickly toward the stairs, Peter happened to see her. He let out a piercing shriek and ran in our direction. Before his mother could stop him, he crossed the room and, arms outstretched and flailing, lunged for Annie. He grabbed her around the neck, screeching and howling, hugging her tightly, his face buried in her fur.

Unperturbed, Annie sat down. She didn't turn toward him or pull away, sniff at him or try to lick his face. She just sat down calmly, faced forward, and submitted to his fierce embrace.

Peter's mother was beside herself. "I'm so sorry," she said. "I just don't seem very good at controlling him when he's like this. He can't tolerate any interruption to his routine." She fussed around, trying to loosen his death grip on the dog, and he protested loudly and refused to let go. All this time, the siren continued to wail in the background. How could the dog remain so unruffled? The chaos had me jumping out of my skin.

"Darling, you need to stop this now. Leave the dog alone. We've got to go down the hall with the other nice people here until the storm passes."

I didn't know what to do. Rita, Peter's usual nurse, was nowhere in sight. I didn't feel confident handling him myself. He didn't know me, and I didn't want to make things worse by introducing something else unfamiliar. I could hear the wind outside battering against the windows and tried to listen for that telltale roaring locomotive sound that precedes a tornado touchdown. How much time did we have?

Annie continued to sit placidly with Peter's arms around her neck. As I watched helplessly, I saw the child begin to relax. He slackened his hold and sat back to stroke her head and shoulders gently. "What a good dog," he said. Then looking up at me, he added, "I have a dog just like this at home."

I smiled and made some bland encouraging comment, and then glanced up at Peter's mother to find her sobbing into her hand.

"It's all right. No harm done," I said, thinking she was embarrassed by her son's outburst.

"You don't understand," she said, sniffling into a tissue and then crying harder. "He doesn't speak. He never speaks. I hardly know his voice."

Goosebumps broke out on my arms as I looked down at this little boy who had just spoken, and to a stranger. I felt my eyes sting. Annie turned her head up to look at me, her eyes wise and patient.

"Wow," I said. I couldn't get any more words out as I choked back tears of my own. I had just witnessed something remarkable that occurred thanks to a calm, unflappable, chestnut-coated therapist — Annie, my dog.

The tornado never did touch down. In an hour, we were back to our normal routine, and Annie was asleep in her crate in the manager's office.

I had always loved her dearly, but I never looked at her in quite the same way after that day. There was an added dimension to our relationship. She was worthy of more than just my affection. She was also worthy of my respect. In Peter's words, "What a good dog."

—Holly Green—

13

Dogs Are the Best Medicine

No animal I know of can consistently be more of a
friend and companion than a dog.
~Stanley Leinwoll

My phone buzzes on the bedside table, pulling me from sleep. I fumble for it in the dark and see a text from my younger daughter. The digital display on my phone reads 3 a.m. I jump to wakefulness. Why is she texting me at this time of night?

I walk into the hallway to avoid disturbing my husband. The text reads, "Mom, I'm so sick."

Jessica, age twenty-four, lives in our basement suite. She recently had to take a break from her university classes but she plans to return to school in the fall. In the meantime, she's been working part-time at a daycare.

She'd come home sick from work a few days earlier. At first, we assumed it was just an ordinary cold virus. This was during the second week of March 2020, and Canada had just announced the first travel restrictions because of the COVID-19 pandemic.

Now, reading her text, the first waves of worry hit me. *Could she have contracted the coronavirus?* I call her. Jess answers in a rough and raspy voice, telling me her chest hurts and she's pretty sure she has a fever. She's worried that she might have COVID-19. I ask if she can manage to call the medical-health line to get advice, or should I do it? She says she'll call.

I wonder what to do. At sixty-one, I'm in the higher-risk age group. My husband has a pacemaker and is sixty-three. Should I risk exposing myself and, indirectly, him? *Staying away would be the safest course of action*, I tell myself, *but this is my baby girl, and she needs me.*

As I walk down to the main floor, I can hear Pepper, our little Cocker Spaniel, whining. I find her pawing at the door to the basement.

I remember reading that pets don't seem to be at risk for getting the virus, but I wonder, *If my girl is indeed infected, could the dog transfer the virus to people she's in contact with?* I do some quick research, but what information I find is equivocal.

The dog continues to scratch at the door, frantic to get downstairs.

Somehow, Pepper has always had the uncanny ability to sense when Jessica is having a bad day. During her worst times, the dog becomes her shadow, following her around, leaning against her and always maintaining physical contact. It's as if she can sense my girl's need.

I've never seen Pepper this anxious to get to Jess, though. I'm torn, but if Pepper wants to be with Jess this much, my girl must need her just as badly. I decide to let the dog stay downstairs for the duration of Jessica's illness.

I open the door. Pepper flies down the steps.

I dig up our thermometer, a box of gloves I'd used when I was a practicing physiotherapist, and an N95 mask I'd used when making glazes for my pottery. Once suited up, I head downstairs to check on my girl.

She's gotten through to the medical line. The nurse's advice is to self-quarantine because she has all the symptoms of COVID-19, but they won't test her because she hasn't traveled or been exposed to a known case.

When I check, Jess has a low-grade fever. Her cheeks are bright red, and a deep, rattling cough rumbles through her chest. Panic flares in my mother-heart, and I jump into action. I fill her water bottle, give her Tylenol, and tuck her into bed. Pepper curls up beside Jess, chin resting on my girl's stomach.

I leave meals for Jess. I check on her constantly but avoid contact as much as possible. This is the responsible thing to do, but it is also one of the hardest things I've ever done. We chat on the phone whenever she feels up to talking, but it's all I can do not to run downstairs and hug her.

Pepper doesn't leave her side for almost ten days. Jess manages to feed her and let her out as needed. Later, she tells me if it wasn't for the dog, she couldn't have made it through the illness. She was so sick and lonely, and she wanted a hug desperately. Her depression reared its ugly head, but whenever she sank into despair, Pepper was there, licking her cheeks and snuggling against her. She was doing what dogs are so incredibly gifted at doing: providing unconditional love.

— Leslie Wibberley —

14

Misunderstood

Therapy dogs visit people in nursing homes, hospitals,
and wherever else they are needed. They cheer people
up who are sad or lonesome and just need
a furry friend to hug.
~Martha McKiever, Finn's Trail of Friends

I was told that Border Collies are rarely therapy dogs. They're too hyperactive, focused, and quirky. I'd adopted my Border Collie, Buzz, from a rescue organization at the age of two, and it was true that he'd been surrendered to the organization for nipping at the heels of the man's mother-in-law in a typical herding maneuver. He wasn't going to bite the woman, but Buzz was sent on his way.

Yes, I knew that some of his tendencies might be problematic, but he also had a deep well of intelligence and sensitivity that was special. I had faith that he didn't need a typical herding job to satisfy his "work requirement."

I trained Buzz on my own and through an obedience class. When it seemed clear that he was ready to take the therapy-dog evaluation, I made an appointment to meet the evaluator at a nursing home. It would be the moment of truth.

After Buzz passed the basic obedience activities, it was time to visit residents. He made his way through the halls, looking aware but unconcerned about the wheelchairs, wires and tubes. He did see the green tennis balls snugged on the feet of the walkers and jerked to attention, but I said quickly, "Leave it," and he obeyed.

He visited three residents in their rooms with happy but controlled attention, but then on the fourth visit, a woman with bright gray eyes sat up quickly in her bed when she saw a dog enter the room. Buzz looked up at her and offered his largest dog smile before bouncing up on the bed next to her! The woman placed her hands on his ruff and tousled him, making him squirm closer as she burst into laughter. "Oh! I've always had dogs, and I've missed being with a dog so much," she managed to say between notes of glee. I was horrified and certain this meant Buzz and I had failed as a team. Jumping! That was a huge no-no.

The evaluator instructed us to finish the test, however. I didn't know what the point was since he'd done something so against the rules, but we would finish what we started.

We found a completely different kind of person in the next room. She sat in a chair, gazing off to one side in an absent way. Her right calf was nearly covered by a large wad of bandaging. One of the staffers told us the resident had an injury that was infected and hadn't healed despite everyone's best efforts. When Buzz saw the woman, he approached slowly and bent his head to sniff the bandaged area ever so gently. His nose never touched the material or her skin. He took a few steps to her left side and sat down next to the chair. Her fingers dangled a bit over the edge of the chair arm close to his head, so he lifted his nose up slowly until the fingertips touched just above his eyes. Her gaze looked vaguely aware, then a bit confused, and she turned to look at me.

"There's a dog who's come to say hello to you today. Do you like dogs?" I asked. She looked down where her fingers touched silky black fur. She nodded and leaned over tentatively so her hand could touch Buzz's head with more definite, albeit clumsy strokes. Although I'm sure it wasn't the most comfortable patting for my dog, he sat completely still as her hand moved and her face brightened a bit. "Dog," she murmured. "Dog."

When we left the room, the evaluator invited us to come back for the expected second set of visits another day. "We aren't disqualified?" I asked, unable to hide my disbelief.

The evaluator shook her head. "He's a remarkable dog. He knows how to read people and offers what they need. You're one of the best teams I've ever had."

It was the beginning of a beautiful career for my once misunderstood Border Collie.

— Tanya Sousa —

15

The Miracle Worker

Love makes your soul crawl out from its hiding place.
~Zora Neale Hurston

"Your son isn't verbalizing as much as he should be at his age," the pediatrician told me, in a way that left no doubt of his disapproval. "You aren't talking to him enough. You aren't spending enough time with him. You need to read to him."

I was torn between indignation and fear. I talked to John constantly. Read to him. Played with him daily. And yet the doctor must be right. This must be my fault.

By the time we discovered he had a condition that had made him temporarily deaf, he was angry and silent. My husband and I knew we had to act. Perhaps a puppy could comfort him, draw him out and teach him to be kind again.

John wanted to name the little Schipperke "Underdog" after his favorite cartoon character. After much pleading on my part, however, he settled for naming her in honor of Underdog's ladylove: Sweet Polly Purebred.

Sweet Polly became John's sole companion. From the time she was only a furry black ball, she loved the High Plains as much as he did. Together, they roamed the long grass, with her bright eyes following him as she wagged her whole body with joy. Polly chased gophers. She chased John. She chased gophers to John, once following one right between his legs, her sturdy body lodging there and giving him his laughter back. Then she showed off her incredible speed by running circles around him to elicit yet more laughter.

A boy raised on the prairie faces dangers that city children don't. To a stranger, the prairie looks benign, only a brown sea of grass. But for a boy and his dog, there is much to contend with — rattlesnakes, stray dogs, and even an occasional ticked-off cow.

John knew that Polly would protect him from those things. She proved it one lazy afternoon when a dog three times her size appeared, growling. She reacted instantly, rocketing toward it, turning the dog into a fleeing coward as she bit its ankles hard — just for good measure.

Proudly, she trotted home, and when I praised her for protecting my little boy, Polly barked loudly — just once — to underscore her fearlessness when protecting John and his home.

In late summer, rattlers often left the fields to coil beside our white clapboard house and warm themselves in the setting sun. One evening, Polly discovered a fat one there, far too close to where John played. The scene rapidly became chaos and noise. The frantic dog was barking and trying to drive away the snake; the snake was angry, rattling and striking, and refused to give ground.

John ran to the house to get his dad. It took four shots before they finally killed that snake. The protected had grown into the protector.

John and Polly filled those summer days with hikes and games of tag, roughhousing, and quiet companionship. She was his. He was hers. They never loved another in those childhood days like they loved each other. In the fall, she wore a deep path in the prairie on the brow of our hill, running to greet him as he got off the school bus. When we'd return from town, she'd be waiting there, a lonely, little sentinel welcoming us home. We'd drive the truck halfway up, and John would jump out, racing his friend from her trail to the house.

But Polly didn't just build a trail on the land. She built a trail to a little boy's heart. John smiled again. He laughed again. He let his mother kiss him again.

When John was twenty-four, the free-spirited Polly began to slip away. Her hearing failed until she couldn't recognize her boy's voice. Her eyes failed until she couldn't see his face. When her body failed too, the vet said we had to let her go. We were beside Polly to see her into the next world.

We don't live at the old place anymore. Another family, with another boy and another dog, live there now. John returned just once more to scatter Polly's ashes over the land she loved best, on a summer afternoon with the hot prairie wind blowing through the long grass.

—Leslie C. Schneider—

16

On the Job

I think the next best thing to solving a problem
is finding some humor in it.
~Frank A. Clark

When we first got him, I had visions of training my dog, Monty, for service. But Monty — short for Monster — had other ideas. He was the sweetest pet on the planet, but it soon became clear that a dog who swiped peanut-butter-and-jelly sandwiches off the counter and then ate our underwear for dessert might not be the best candidate to become a therapy dog. After all, he barked at the laundry basket and was afraid of helium balloons and grocery bags. I thought it was more likely that he would *be* in therapy than become a therapy dog.

But not long after he turned two, he suddenly mellowed. Sensing an opportunity, I brought back the trainer who had given him a failing grade in puppy kindergarten.

"I'd like to get the dog to help me do the laundry," I told the trainer.

"Does he sit, lie down, and stay when you tell him?" she asked.

"No," I replied.

"Do you think maybe we should start with the basics before you have him cooking the dinner and picking up the dry cleaning?" she asked.

"Okay," I agreed, not because I thought it was necessary, but because I had already picked up the dry cleaning that day.

She said the first thing we needed to do was establish dominance. I told her I wasn't into that kinky stuff.

She said dogs are pack animals and need to know their position in the pack. I told her his position was smack-dab in the middle of the kitchen floor while I was making dinner.

"Your dog won't do anything you tell him to until he knows you're the leader of the pack," she said.

"Just like a man," I mused.

"The leader of the pack always eats first, so when you feed him, he needs to see you eat before him," she explained, as she handed me his bowl of food.

"Let me get this straight," I said, inhaling the savory aroma of chicken and salmon kibble. "If I eat his food, I'm in charge?"

"Right."

I wondered if I would lose points if I threw up after eating the kibble.

The trainer demonstrated how I could pretend to eat the food.

Eventually, the dog learned to sit before he could eat. He learned to sit before he could go outside. He learned to sit before he jumped up and knocked people over when they came in the door.

"Clearly, he's good at sitting," I said. "Can you get him to sit on the toilet?"

She growled at me.

"How is his leash-walking?" she asked.

"I don't walk him," I said. "He takes me for a drag."

She told me we needed to get him to walk nicely on a leash. I asked if I needed to eat more dog food for this to happen.

Many dollars later, the dog could sit, stay, and fetch a can of diet soda from the fridge. It seemed the only thing I couldn't get him to do was go food shopping for me, and that had more to do with the fact that he was afraid of the grocery bags than that he couldn't drive.

Once the dog seemed relatively well behaved, I contacted the local pet-therapy organization and arranged for an obedience test. We worked on some special skills he would need to be able to go into hospitals, schools, and nursing homes, and then I brought him in for his test. Since we would be working as a team, I had to take a test, too. Although I was not as good at "sit" and "stay" as he was, we both passed.

Monty loved being a therapy dog. His favorite thing in the world was to have his belly scratched, and there were many people willing to do that for him all day. We visited children battling cancer, seniors with dementia, and even worked the airports when flights were delayed or canceled, and passengers needed a way to blow off some steam. On the job, he was the center of attention. For a dog, that's about as good as it gets.

But then the COVID-19 pandemic struck, and Monty the Therapy Dog was benched. With social distancing in place, I couldn't take him to any of the places we used to go. He couldn't do his job, go on his morning group dog walks with his canine friends, or even chase a ball in the local dog run. Soon, I got the feeling that he was more depressed about the isolation than my husband and I were, and I realized I needed to do something to stimulate him or risk the chance that he would start snacking on our underwear again.

"The dog is making me feel better in the midst of this crisis," I said to my husband. "But I think he needs something to cheer him up."

"What did you have in mind?" he asked.

"What if we played pretend therapy visit?" I said. My husband gave me the look he reserves for my kookiest ideas, which is something like a cross between an eye roll and a stroke.

"How do you plan to do that?" he asked.

"Well, you can be a patient, or a student or a senior, and I will bring Monty on a therapy call," I explained.

"I think he's going to know it's me," said my husband. "You know, because I stand in front of him and eat his food before he does."

"Let's just try, okay, honey?" I said. "I think he'll appreciate it."

I went and grabbed the dog's therapy attire. I put him in his official vest and bandanna and clipped his badge to his collar. Then I put on my official sweatshirt and badge and slung my therapy backpack, which held the dog's certification papers and some dog biscuits, over my shoulder. Immediately, Monty seemed to perk up and struck his therapy-dog stance. I took him outside, closed the door, and knocked on it. The dog sat next to me and waited patiently.

"Hello," I shouted as I opened the door and stepped in. "We're here for your therapy visit."

"Up here," yelled my husband from the top of the stairs.

I turned to the dog and said, "Monty, therapy," so he knew he had to behave and also get his belly rubbed.

We walked up the stairs, and when we got to the top, I saw my husband lying on the floor pretending to be in pain. Monty walked over to my husband, lay down next to him, and rested his chin on my husband's leg.

"Good job, Monty!" I said. "And good job to you, too, honey. You really look like you're in pain!"

"I really am in pain," he said as he massaged his leg. "I tripped over the dog's toy and slammed my shin into the coffee table."

"Well, you did it for a good cause," I replied. "See how happy he is!" The dog did, indeed, appear to be grinning.

"Great," he said, and then looked at his watch. "Now if you wouldn't mind helping me up, I need to go eat some kibble."

— Tracy Beckerman —

17

Small Victories

I have found that when you are deeply troubled,
there are things you get from the silent,
devoted companionship of a dog that
you can get from no other source.
~Doris Day

Deep in the throes of my bipolar depression, I had spent the night in the hospital on suicide watch. There is no place lonelier than the sterile white observation room with a night nurse assigned to keep an eye on you through a glaringly obvious camera positioned in the corner.

"Maybe your mom was right. Maybe what you really need right now is a puppy," my husband said in the car on the way home from the hospital. Until he said this, I had been slumped into the passenger seat, eyes half-open. The nurses had kept me awake all through the night with requests for more vials of blood and long sessions with counselors.

"A puppy?" I asked, wary of becoming too enthusiastic. "I guess we have been talking about getting a new puppy for a while."

It was true. The topic of adding a new dog to our small family had been on the table for quite a while, but it never seemed like the right time. I was constantly struggling just to keep myself afloat. How could I possibly be expected to take care of another living being?

"I don't know what else to do for you. The medications aren't working. The therapy is helping you make progress, but it's so slow.

You need something to work right now. You need a reason to get out of bed in the morning."

I could hear the resignation in his voice. Something small shifted inside me. I realized what a tremendous weight he was carrying on my behalf. This puppy idea was his last Hail Mary attempt to catapult me out of this despair and back into the land of the living. He knew better than to believe that a four-legged friend would be the cure-all for my condition, but certainly it couldn't make things any worse.

"Okay," I conceded. "Let's get a puppy."

We went home so that I could shower away the terrible memory of the hospital. Then, we headed back out to the animal shelter. My heart was set on a Poodle, but it felt more important that we get a new dog today. The animal shelter would have to do.

We walked through the glass doors and into the cacophony of barking. Before we arrived, we hadn't really talked about what we wanted in a new dog. Should it be little or big? Would it be a male or a female? I had this idea that we would know automatically when the right dog came along. It was how I had picked all our animals to date. The right dog always showed up at just the right moment.

For a solid half-hour, we wandered through the kennels, winding our fingers through the wire to pass treats in exchange for licks. I had all but decided that it was a loss until we ran smack-dab into the last kennel on the left-hand side. Inside was a midsize black dog with beautiful butterscotch eyes and brindle paws. She jumped up on the fence to get a closer look at us as we passed. Out of all the dogs we had seen, she was the one who seemed most eager to head out to a new home. I knew immediately that she was the one.

We filled out all the paperwork, grabbed her new leash from the car, and happily loaded her into the back seat. I named her Cricket, a name that I had been secretly saving for quite some time. It fit her personality and rambunctious leaping with all four paws off the ground.

She was enthusiastic about leaving the shelter, and it brought a smile to my face even though I still felt like I was moving through water. She was a silver lining on an otherwise dreary day, the same type of dull existence I had been living in for months. Bringing her home took up an entire day and kept me from crawling back underneath the sheets of our comfortable bed. My husband counted this as the first small victory in favor of the new pup.

When the light of the next morning pried my eyes open, I was faced with the butterscotch eyes and gentle whine of my new canine companion. I could spend hours lying in bed doing nothing more than staring at the wall, but she needed to go outside. Faced with the first problem that would force me out of bed, I made the decision to take care of her. I groaned as I shoved back the covers and felt the floor steady beneath my feet. It was my second victory.

Day after day, we followed this new routine. My alarm would go off, and Cricket would plead gently with me until I finally shuffled my way to the front door. By the time she was taken care of, I no longer felt like going back to bed. I began to spend more and more time with her, teaching her basic commands. She flew through them at lightning speed, and we moved onto learning more advanced commands. She was my partner, and I was marking off small victories each and every day that I was able to get out of bed and work with her.

Eventually, we realized that she was capable of doing far more than just shoving me out of bed in the morning. The training process had become therapeutic for me, a familiar rhythm that steadied my days. We set higher goals and began to establish the framework for Cricket to become my service dog.

More than a year later, Cricket accompanies me everywhere I go. She lies at my feet when we go to restaurants, knowing that she will score a few French fries from my plate for a job well done. She soothes my anxiety and panic attacks when we wind our way through crowded stores. When my bipolar depression flares up and I struggle to get out of bed, she presses her cold nose beneath the blankets until I remember that I have something to live for.

In the end, it turns out that my mother was right, as she so often is. A dog may not have cured my bipolar disorder, as nothing can take away the ebbs and flows of my madness. However, she was a balm to my soul when I could not imagine ever getting better, and she continues to be the cure for my sadness. Faithfully, she pushes me to take those difficult first steps day after day. We win together, one small victory at a time.

— Ashley Simpson —

Witten's Story

Dogs die. But dogs live, too. Right up until they die,
they live. They live brave, beautiful lives.
They protect their families. And love us.
And make our lives a little brighter.
~Dan Gemeinhart, The Honest Truth

I remember the post like it was yesterday: "Pathetic Pekingese in Denton Shelter." Judging from his photo, the description was accurate, maybe even an understatement. The poor little guy had almost no hair, and his wrinkled, naked skin was plagued by mange. Even worse, the condition of his skin revealed malnutrition and dehydration. The scant wisps of hair poking out from the skin were white, so I assumed he was a white Peke in his better days. I wasn't sure he would survive, but I decided he should be given a chance to live. If that was not to be, at least he could die in the comfort of a soft, warm bed after a comforting bath to soothe his tortured skin. So, off to Denton I went. I signed his release papers, taking him into our Pekingese rescue group.

His vet exam confirmed my initial impression that he had mange. In fact, he had both types: the contagious and non-contagious type. There was more bad news. The poor boy was heartworm positive, but not well enough to treat.

It took months of TLC to bring his physical status up to treatable. Then, the mange yielded to medication and his improved immune system. He regrew his hair. His thin body filled out.

Throughout those months, he never lost the light in his eyes or his sweet, calm disposition. After a while, a handsome, pure-white Pekingese emerged from the shattered, diseased boy we had pulled from the shelter.

When it was finally time to treat his heartworms, I was afraid. Our group had lost dogs to the treatment before. But there was no question he needed it, so with my hand shaking, I signed the consent.

He had no trouble staying sedentary during the long months of treatment with antibiotics and anti-inflammatory medication. Finally, he was given a clean bill of health; after almost a year and more than a thousand dollars in vet bills, he was ready to post on our adoptable dogs' site.

A few weeks before Christmas, I was contacted by a family that wanted to give their dad a dog for Christmas. Usually, rescue groups do not adopt out a dog for a gift, but this was a different situation. They explained that their dad — a strapping, healthy man until a few months earlier — had gone to the emergency room for shortness of breath, expecting a diagnosis of an upper respiratory infection. He was given a devastating diagnosis of pulmonary fibrosis instead. The cause was unknown, and it had no cure. Treatment was aimed at providing comfort to lungs that would stiffen progressively, making breathing nearly impossible.

Forced into sudden, unexpected retirement by his diagnosis, the dad was alone at home, and his wife and children wanted to provide him with a canine companion who was calm and not too active. Our boy fit the bill, and they fell in love with him.

The pathetic Peke from Denton was named Witten after his soon-to-be owner's favorite football player, and the children took him home to hide out until Christmas morning. They had his now luxurious white hair shaved down to avoid shedding that might impede their dad's breathing and fitted him with a Dallas Cowboys blue jersey with Witten's name on it. Barely able to contain their excitement, they presented Witten to their dad on Christmas morning.

Witten knew instinctively who he was there to care for. He climbed carefully into his new dad's lap and lay his head on his chest, careful to avoid the oxygen tubing that allowed his dad to breathe. Their eyes met, and Witten never wavered in his devotion to his man.

A few days later, Witten's dad tripped on his oxygen tubing and fell to the floor. Witten alerted his dad's wife and stood guard until his dad's feet were cleared from the tangle of tubing and he was helped to his feet. He remained a faithful protector until his dad died a mere four months after they first met. Witten had played such an important role in his dad's final months that the family honored him at the funeral. His photos with his dad were displayed at the memorial, along with the human family pictures, and his role in the family was mentioned in the eulogy.

Immediately, Witten assumed the role of comforter and protector for his dad's widow. He stayed by her side, sat beneath her chair, and went for walks with her. The acute bereavement period for a spouse who loses a loved one is often between two and three years, and so it was for his mom. As she grieved and healed gradually, her Peke comforter was by her side, offering companionship and comfort.

Then, almost as quickly as it started, it ended. One day, after a short walk outside, Witten lay down and died quietly. His heart just stopped beating. His mom was devastated. But in his memory, she adopted another orphaned rescue dog in need. Witten's legacy continues with a new dog that now has a life rather than confinement and possible euthanasia in a shelter.

—Judy Quan—

Hershey's Visit

*A dog can show you more honest affection with a flick
of his tail than a man can gather through
a lifetime of handshakes.*

~Gene Hill

Mrs. Bea, as we called her, was unusually quiet that day. She was the last patient of the morning. Doc talked to her about her diabetes and high blood pressure, and then left me with her to write up prescription refills.

"Is this everything you need then?" I asked. "I'll have Doc sign these, and you can be on your way." I got up from the little desk in the exam room and opened the door to leave.

Without any explanation, she burst into tears. Hunched over, hands to her face, she shook with muffled sobs. I did a mental review of the visit. Had she gotten bad news from Doc? Was she going to tell me she couldn't afford her medications this month? Might I have inadvertently said something to upset her?

I sat back down across from her. "Mrs. Bea, what's wrong?"

"I'm sorry," she said. "I'm just not handling this well at all."

I waited.

"My little Patsy died this week."

"Oh, no," I said, completely mystified. Who was Patsy? I knew the woman's family. She was a widow with two grown sons. I knew of no Patsy in her life.

"And it was all my fault. I as good as killed her."

This was bad. "Can you tell me about it?"

"I was just inexcusably careless. I let her out a couple mornings ago. It was chilly, so I didn't go with her. The back yard is fenced, you know. What trouble could she possibly get into?"

"Patsy's a pet?"

"She's — she was — my little dog, the best friend I ever had, my only companion now that I live alone. I even sometimes pretend — pretended — she was my daughter." At this, she burst into a fresh round of tears, and I felt my own eyes welling.

"Did you tell Doc?" I asked.

"Oh, no, he's so busy. But I knew you'd understand."

"If anyone would understand, it's him," I told her. "He's quite the animal lover. Do you know he even brings his own dog to work?"

"He does?"

"Uh-huh. Tell me about Patsy. What happened to her?"

I dreaded hearing that the dog had been carried off by a coyote or run over by a car. All kinds of gruesome outcomes flashed through my mind.

Mrs. Bea told me, between bouts of uncontrolled crying, that her little Poodle, left unattended, ate a bellyful of mulch from the landscaping while she relaxed inside with her morning coffee. The dog died in terrible pain. The vet couldn't save her. By the end of the story, we were both in tears. We held each other's hands and wept for Patsy.

I was feeling helpless to comfort her when I caught a faint noise coming from down the hall, a sound I definitely should not have been hearing. It was the jingling of dog tags. Hershey's.

Doc's chocolate Lab, who spent the day in an office in the back, never ventured into the patient area. Hershey was a wonderful dog, a nearly perfect dog — gentle, joyful and, above all, obedient. You could give that dog a command and he would follow it until you released him. Every morning, Doc settled him in his office and told him, "Stay." And he did. Without fail. But he was loose now. What was going on? I listened in dismay as the sounds got closer and closer. He was coming down the hall. Doc would be furious.

I looked at Mrs. Bea, who was still crying and didn't seem to notice anything unusual. Then, to my horror, Hershey's lovely brown face appeared in the open doorway. I held my breath, put up a palm-out "stop sign" with my hand, and tried to telegraph a message to him: "Don't come in here. You're not allowed."

The message didn't get through. Hershey walked into the room and headed straight for the grieving woman. He put his head in her lap and stood silently beside her, minus his usual goofy smile and wagging tail. I watched in wonder as Mrs. Bea took her hands from mine and stroked the dog's velvet head and silky ears.

"Patsy slept curled up beside me on the bed every night. In the mornings, she'd hop onto the couch, and we'd watch the TV news together. Whenever I went out, she'd be waiting by the door when I got back, her little tail going a mile a minute. I miss her so much," she said. "How could I ever replace such a dear little thing? She was only twelve pounds, but she was smart as a whip. She'd balance a little dog biscuit on her nose until I told her it was okay to eat it."

I listened in silence as the woman painted a picture of her life with Patsy. She trailed her hand along Hershey's back and chucked him under his chin, never once commenting on his presence. As I watched, she got calmer and more composed. Her sobs subsided. She pushed Hershey gently to one side to reach into her purse for a tissue, and then resumed patting him, her whole body relaxing a little at a time. He remained patiently at her side.

After a few more minutes, she drew in a deep breath and took my hand in hers. "You are so sweet to sit and listen to an old woman like me. I'm sure you have other things to do. I'm sorry I took up your time, but I always know I can tell you anything and you'll make me feel better. Doc is lucky to have you as his nurse."

I wanted to point out that she was giving me credit for what Hershey had accomplished, but then thought I'd better not. He stepped back as if aware his work was done. In a graceful sweep, he turned and left the room. I listened to his tags jingle as he retreated to Doc's office. What had I just witnessed? Had the dog sensed an elderly woman's suffering from down the hall and come to comfort her? I think he had. Amazing.

Mrs. Bea never mentioned the dog who'd visited her in the exam room that day. In fact, I don't think it registered consciously at all. She absorbed the compassion he showered on her without really knowing he was there.

To my knowledge — and I worked in that office for many years — Hershey never entered a patient room again. But he was there that day when he was needed, and he did just the right thing.

— Holly Green —

20

A Golden Opportunity

When you feel lousy, puppy therapy is indicated.
~Sara Paretsky

"Gibbles is dead," whispered my friend Laura into the phone. Laura is the most over-the-top pet lover I know, so I'd assumed that Gibbles, our pet guinea pig, would be safe at her menagerie like house while we were on vacation. But he had died mysteriously in his cage.

I knew I had to find Fido fast. I wasn't just making good on a promise that someday we would be a dog family; a month before, my eleven-year-old son had been diagnosed with a severe case of Tourette syndrome. He had already missed three weeks of school because we were still looking for the right doctors to treat him, and he couldn't control the sounds and words coming out of his mouth. He barely went out in public because he was so embarrassed by these involuntary tics.

When I shared the news about Gibbles, Michael sobbed. I was in a condo in Vermont with a crying child, so I did what any mother would do: I went online to find a dog. I knew that would cheer up Michael even if it made me miserable!

I had spent the first forty-seven years of my life disliking dogs. I attribute this to my mother — who readily accepts the blame. My parents were incredibly loving, but they did not raise my three siblings and me to be pet lovers. While we had a dog named Patches when I was growing up, he slept at my aunt's house across the street.

My husband grew up with dogs and always wanted one, but I dodged the subject for years. Once we had children, it seemed impossible. Both Michael and his younger sister, Katie, love animals and begged for a puppy, but to stave off getting a dog, we acquired many goldfish, hermit crabs, a gecko, and that guinea pig.

Several months before, when we researched what type of dog we wanted someday, I decided that I needed to be sympatico with this dog, given my history. After taking doggie quizzes and reading about different breeds, we decided on a Golden Retriever because they are easygoing and active. It felt a little like online dating, but our family would be wed to the match after just one meeting.

The day after Gibbles died, I sat in my pajamas until noon, sipping coffee and looking for a puppy online. I had looked at a few adoption sites, but I decided that a breeder with a solid track record would suit my family better since they would offer lots of helpful tips and tricks after we brought the puppy home.

Finally, I found a breeder with a new litter. When the kids came back from skiing, I showed them pictures of several puppies, and they agreed on a female tagged "Orange Girl." The next morning, I put down a deposit on our pooch, but we couldn't pick her up for six weeks because she needed to get all her shots.

Finding out you are getting a puppy in six weeks is like getting excited for Christmas a week or so after Halloween. It was enough to allow Michael to take his mind off Gibbles. And I had enough time to prepare myself and our house. At night, the entire family read dog-training books aloud.

Meanwhile, Michael was taking medication, although some days he still had tics ten times a minute. He refused to talk about going back to school. He wouldn't see his friends. He still saw himself as a freak.

I was terrified of launching my son into a world where Tourette's is the butt of jokes on late-night TV. Desperate for answers, we saw a dozen healers, switched schools, and tried vitamins, acupuncture, and fad diets. I wasn't just looking for something to control his symptoms; I wanted an all-out cure, something that would build his self-confidence and restore his spirit. I wanted a miracle.

Then, in April, Michael and I drove from our home in Connecticut to Vermont to retrieve our Retriever. When I saw the puppy in his arms, I knew I had made the right decision. What surprised me was my reaction. When I saw our new puppy, it wasn't quite the same flood of emotion I felt when the doctor handed me my babies, but it was still love at first sight.

When we got into the car, Michael sat in the back seat with his new puppy, named Bailey, on his lap. He petted her lovingly, as if he had been waiting for this day forever.

Bailey brought added chaos to our home, but also unconditional love. Having a puppy also gave Michael a job — helping to walk the dog — and it got him out of the house a bit. She was not a complete panacea, but she was a distraction.

By the time we brought Bailey home, Michael had missed three months of school, although his public school paid for tutors once a student missed two weeks of school due to a medical problem. He had become bored and restless, but now my boy had a best friend. He cuddled with Bailey, sang to her, and even wrote a poem about her. By the time he went back to school, he was not completely healed, but he was happy again.

Nine years later, both Michael and Katie refer to Bailey as their "sister," and my husband calls her his therapy dog. In reality, she was everyone's therapy dog.

If you ask me what helped Michael's symptoms improve by that summer, I will give you a litany of answers — from prescription medications and vitamins, to taking guitar and drum lessons. But if you ask Michael, he'll give you one answer — Bailey.

— Michele Turk —

21

Puppy Power

When the world says, "Give up," Hope whispers,
"Try it one more time."
~Author Unknown

I n 1969, I had recently graduated from high school and secured a job as a nurse's aide at a local nursing home. The first day on the job, they took me to the ward that I'd been assigned to, introduced me to everyone, and gave me a brief medical history on each resident along with their daily routines.

It was an eye-opening experience. The residents seemed bored and unhappy. I decided to try to find things that might spark their interest in life again. I always struck up a conversation the minute I walked into their rooms to get them up for breakfast. Many of them never spoke but I knew they could hear me, and they knew I cared.

One of the ladies on my ward had gained the reputation of being "Houdini's mother." They didn't explain why, but they told me that when I got her up, I should tie her securely to her chair before I went to get her breakfast because she might fall down. She never spoke, so I had no idea whether she was in a stable frame of mind or not. I simply did as I was told. After all, I didn't want her to fall and get hurt.

The first day, I sat her down in her chair with a couple of comfy pillows and proceeded to attach the restraints as I had been shown. The first one had armholes like a vest and secured her upper torso to the back of the chair. Now, as far as I was concerned, that looked like it would've been enough, but they insisted that she needed elbow, wrist and ankle restraints, too. She never said a word while all of this was taking place. She just watched me intently as I set about the task at hand, talking to her the entire time.

When I was sure that she was safe and comfy, I explained that I would be right back with her breakfast. I stepped out into the hallway to the breakfast cart. It took a couple of minutes to find hers. I grabbed it and started back down the hall to her room about fifteen feet away. As I approached the door, I heard some shuffling noises coming from inside. I looked in and saw an empty chair with all the restraints still tied in place but hanging uselessly. My patient, "Houdini's mom," was back in her bed, all covered up and cozy, acting like nothing had happened. Right then and there, I realized that there was a lot more going on in that gal's head than any of us had imagined. I had to find something that would spark her interest in life again.

Every day for the next three months, we went through the same morning ritual. I would talk about everything I could think of. Did she sew? Crochet? Knit? Garden? Did she have children? What had she done for a living? Then one day as I opened the curtains, I said, "I bought a Great Dane puppy, and I'm going to go to the coast this weekend to pick him up. I'm so excited. He is so cute!"

I was shocked and astonished when I heard a tiny voice from the far corner of the room say, "I used to raise dogs. Samoyeds."

"Oh," I said, trying not to sound shocked and astonished. "I had a Samoyed when I was growing up. Jada was her name. They are so beautiful, all white and fluffy, and they are such nice dogs."

From that day on, we spoke every day. There was nothing wrong with her speech or her brain. When I asked her if she would like me to bring my puppy by to meet her, her face lit up at the thought of being able to cuddle a puppy again. I explained that they wouldn't let me bring the pup into the building (this was way before the acknowledgement of the value of therapy dogs), so we would have to make a plan to sneak her out to the pup. Finally, she was starting to look forward to life again.

Every day after breakfast, she wanted me to take her for a walk. She had to be strong enough to sneak out to see that puppy. It wasn't long before she didn't need any help; she could walk all by herself. That was when we knew she was ready. We decided that I would bring the pup the next day at about ten. Breakfast would be over, and most of the staff would be on a break. She would go to the back door of the ward that was the farthest away from the break room and open that door for us. She was so excited that she could hardly stand it.

Finally, the morning of our clandestine K-9 operation arrived. The look on her face when she opened the door and saw us standing there was priceless. We sat in the yard for about an hour that day, playing with the puppy while she told me happy stories about her experiences while raising her dogs. When I left that day, I felt good knowing that a little visit with a therapy dog had brought that wonderful woman back from the brink of no return. The last I heard, she had gotten strong enough to return home.

— Cheri Bunch —

22

In Times of Trouble

Smile, it's free therapy.
~Douglas Horton

Sitting in my home office wasn't a new phenomenon for me. I'd been working from my house for years. It was one of the few activities that hadn't been altered by the sweeping changes related to the COVID-19 pandemic. My dog, Winston, slumbered at my feet as he nearly always did, breaking the silence with occasional snorts and snores. For a short while, I could almost forget about what was going on and that the quarantine had changed nearly everything.

I couldn't see my children or grandchildren. Face-to-face gatherings were off the table. Church services had been canceled. Stores and restaurants were closed. When it became evident no one would be going anywhere for quite a while, virtual meetings became the new norm. I hustled to learn the new technology.

The first time I joined a meeting the voices of the participants filled my office. Winston's chin lifted, and his ears perked up. He looked at me with his head tilted to one side in bewilderment. Utterly confused by my interaction with people he couldn't see, Winston pawed my leg. Worried he might disrupt the meeting with a whine or bark, I picked him up and plunked him on my lap to calm him. When my gaze rose to the computer, there was Winston's face, plain as day, much more prominent than mine since he was closer to the camera than I was. He stared at the screen intently, just like all the other participants.

Embarrassed, my first instinct was to put him back on the floor, until I noticed something. The previously grim expressions on the faces of the other people I saw had softened into grins. I could feel the tension in my own shoulders begin to ebb and melt away. I felt more relaxed than I had in some time. Winston was a hit.

Perhaps it goes without saying, but from that moment on, my dog has become a popular attendee at almost any meeting I join. He's been transformed into a virtual therapy dog, bringing much-needed relief as he perches on my lap for workshops, family get-togethers, and church services. He'll even give (with a little help from me) an occasional wave of his paw. In a time of extraordinary fear and anxiety, when life is anything but normal, the simple act of inviting a dog to join us in this unexpected way has become a source of comfort and visibly reduced the stress on our calls.

The experience has been a powerful reminder to me that there are two things we truly need in times of trouble — a dog and a smile — both coming to you now via the Internet.

— Pat Wahler —

Chapter
3

Meant to Be

23

And Ringo Was His Name-O

*Engagement marks the end of a whirlwind romance
and beginning of an eternal love story.*
~Rajeev Ranjan

e had just arrived in Italy for our wedding. Finally, we had managed to plow through all the complicated paperwork needed to get married in a foreign country. Now, we just wanted to relax and enjoy our time there. We imagined a week of unequaled bliss.

I had been dreaming a lot about dogs lately. The dreams were jumbled, so there wasn't much clarity to them. However, the lyrics to a children's song would remain on my mind afterwards. "There was a farmer who had a dog, and Bingo was his name-o. B-I-N-G-O, B-I-N-G-O, B-I-N-G-O, and Bingo was his name-o." The dreams were perplexing, leaving me wondering what they meant. But I had a wedding to think about, so I didn't worry too much about my weird dreams at the time.

My fiancée and I had also been discussing the adoption of a dog from our local animal shelter, but we had put the plans on hold until we plowed through our matrimonial paperwork. That probably explained the convoluted dog dreams I was having. We planned to resume doggie discussions when we returned home after our honeymoon.

Coincidentally, at the same time, a scruffy-looking little Terrier was hanging around the hotel parking lot in Italy, watching our every move as we unloaded the luggage from our rental car. We had a few snacks left over from our road trip, and he looked hungry, so we put them on the ground where he would see them. As we rolled our bags inside, we saw him dash between the parked cars and scarf up the goodies. We made a mental note to give him more food if we ran into him again.

Our wedding was going to be a small, uncomplicated affair with just a few friends. There wasn't much planning to worry about at that point since we had already gathered all the documents we needed. So off we went to enjoy a delicious Italian dinner on the terrace of the hotel where we were staying—the same place that was organizing our wedding reception. As we were enjoying after-dinner drinks, my thoughtful future wife presented me with a trio of gifts.

I unwrapped each tiny box and was delighted to find a different ring in each one. I had always loved rings, but I hadn't worn any since I was a teenager because I kept losing them. This seemed like a good time to start wearing one again.

My fiancée is a planner, so I got a simple band for everyday use, a second ring with a beautiful ruby for dressy events, and a third ring for really special occasions. The last ring was custom-made from old gold jewelry she had melted down to form a new family crest that she had designed especially for us. It was original and irreplaceable. We would use it during our ceremony.

Meanwhile, we heard a commotion as the hotel staff shooed away a dog that had gotten inside the hotel. It was the same scrappy-looking one that we had fed in the parking lot. Apparently, he had seen us enter through the automatic sliding door and discovered that it would open for him, too. He scurried away from the terrace and hid in the bushes nearby. When the staff went back into the hotel, we furtively left him our dinner scraps.

The next day, when we were organizing our things, I decided to have a closer look at the rings my wife had given me during dinner the previous evening. Ring number one was lovely. Ring number two was stunning. And ring number three was... GONE! Trying not to panic, I checked through our things to see where I might have accidentally misplaced it. I couldn't find it anywhere.

I mumbled to my fiancée that I was going to get more stuff from the car, and then I dashed through the hotel, retracing our steps to the terrace from the night before. I stopped at the front desk on my way, explaining the situation to the clerk and mentioning that I didn't have the heart to say anything to my fiancée yet. "As you can see, I don't wear a wedding ring," he said. "After losing three of them, I stopped wearing them altogether." Behind him, the hotel manager piped up, "I lost mine the same day we were married, so you can imagine what my honeymoon was like."

A community brunch was being held at the hotel that morning. A woman standing in the reception area overheard our conversation and spoke up. "We can organize the children into a search party. If we make it into a game, it'll be fun for them to help out." So, the next thing I knew, dozens of kids were scouring the hotel and grounds. I was more than willing to offer a reward for the return of the ring. With great enthusiasm, the children searched and returned with all kinds of things, including metal nuts, spacers and even a ring that wasn't mine. I bought the kids a round of ice cream to reward them for their efforts, but I was back where I started.

I decided that I'd better come clean and 'fess up to my fiancée before she became my future ex-wife. I invited her back to the hotel terrace for a glass of wine and some lunch. There, I laid out the whole story of the loss of the ring and the fruitless search. As always, she was very understanding. However, I knew that she was disappointed and upset, notwithstanding the explanation. I felt awful about the whole thing.

Like the previous evening, we saw the little wirehaired dog skulking in the bushes. We hadn't noticed him earlier since we'd been absorbed in conversation. We hadn't eaten much of our lunch because we'd lost our appetites along with our ring. So, we gave him a generous amount of leftover food, cheering ourselves up with the thought that at least he would be having a great meal.

Once upstairs, we consoled ourselves by sitting out on our room balcony, romantically holding hands while gazing at the scenery. To my relief, it seemed like the wedding was still on.

As we relaxed, I thought I heard a slight noise at the door to our room. Listening closely, I definitely heard a whine and some scratching. Crossing the room quickly, I opened the door with a flourish, only to find no one there. Looking down, I saw the scruffy Terrier who had been stalking us for days. He had managed to sneak into the hotel again.

He looked up at me soulfully with his deep liquid eyes and dropped something out of his mouth. Incredibly, it was my ring! That night, he got some extra treats and stayed with us in the hotel. He attended our wedding and has been a family member ever since. In a variation of the song from my dreams, we named him after the ring he brought back to us.

And Ringo was his name-o.

— Sergio Del Bianco —

24

Tundra's Clone

*Rescuing dogs will tear your heart out, stomp on it
and bury it where you never think you will find it…
Then along comes another dog that digs it up
and gives it back to you.*
~Author Unknown

I rested my forehead against the cold window glass and stared at the weathered wooden cross in our back yard. It was a memorial for my dog Tundra who had been my constant companion. As I cried, I closed my eyes and pictured the companion who'd spent so many years by my side.

Golden fur. Alert ears. Smiling muzzle. Wise brown eyes shining with love.

My husband Jake walked into the room and pulled me into his arms. "Honey, I'm sorry you're hurting, but Tundra died last year. Maybe we should get a new dog."

I jerked back and wailed like a two-year-old throwing a grocery-store tantrum. "No dog could ever replace Tundra."

My daughter Patty tiptoed into the room holding out a tissue box like a shield. "Mom, I miss Tundra, too. But maybe looking at puppies will make us feel better."

Despite my protests, we drove to our local Humane Society. When we went inside we were greeted by a chorus of barking from the chain-link kennels lining the long room. The scent of damp fur and fresh doggie poo competed with the pungent disinfectant one of the volunteers was using as she cleaned.

Patty dashed from one dog to the next. A monstrously large Akita attracted my tall, weight-lifter husband. "Hey honey, the tag says he came from Japan." Jake reached into the cage and petted the huge beast.

I forced a smile, but my heart ached for my precious Tundra. To hide my rising tears, I walked to the end of the row.

There she stood.

My Tundra's clone. In miniature.

Same golden fur.

Same alert ears.

Same smiling muzzle.

Same wise brown eyes shining with love.

"Lord, am I losing my mind?" I whispered.

Tundra's tiny double pawed the kennel door as I knelt down. The force of her wagging tail shook her entire body. I knew this wasn't my dog. Still, I couldn't help whispering, "Tundra?"

The pup transformed into a bundle of canine craziness. Jumping, spinning, barking — she was the epitome of puppy joy.

Jake hurried over to see the commotion. His eyes widened. "Holy smoke, it's Tundra. Pint-sized."

Patty ran over and screeched to a stop. "It's a tiny Tundra!" She squatted next to me and gawked at Tundra's double.

The kennel attendant walked over, smiling. "Hi, I'm Frances. I'll bring her out."

She grabbed a leash and opened the kennel door. I crouched down, and the Tundra clone raced into my outstretched arms. A second later, I sat on the chilly concrete floor with the exuberant puppy commandeering my lap.

Jake watched the pup lick tears from my grinning face. My husband cast a longing glance at the Akita, sighed, and pointed to the pooch in my lap. "Frances, we want to adopt this puppy."

Frances bent and tickled the pup under her chin. "We found this little girl crouched in a drainpipe, shaking and sopping wet. Her owners have three more days to claim her. If not, she goes up for adoption on Monday."

I cuddled the pup closer. "Okay, we'll pick her up Monday."

Frances shook her head. "We adopt out on a first-come, first-served basis."

Realization dawned with sickening clarity. I asked, "You mean, someone else might get her?"

She nodded. "I'm sorry, but that's a possibility. The new owner must meet our adoption criteria, of course."

Patty jumped to her feet. "My mom needs this puppy so she can quit crying over her dead dog. This puppy is his clone!"

Frances patted Patty's shoulder. "I can tell your mom really likes this dog, but it's out of my hands. This puppy is exceptionally popular. If her owner doesn't claim her, the first qualified person here Monday gets her."

Frances lifted the pup from my lap and winked. "Fill out our paperwork and check back Monday morning."

I'd already lost my Tundra. Now, the thought of losing this puppy had me bawling. Patty groaned. "Sheesh, Dad, there she goes again."

The next day, Saturday, I risked a ticket speeding to the animal shelter. Tiny Tundra leapt up, pawing the chain-link door when she saw me.

Frances noticed and brought out the pup. I spent the morning playing with her while rivers of people flowed past. When potential rivals ogled Tundra's double, I tried projecting a "This Dog Is Taken" ray into their brains.

Sunday after church, I hurried back to visit my duplicate Tundra. A middle-aged woman cooed to her through the cage mesh. I sent up a panicked semi-prayer, "Lord, smite that woman with dog-fur allergy. Or turn her into a cat lover." Jerking out my wallet, I raced into the kennel's office and found Frances. "I'll pay extra to take her home today."

She lifted her hands. "I'm sorry, we have to follow protocol. The owner has until tonight to claim her. Call us tomorrow." At my stricken look, Frances said, "If this doesn't work out, there are plenty of other dogs available."

"Not for me."

Frances tapped her finger against her chin. "Get here tomorrow before we open. If you're the first approved applicant, she'll be yours." Frances held up a cautioning hand. "Even so, you can't take her directly home. We'd transport her to your veterinarian to be spayed. You'd get her from there."

Giddy with happiness, I rushed home to share the news, and then I called my boss to request Monday morning off.

He answered after multiple rings, and I explained my dilemma. He said, "Half of the office is sick. I'm sorry, but we need you at work."

Panic set in. Someone else would get my dog.

Jake stroked my back. "Calm down. I'll go there tomorrow morning after work."

"You work nights. By the time you get there, it'll be too late." I pictured tiny Tundra with the middle-aged, cooing woman. My overactive tear ducts sprang into action.

Patty strolled into the room. "Sheesh, Dad, not again!"

At her father's "Not now" signal, Patty sighed and wandered out.

Jake lifted my chin. "Everything will work out. You'll see."

I worried all Monday morning. Would Jake reach the shelter before someone else claimed my puppy? I drove to work trembling. Jake called soon after, sounding cheerful. "Swing by the vet tonight to pick up your dog."

I choked out, "Jake, you're the best," before bursting into happy tears.

That evening, we sat on the living room floor while Tiny Tundra romped across our legs. I snuggled against Jake. "Sorry for acting so crazy after Tundra died."

"You acted pretty crazy about Tiny Tundra, too, Mom," Patty chimed in.

Encircled by the precious family who'd supported me through the challenging past year, my tears welled up again. Patty scooped up Tiny Tundra and settled her in my lap. "Mom, enough blubbering!"

Laughing, I kissed Patty's cheek and cuddled our energetic pup. "Happy tears, honey. Only happy tears from now on."

— Jeanie Jacobson —

25

A Visit to the Scrappy Yard

Here, Gentlemen, a dog teaches us
a lesson in humanity.
~Napoleon Bonaparte

've always had a soft spot for Collies, and I was ready to bring another one home after losing my thirteen-year-old Collie to cancer. When a local rescue group advertised a Collie named Scrappy who they had saved from a high-kill shelter, I was ready. I arranged to meet him in hopes that he'd be a good match for our family.

As Scrappy circled the yard, he stopped to scratch every few seconds. "Why is he scratching so much?" I asked the rescue worker.

"Oh, it's just dry skin," she said. "He had a bath when I brought him home from the shelter, and his skin's still irritated. He also had his hair shaved around his ears because of mats the size of baseballs, and the new stubble can be itchy."

My husband Michael and I watched the gangly, malnourished, patchwork dog hobble around the yard on three legs as he attempted to scratch every which way with one of his back paws.

"Does he have any medical issues?" Michael asked.

"He had flystrike," she said.

"What's that?"

She cleared her throat. "Um... flies laid eggs in his ears and hatched." She must've seen me wince, so she added, "Antibiotics did the trick."

"Well, thank goodness." I glanced at Michael, who gave me the you-can't-still-be-interested look. I had to admit, my interest was waning a bit. But as I gazed into Scrappy's large amber eyes, I saw a dog who deserved a second chance.

"Oh, and a bladder infection, but it's being treated," she added.

"Hmm…" I nodded.

She turned to me. "One more thing. He's prone to hotspots."

"Is that all?" Michael asked, as I prayed that was it.

Meanwhile, Scrappy was zooming around the yard having a great time despite his various skin irritations and ailments. We decided it was like a scrap yard, but for unwanted dogs like Scrappy.

Michael turned to me and said, "Let's think about…"

"We'll take him," I blurted before Michael could object.

After we completed the adoption paperwork, Michael whispered, "I hope you're right about him. He has a lot of issues."

I smiled. "Don't we all?"

We loaded Scrappy into our van, and I sat beside him to comfort him on the ride home. I started stroking his hair with my fingers and discovered the real reason for his frenetic scratching: fleas. Hundreds and hundreds of them. Worried that my husband would turn the car around and heave the dog back into the Scrappy yard (from which he was salvaged), I waited until we reached our driveway to deliver the bad news.

"Um, honey, we have a little problem."

"What's that?" he asked.

"It seems the dog has a few… um… fleas."

"A few?"

"Well, maybe more than that. But don't worry, I've got this."

Michael wrinkled his brow. "You know, we could've waited for the right dog to come along. We didn't need to rush this."

"He is the right dog. You'll see." I marched into the house and drew a bath, convinced that Scrappy just needed some loving care. While I watched the fleas dive into the tub as if competing in an Olympic event, I sent Michael to the store to gather flea powder for the carpet and spray for the house. Thankfully, we already had preventative for our other two dogs. We'd attack the problem on all fronts.

Exhausted from the day's battle, we lay in bed that night while Scrappy scratched, licked, whined, moaned and rolled. Awakened numerous times by the dog's serenade of misery, Michael leaned in and asked, "You still think he's the right dog?"

"Of course," I said, resisting the urge to scratch my leg, knowing I'd become a host to the bloodsucking parasites.

After a few days, the flea infestation was under control, but then Michael discovered a new surprise. He pointed toward the grass. "Look."

"Do I want to?"

"Probably not."

I looked and grimaced. "Eww. Now we have our own Scrappy yard."

Off to the vet we went. Scrappy was living up to his name, both inside and out. A hookworm infestation required us to place all three of our dogs on medication. A bit later came the tapeworms, a byproduct of the fleas. Scrappy was spreading a whole lot more than love during his first month at our house.

Michael waved the latest vet bill in the air. "Do you realize we've spent over $700 on Scrappy already?"

"I know, but he needs us. He's had a rough go of it," I countered. "I think the name Scrappy has bad mojo. Maybe that's why he keeps getting sick." The dog walked beside me as he always did from room to room, a true Velcro dog. "Just wait…" Scrappy came to a halt and sat down immediately. He did not move as I walked away. I looked at Michael. "Did you see that?"

"What?"

My intuition told me that our rescue was about to show us his well-mannered side. I commanded him to come, and he did. He sat in front of me and looked upward, waiting for his next command. "Down," I said. And he lay down. "Over." He rolled over before sitting back up. "Shake." He offered me his paw. Unsure of the extent of his training, I asked, "High-five?" He tapped my hand with his right paw. "Go," I said, and he slinked away. "Come." Obediently, he came back and sat before me with his eager eyes. He licked my hand, and I tweaked his ear.

"Well, look at that," Michael said. "He's not so scrappy after all."

"He's not scrappy at all. I've been thinking, and I think he looks like a Watson."

"Much better," Michael agreed.

"My Dear Watson." The dog leaned against me as if to approve.

After several weeks of love and proper medical care, Watson started to resemble Lassie, with his robust energy and undying loyalty to our family. His wounds healed, and he settled into our home as if he'd been there all along.

Snuggled up with Michael on the sofa, My Dear Watson lay his head across my husband's lap, and I recalled the dog we'd nearly left behind—a dog so worn and broken, tossed into a shelter through no fault of his own when his eighty-year-old owner moved into a nursing home.

I glanced over at his revitalized Collie coat as he buried his muzzle deeper into the throw blanket and sighed. A little polishing was all that he needed to shine. Watson blessed our house for the next eleven years with his love and loyalty, and we continue to treasure the dog who taught us that gems can be discovered anywhere, even in a Scrappy yard.

— Cathi LaMarche —

26

From Puddle to Poodle

*The gift which I am sending you is called a dog
and is in fact the most precious and
valuable possession of mankind.*
~Theodorus Gaza

As a single mom, it took all my energy to guarantee my sons, ages eight and six, had food, clothes, and a roof over our head. When they asked for a dog one Christmas, I said, "Wait until you're older."

A year later, they asked again. I explained we had to solve two problems first. I worked full-time, and dogs were happiest with someone at home. Dogs also needed a fenced-in yard. Owning one meant spending money for new necessities like a license, food, and veterinarian fees.

My older son offered to donate his allowance. His brother said he would deliver newspapers. They had me in tears.

Meanwhile, our car was wearing out. Its engine still ran, but its body was so rusted that when I drove along rainy streets, water from puddles splashed through tiny holes in the car's floor and into the back seat until we had a couple of inches of standing water. My boys were not in danger, but they had to lift their feet to keep from getting splashed with mud or water. They laughed, but it wasn't funny.

We cut costs by sharing a rental home with another single mom with two sons. Our kids had fun, and Judy and I did our best to take turns getting home to watch the kids, start dinner, and keep things normal. Soon, her boys wanted a dog, too.

"We need our own place first," I told my boys. "Once I buy a car and get a better job, then we can get a dog." Their smiles drooped. Clearly, we'd have this conversation again.

Meanwhile, I started looking for a reliable car that wouldn't have a puddle inside it on rainy days. We lived in Texas. My dad sold cars in Oregon, too far away to help, but he sent suggestions.

"Don't go to a dealership. Decide what year and model you want and search the classifieds for sale by owner. Sometimes, people have to move suddenly or settle debts. Hunt for a good deal."

I bought the weekend newspaper and crossed off ads. I had worked overtime and saved enough so I could offer cash, but probably not enough to buy a newer car. But then I read: "Must sacrifice two-year-old Ford Galaxy, top condition, low miles."

Wow! That night was the ad's first run. Judy offered to drive me over there in case I got the car and needed to drive it home.

I hired a babysitter and off we went. Thirty miles later, the address led to a pleasant brick home with a real-estate "Sold" sign out front. A large RV filled the driveway next to a shiny, late-model blue Ford Galaxy.

"This might be too good to be true," I told Judy. A pleasant-looking young man answered the door. He and his wife had sold their home to travel nationwide to develop the next stage of their business. Their car ran like a dream and was still under warranty. They accepted my cash offer.

As we signed papers, the seller asked, "Do you have kids?"

"Two boys. So does Judy. Why?"

"This car has a bonus." He left the room and returned with a miniature white Poodle in his arms, petting her soft, curly fur. "We love Lacy Brooke, but we can't take her with us. She's yours."

His wife said, "She loves children, and her shots are up-to-date. Here are her toys, leash and collar, two bags of dog food — everything you need.

Judy and I exchanged glances. "How can you resist?" she asked. "She's a cuddly, living stuffed toy."

"Nothing like my sons and I imagined," I said, "but still…" When I petted her, her perfect pink tongue rasped my fingers.

We drove home in two cars. "Boys, come see what we've got." Once they inspected the outside of the car, I opened the door to show our surprise. "Meet Lacy Brooke; she's ours." I held her out for them to meet, and they erupted in happy shouts.

Lacy Brooke thrived. We all adored her. Animals know when they're loved, and she returned every bit of affection with constant licks and tail wags.

We found what our family really needed — no puddles and a new Poodle.

— Delores E. Topliff —

27

Destiny Dogs

Dogs come into our lives to teach us about love;
they depart to teach us about loss. A new dog
never replaces an old dog. It merely expands the heart.
~Author Unknown

Morgan, a Golden Retriever puppy, was part of the package when I started dating his owner, Steven. After a few years, Morgan stood with us as the ring bearer at our wedding. The three of us set up housekeeping in a cozy, two-bedroom apartment. Steven worked long hours as a chef, and Morgan and I became inseparable.

Before long, Steven wanted to get another dog so we could each have one. The three of us went to pick out a Labradoodle from a litter of new puppies. It was easy to decide on Cuervo because he picked us, following Morgan around the second they saw each other. The four of us were one happy family.

"Stop growing older," I would scold Morgan playfully but a little sadly, as I pretended to rub away the white that inevitably grows through a Golden's facial hairs with time. But Steven's previous Golden Retriever had lived to be fourteen years old, so I looked forward to many fun years ahead of us.

No one is guaranteed even one more year, though, not even the sweetest, most loving Golden Boy. Morgan was granted only half the average Golden lifespan. Weeks before his seventh birthday, his usually stocky body began to lose some bulk, and I detected a mass on his stomach. The vet ruled out cancer but advised that surgery to remove the benign tumor was risky.

Over the next two months, we hoped a low-carb diet might shrink the tumor. I fried up vegetables in coconut oil for him that seemed to help, but one morning when he went outside to use the bathroom, he lay down and never got up again.

I didn't think I would ever stop crying. A week after losing Morg, Steven encouraged me to go to the local animal shelter to pick out another dog, hoping that would stem the tide of tears.

"I miss Morg, too," he said kindly, "but there are many dogs that would love to share our wonderful home."

"No. Morgan was irreplaceable."

"Of course, he was," Steven agreed. "Another puppy wouldn't be a substitute for Morg. It would be a brand-new relationship for you to enjoy."

I buried my face in the sofa cushion.

Our friends began to worry about me. After a month, my friend Gabby coaxed me into coming to her apartment for pizza and a movie. I hadn't left home for anything besides work and knew I needed to.

After an evening of escapism watching *Mamma Mia!* I grabbed an Uber home.

"Headed home early on a Saturday night?" the driver asked, glancing at me in his rearview mirror.

"Yes, I need to get home to my Labradoodle," I said, staring blankly out my window.

"Yeah? I have a Labradoodle, too. They're cute!"

I like anyone who likes dogs and managed a smile. "Yes, we love our Cuervo."

"My Murphy is a handful, though! And expensive — well, you know. He's almost a year old now, so he just recently got clipped, got shots, dewormed, neutered, and then the food, snacks, toys…"

"Yeah, it adds up."

"I love Murphy, but we don't get to enjoy each other much. It's not fair that he's been lonely. I've even had to hire a dog-walker," he sighed. "I've been thinking about finding a better home for him."

"Our home needs another dog," I said softly before I could stop myself.

"What?"

"We used to have two dogs, but we lost the older one to a tumor. It killed me." My eyes filled with the tears that had become a part of my daily existence. "I mean, if you ever do look for a home for Murphy, we'd love to meet him."

The car arrived at my driveway, and I started to get out. "I know it's a big decision, but you have my number if…"

"Can I see Cuervo?" the driver asked.

He followed me up the walkway, and we paused on the front step. Through the picture window, we could see Cuervo surrounded by dog toys, trying to pull his favorite stuffed shark out of Steven's hands. Steven wouldn't let go, so Cuervo pulled him from the sofa onto the floor, with Steven laughing the whole way down.

"Here's my card," the driver said. "I'll bring Murphy by tomorrow afternoon for a playdate, and we'll see how they get along if that's okay."

"Wow. Yes! Thank you… I never pictured having two Doodles. But now that I am, I can't stop! I have such a good feeling about it, and I hope you do, too — Rick," I added, glancing at his card.

Rick did have a good feeling about it. He and Murphy showed up the next day, and I held my breath as the rambunctious pup bounced toward Cuervo. The dogs sniffed each other, and I pulled out my bag of Milk-Bone biscuits.

"Who wants a treat?" I asked, and the dogs ran to me.

"Sit," I said, knowing Cuervo would. I was pleasantly surprised when Murphy did, too. They each took their treat.

"Shake, Murphy," Rick added, and Murphy lifted his paw. I shook it, stared into his big brown eyes, and started to cry. It was just too perfect an introduction after everything had been so wrong.

"So glad to meet you, Murphy," I whispered.

Rick sat and watched the ballgame with Steven while I sat on the floor, watching the puppies play together happily and telling myself I wasn't dreaming.

"Well, I have to go," Rick said after twenty minutes had passed without incident, walking toward the door.

"Okay, we'll be here. Let us know what you decide," Steven said.

Rick glanced at Murphy, who was following him. He bent and scratched the pup's ears, and then asked him to sit.

"This is a doggie dream home." He smiled sadly. "I knew it last night. Let's just rip the Band-Aid off right now. I have all his stuff in the car; I'll go get it."

When he returned, Rick placed a huge box in Steven's arms and passed me a bag of dog food. With my free hand, I held out a $100 bill.

"Thank you so much," I said through tears, finally happy ones. "I am never replacing my Morgie, but I needed this little guy and didn't even know it until now."

"Keep that. You'll need it. Murphy's a big eater!"

"Thanks, Rick, really. Come visit him any time," Steven said. Rick waved and got in the car without looking back.

"Wow. It's meant to be." I glanced at Steven, a huge grin on my face. I dropped to the floor between Murphy and Cuervo, and they both started licking my face.

"I think I see the old Jan coming back," he said with a grin.

Steven snapped a quick picture of me and the pups as I smiled a real smile for the first time in weeks. When he showed it to me, I saw that Morgan was in the framed picture above me on the mantel, smiling down on us. He will forever be my first and favorite puppy love, but there is always room when destiny provides another dog.

— Janette Aldridge —

28

A Puff of Magic

*Acquiring a dog may be the only time a person
gets to choose a relative.*
~Author Unknown

I have decided that nothing happens by chance. I am sure of this because of how Puff and I met one hot Saturday afternoon. I was about to go into the music store on Whyte Avenue when I saw her standing in front of the entrance. As I moved toward the door, she suddenly flopped down on the ground and lay still, exposing a smooth pink belly.

"That dog has heatstroke," said a man behind me. I bent down and picked her up. She was more puppy than dog and lay like a baby in my arms, staring up at me with large, trusting eyes. I opened the door and walked inside. "Do you have some water I can give this dog?" I asked.

The clerk shook his head. "Just leave it. It doesn't belong here. Someone will come back and fetch it."

I knew I had never seen this dog before, but something about the way she looked at me gave me a sense of déjà vu, a memory from some past time. She needed me.

I carried her along the street back to my car and placed her next to me in the passenger seat. As I drove, I could feel her gaze on me. I snatched a quick glance every so often, but each time she averted her eyes, as if it were discourteous to stare. In comfortable silence experienced only with a close friend, I drove her to my home.

Strangely, she took no water when she arrived inside. But she did allow me to bathe and towel-dry her long, curly white fur until it looked as fluffy as a powder puff.

Puff, I thought. The perfect name.

In the kitchen, I placed an old quilt inside a box. Puff seemed to know it was for her. She walked straight past the cat, who regarded her first with curiosity and then disdain, and climbed inside. She rested her head on her paws, regarding the cat and me until the children came home.

"She's a lamb," they both said and hugged her. She turned over onto her back, and they rubbed her shiny belly. She needed no enticing into the garden to chase a woolen sock rolled into a ball. Through long blades of grass, she gamboled, barely visible.

"We're glad she found us," the children said.

Three days later, the advertisement appeared: "Lost. One white Terrier-Poodle. Answers to the name of Augy. Reward."

The address was for a used clothing shop four doors away from the music store.

When I arrived at the clothing shop later that evening, I had an uneasy feeling. The young man behind the counter greeted the dog warmly, ruffled her fur, and thanked me profusely for taking such good care of her. I knew this man loved his dog. He had paid for an ad and offered a reward — even if it was used clothing. I had been sure I was doing the right thing bringing her back, but I had a nagging feeling that something was wrong.

I declined the reward and left the shop alone, wishing immediately I had kept Puff.

The next two weeks, I could not keep Puff out of my thoughts. Then one evening when I returned late from work, my son was waiting for me at the door. "That man phoned," he said.

It could have been any number of men who had called, yet I surprised even myself when I said, "You mean the man from the used clothing shop?" I phoned back immediately.

The young man's words were totally unexpected.

"We have to move to an apartment and can't take the dog. My

wife and I thought that since you took such good care of her, you might like to keep her."

Puff was waiting at the door when I reached the shop. She stood up, wagged her tail and gave me a knowing look. Then she rolled over onto her back for a tummy rub.

As they say, nothing happens by chance. Some things are just meant to be. I think Puff knew that all along.

— Lesley Belcourt —

29

Finding Bleu

*Before you get a dog, you can't quite imagine
what living with one might be like; afterward,
you can't imagine living any other way.*
~Caroline Knapp

Isabella wanted a dog. Desperately. Being twelve-and-a-half meant she was able to assume responsibility. She would feed, walk, and bathe the dog, she assured us repeatedly.

I was easy to convince. If Isabella wanted a dog, well, why not? Isabella was a great student, working hard at ballet and piano, and reading constantly.

I expected Nick to be in our corner on the great dog debate, but alas it was more complicated than that. Nick was eight and more concerned about his stuffed pigs. Would the dog eat them? Would they be mistaken for toys and shredded as if destined for a pulled-pork sandwich? Nick was on Team Pig, not Team Dog.

The big barrier to getting a dog, though, was my beautiful wife Dawn. If there was one aspiration that drove Dawn, it was cleanliness. She kept the house immaculate. And if she knew one thing about dogs, it was this — dogs are messy. They bring in mud from outside. They pee; they poop; they throw up; they shed; they tear up furniture. And what about Nick's pigs?

Despite all those concerns, after months of debate, Isabella got the green light. We could get a dog. But not just any dog. It had to be small, but not *too* small. Also, it had to be male. Dawn was concerned about the dog having periods. Is that a thing? Anyway, male it would be. Also, it could not shed. Well, what dogs don't shed? There were several apparently: Scottish Terriers, Yorkshire Terriers, Poodles.

But I had my own requirement. It had to be a rescue. I wanted to give a home to a dog who needed one.

After asking all the dog lovers I knew, I learned that PAWS was a top shelter in the Philadelphia area. They had a strong reputation for treating their rescues (dogs and cats alike) with love and affection. Serendipitously, after checking their website, I learned that the very next day was the Mutt Strut at the Philadelphia Navy Yard. What a great opportunity to find our dog! Surely, there would be dozens to choose from and we could leave with our perfect match.

But the forecast called for possible rain. And the PAWS website said one needed to be pre-approved to take a dog home from the Mutt Strut. Discouraged, I decided that fate had intervened. Our dog must not be there. So, I stayed home, paid bills, did some chores, and went to work on Monday.

The best part about going to work on a Monday is I get to exchange my standard, "Hey, how ya doin'?" with a "Hey, how was your weekend?" That Monday, I got an unexpected response from a young co-worker.

Amanda explained that she had spent the day before at the Philadelphia Navy Yard volunteering for PAWS. It had been the biggest event of the year. Exasperated, she explained that she spent the whole day with a single dog, and she had really messed up. Because she had given this one dog so much attention, he hadn't gotten adopted. People must have thought that she was adopting him! Amanda was heartbroken. She was completely in love with this dog and had inadvertently ruined his life. She was beside herself. And a little obsessed, to be honest.

"So, what's he like?" I asked.

Amanda explained that he was the most affectionate dog ever. She was sitting in the grass with her legs crossed, and he came right up and put his little head on her thigh, looking up at her with his brown eyes. She scratched his belly, and he rolled over and just lay there, enjoying the scratch. Then he crawled between Amanda's legs as if they were his doggy bed and fell asleep as she stroked his furry white body.

"So, why didn't you just adopt him?" I wondered aloud. Amanda explained that she was not allowed to have dogs in her apartment. She had left her own dog at home with her parents when she moved to Center City. There was nothing she could do for him.

"So, what breed is he?"

"He is a little Poodle mix, about a dozen pounds maybe." Amanda was confirming all my hopes. He was the right sex, right size, right breed. It was eerie.

"I am going to go meet him," I said. Amanda was thrilled. I was thrilled, too.

I showed up at PAWS and filled out an adoption application. There was some barking and lots of activity, but every animal looked healthy and cared-for.

Then, I got to meet him. I sat on the floor, crossing my legs, and sure enough, this adorable, fuzzy white Poodle mix came and rested his little head on my thigh. Was this just his shtick or was he really this affectionate? I scratched his belly for a bit, and I was sold. Hassan was going to be our dog.

Yes, his name was Hassan. The worker explained that they had to come up with creative names for the rescues. Not everyone could be Fluffy and Snowball.

I went home that night with big news. I had found our dog! I told my wife the story excitedly, committed to making Hassan part of the family. Suddenly, her prior agreement to get a dog seemed like a tentative maybe instead of a definite yes. She would need to meet Hassan.

That Wednesday, Dawn, Nick, and Isabella piled into the car and met me in Philadelphia after work. When we entered PAWS, I could tell Dawn was hesitant. It smelled like animals. Did she want her house to smell like that?

When we met Hassan, the kids loved him immediately. He snuggled up to them, accepting their gentle strokes docilely. Dawn wasn't so sure. Feeling the pressure, she relented eventually, but insisted on naming rights. "I want to call him Bleu as in bleu cheese." We took Bleu home.

That was two years ago. Bleu is such an important part of our family now. He still enjoys his belly scratches and walks with me every morning to see the kids off to school. He sits with Dawn during the day and guards the door as she works in the house.

The pigs survived without a scratch. Nick is even ready to get another dog. He wants to name him Rojo since that's a color in a foreign language, just like Bleu.

I wonder a lot about what role fate had in bringing Bleu into our lives. Was I supposed to go to the Navy Yard that Sunday? Was I supposed to have met Bleu there? Or would that have somehow interfered in what now seems to have been destined.

Sometimes, I suppose, if you keep your eyes, ears and heart open, and if you are lucky, fate will find you. Just like Bleu found us, and just like we found Bleu.

— Tim Law —

30

My Beloved

*Falling in love consists merely in uncorking
the imagination and bottling the common sense.*
~Mandy Hale

I t was a long-distance love affair. He was from cosmopolitan Toronto, and I was from small-town Regina. In many ways, we lived worlds apart. I knew at the outset that I was several years his senior, but I dismissed the gap as relatively unimportant. I was never one to be easily discouraged in such matters of the heart.

Admittedly, our lifestyles were also as different as night and day. With Tibetan roots, Keiko's ancestors were raised royally in temples amidst snow-capped mountains at the "Roof of the World." His name, pronounced "Kee-ko," translates to "beloved." With the best life had to offer, including guards on the premises, his family was accustomed to a life of great privilege and rich culture.

On the other hand, I am a simple prairie girl from Saskatoon, from a farming background, and a combination of German, Austrian, and Irish.

Our chance encounter was interesting, to say the least. I was first introduced to Leah, a friend of a friend who had an array of great photos of him on Facebook. I was drawn immediately to his beautiful, jewel-like brown eyes and a smart-looking, full moustache that framed a warm smile. He had a noticeable overbite, but then, so did I. His chest and broad shoulders appeared to be muscular. He was definitely appealing. I was excited to meet him!

I hadn't had anyone quite like him in my life for some time, particularly since my children had gone. But with winter coming, I felt ready for meaningful companionship. The prospect of doing some travelling and sightseeing together up the road was also exciting.

Several e-mails and telephone conversations followed. Early on, I learned that Keiko was very bright and well-mannered, although somewhat shy, whereas I was the outgoing type. We were both short in stature but had attitude to make up for any deficiencies in height. He was athletic and loved fast-paced runs and workouts. I shared his enthusiasm for invigorating daily walks through nearby tree-lined streets and parks. Fresh air, the delight of birds flitting in the branches overhead, and the cool ground beneath one's feet were all a magnificent part of embracing the beautiful, natural world around us. Biking was also on my list of enjoyable physical activities, as well as swimming and whirlpooling. He wasn't especially fond of water sports, but relished a good neck rub or full-body massage.

Luxury vehicles had become part of Keiko's life. Leah, his socialite adoptive mother, was equally at home in her late-model Z4 M roadster or their shared lipstick-red BMW convertible.

In contrast, I was driving a ten-year-old Ford Contour with a rear spoiler and a tight-fitting black leather bra. However, of late I'd been giving serious thought to upgrading to a newer Ford Escape 4x4 with heated seats and sunroof, or a snappy Jeep Liberty. Certainly, there would be adjustments to make if we were to become an "item."

Our epicurean delights also varied. He was accustomed to regularly savouring tasty appetizers and being served a wide variety of gourmet meals, including hearty rice and lamb, and beef with plenty of thick gravy. I was a meat-and-potatoes kid at heart, but often chose to whip up a no-fuss toasted tomato or grilled-cheese sandwich at lunch hour. Being a busy working woman, I was also fond of patronizing a local drive-thru restaurant such as Arby's and having a bite on the run to save precious time. Over the years, I had mastered the fine art of ingesting a roast beef "bunwich" at a red light!

Arrangements were finally in place for Keiko to come to me in the "Land of the Living Skies." His flight was booked to arrive right after

Canadian Thanksgiving weekend, which seemed most appropriate. Happily, I made preparations to meet him, hoping that everything would work out. Several "what ifs" loomed in my mind all the same. Would he want me as much as I wanted him? There still seemed to be many unanswered questions. It would be a drastic change for both of us.

Finally, October 12th arrived — a day that was indelibly marked on the calendar and in my heart. I dressed, fixed my hair, put on make-up, and headed for the airport to meet him. After locating a parking stall near the terminal, I entered and waited alongside many others gathered to "meet and greet" loved ones. I could hardly wait to be face-to-face with my new sweetheart for the first time.

The crowd had all but cleared when we finally made eye contact. Keiko was even more handsome than his Facebook photos. He looked in my direction and appeared to be pleased. I was overjoyed! He was affectionate when I gave him a big hug before we headed for my vehicle.

I could hardly wait to introduce my husband to Keiko. After all, he was an almost perfect little Shih Tzu.

— Kathryn Leier —

31

A Senior Dog Named Ernest

A really companionable and indispensable dog is an
accident of nature. You can't get it by breeding
for it, and you can't buy it with money.
It just happens along.
~E.B. White

The big, scraggly Golden Retriever burst into our home, pulling the rescue worker at the end of the leash. He shook his head vigorously and lunged toward everything he set his sights on. Clearly, he hadn't had a bath in years. His dingy reddish-gold hair lay matted on his neck and back. His warm eyes and goofy grin, however, stole my heart. I glanced at his graying muzzle. Another senior dog. Could we really do this again?

Years ago, my husband Mike and I had adopted our first senior dog—an eleven-year-old Golden Retriever. He'd been abandoned and on his own for who knows how long. I'd hesitated. What if he had expensive medical concerns? What if he had behavioral issues we couldn't correct? And… what if we fell in love with him and he broke our hearts?

But we took a chance. We adopted him and we did fall in love. And he did break our hearts. But then one day, another senior dog who needed a home found us. And another. By then, we realized that our first old Golden had come to us in order to open our hearts and set us on our mission of rescuing senior dogs.

We discovered that there is so much we love about senior dogs. They are already housebroken. They lounge at our feet in the yard and are happy with our leisurely pace when walking around the block. Sunday strolls are just our style. Senior dogs are happy to nap while I work at my desk. And they are eager to please and already know the rules. Living with a senior dog fits our lifestyle.

Then we lost two beloved old friends within a week of each other. Saying goodbye to them was one of the most difficult things I've ever had to do. We missed them terribly, but we also didn't want to wait too long to fill our home with a dog to love again. I barely knew how to navigate my morning without a pooch to let out the back door and a bowl to fill with kibble. It was too sad coming home from an errand without a furry friend greeting us at the door, jumping for joy at our arrival. There was no warm companion to snuggle with me on my living room chair. Still, my heart reminded me, loving and losing are hard.

Then this big, messy Golden Retriever bounded into our home. "He's been kept in a cage," the rescue worker said, shaking her head. "He's a little wound up!"

"Kept in a cage?" I asked. "How did this happen?"

She told me that the previous owner had no interest in the dog, so she kept him caged up. "Fortunately, she finally agreed to surrender him. She told us, 'I didn't take good care of him, but who cares?'"

I gasped. How could anyone feel that way about another living thing?

"Can you imagine, she let us lead him away… didn't even say goodbye."

The dog sat down and scratched hard at his neck. Poor guy was uncomfortable. Then he ran up and pushed his head under my arm to pat him. As I rubbed him all over, I discovered that he'd been let outside just enough to become covered in ticks.

"Looks like he needs us," Mike said, and there was no question in our minds that this unruly, unkempt, sweet dog was our new best friend.

We named him Ernest because he seemed so sincere. We always re-name a rescue dog when we get one — new life, new name. We didn't want him to associate his name with anything negative. We gave Ernest a good grooming, removed six ticks, and trimmed his nails. Ernest just looked at us, grinning the whole time.

Ernest was so excited to be out of a cage that he ran around the whole house and yard. "You don't have to worry about being locked up now," I said. He was so happy to be free; he couldn't get enough of the human touch. He loved to be patted. He loved it so much that he developed a bad habit. Any time we stopped patting him, he barked, loud. The minute we resumed, he relaxed and remained quiet. I figured it would just take time for him to feel secure that we'd always pat him whenever he wanted. I was right. After several weeks, he stopped the barking habit. But he still loved to be patted all the time.

I knew right away that Ernest would make a great therapy dog. Sometimes, when a dog we adopt seems like a good fit, we take him for therapy-dog training. Ernest seemed perfect.

He walked into class calmly, unlike the first day when he had bounded into our house full of pent-up energy. He was friendly to people and polite around other dogs. He didn't react to loud noises and sudden movements. He wasn't afraid of wheelchairs and walkers. Ernest passed his test with flying colors. He's now certified with Therapy Dogs International and proudly wears his red therapy-dog bandanna. He works at nursing homes, libraries, colleges, and elementary schools. He even went to the New York State Capitol to help employees there during stressful times at work.

Rescuing Ernest hasn't been without its challenges. Sometimes, he has trouble managing the stairs when he's tired. He's had issues with food and seasonal allergies. And he was diagnosed with cancer, but he had surgery and is more than two years cancer-free!

Living with and loving a senior dog aren't always easy, but we've realized we wouldn't have it any other way. Ernest fills our hearts with love and is living out his golden years with a family that cares about him. The dog who lived most of his life locked up in a cage is now free to enjoy the life he was meant to live. And he gets patted just as much as he could ever want.

—Peggy Frezon—

32

Prayer and Garage Sales

A dog teaches a boy fidelity, perseverance,
and to turn around three times before lying down.
~Robert Benchley

I was midway through my eighth pregnancy when nine-year-old Josiah's prayer life changed. Every night, I gathered the children to pray before going to bed. Beginning with the youngest, each person prayed aloud. I finished the round.

On this particular night, after three-year-old Hannah and six-year-old Estee had said their prayers, Josiah began his request. "Lord, could I please have a black Lab puppy and a set of drums?"

My eyes popped open. Though I didn't say anything, a black Labrador puppy and a set of drums were not on my prayer list. Over the next four months, as I inched toward my due date, Josiah prayed for a black Lab puppy and a set of drums every night.

In March, we welcomed Lilyanna Faith into the family. The following week, my husband left on his first business trip since the birth of the baby.

"How are you doing?" he asked me the Saturday morning after he returned.

"Life is galloping way out in front of me," I reported. "I feel completely overwhelmed."

"That's understandable considering you just had a baby, and I was away for a week. I have a handful of errands to run. How about I take the children with me while you and Lilyanna take a long nap," he suggested.

"Hot dog," I agreed.

Twenty minutes after the happy band hit the road, the phone rang. It was Josiah. "Mama, can I keep this black Lab puppy I'm holding? I promise to eat all my vegetables, clean my room, and do my chores."

"Put your father on the phone," I said through clenched teeth. Josiah handed the phone to his father.

"What," I asked, "are you doing?"

"It's like this," he explained. "We were driving past a farm, and there was a big sign in the yard that said, 'Free Puppies.' Knowing how overwhelmed you're feeling, I looked the other way and pretended not to notice the sign. But the children spotted the sign. 'Look, Dad,' they announced, 'free puppies! Black Lab puppies! It's the answer to Josiah's prayers!' So, what's a dad to do?"

"What's a dad to do?" I echoed. "Put Josiah back on the phone."

"Hi, Mama," Josiah said hopefully.

"Look, son," I outlined, "are you going to train this dog so it's a good, obedient dog?"

"Oh, I will," Josiah promised.

"And clean up?"

"I'll clean up after the dog," Josiah assured.

"I don't need another project, son. I have plenty to do. If you bring this dog home, it will be your dog to train, care for, and clean up after. Deal?"

"Deal. I'll take care of the dog."

"Okay, son, bring home your puppy. I can't wait to see him."

Josiah named the pup Old Dan after the male puppy in the book, *Where the Red Fern Grows*.

The following weekend, I went garage sale-ing. It was Josiah's turn to have some alone time with me, so he scratched Old Dan behind his floppy ears, jumped into the passenger seat of the van, and away we went. At the first garage sale we came to, we spied a complete set of drums, assembled and ready to play. I looked at Josiah.

Josiah looked at me.

I grinned. "What's a mom to do?"

Josiah emptied his savings and proudly brought home his Roxx drums. A week later, he played those garage-sale drums in a fiddle show.

Under Josiah's training, Old Dan went on to become a 4-H grand champion dog in obedience. Old Dan played with the children, minded his manners for the most part, and barked when someone came to the house. He also had a singsong way of verbalizing his feelings.

Neither the drum set nor the dog was on my prayer list, but they were on Josiah's. My son learned that all good things come to those who pray and go to garage sales. Several years later, Josiah again scratched Old Dan behind the ears before leaving for the military.

On Thanksgiving, the girls and I watched the road. Josiah had gotten leave to come home for the holiday. At last, his car turned into the driveway, where he parked and got out.

There stood my grown son, tall in his uniform, grinning at all of us pouring out onto the front porch. But we stood back and let Old Dan go first to meet Josiah. Hesitant at first, Dan got close, and then his tail wagged, and he whined his singsong welcome. In a moment, Josiah was sitting on the ground, and Dan was in his arms, the two lost in the joy of each other's company like they had done throughout Josiah's growing-up years.

While his mother and sisters saw the man who had come home to us, Old Dan recognized his boy.

— PeggySue Wells —

33

For the Love of Greta

There are two ways of spreading light — to be the
candle or the mirror that reflects it.
~Edith Wharton

For months, I moped around the house depressed. My dog had died, and I missed her terribly. My boyfriend Brad said, "Maybe you should adopt another dog. It will make you feel better. And there are some really nice pups at the SPCA right now that desperately need good homes. I know, I looked. Why don't you go get one?"

"I'm not ready," I said. "Maybe next year."

Brad knew I was in the habit of making donations to the local animal shelters. One day, he stopped by the house with a trunk full of dog food. "C'mon," he said. "We're going for a ride. And while we're there, we'll have a look around."

"I told you I'm not ready."

"Yeah, I remember," he said. "I didn't say you had to adopt one. But maybe just looking will help you come out of your funk."

"I doubt it," I said. But I was wrong. While we were looking, an adorable dog — a German Shepherd type — came out of her pen and put her head against the gate so we could reach in and pet her. After one look into her sad brown eyes, I was hooked. "Let's take Greta home," I said.

Although almost fully grown, Greta was still a mischievous, un-housebroken, lightning-fast puppy. She loved going to the dog park, where her favorite activity was scaring me half to death. During her first disappearance from the park, she broke into a man's home and fell asleep on his bed. The second time, he found her in his garage with her tail sticking out of a huge bag of dog food. And one day, she swam downstream to a farm where she terrorized the horses.

Despite all her antics, I loved her dearly.

But suddenly, Greta changed. One snowy night while out for our walk, a mammoth snowplow drove past us. Greta ducked for cover under an SUV. Then she refused to walk at that end of the street. The first springtime thunderstorm sent her running into the closet. And the fireworks my neighbors lit in their back yard on the Fourth of July sent her into a panic. After that, she wouldn't walk at night at all.

Night after night, I tried in vain to get her to go outside with me. "C'mon, baby girl. You can do this," I said enthusiastically. And each night she ran into the closet. But one night, she stood at the top of the stairs for a long time. Little by little, I made progress. Six weeks later, she walked out the front door with me. But her triumph was short-lived. We got to the end of the street, and she froze. *She remembers the snowplow,* I thought. We were back to square one.

The following summer, I enrolled in a five-day workshop. Being gone all day made me nervous. I hoped the drone of the air conditioner would diminish any loud noises enough for Greta to stay calm. But on the last day of class, it was breezy, and I forgot to close the windows. Halfway through class, I grabbed my books and made a mad dash for the door.

"Everything all right, Ms. Lush?" the instructor called out.

"No," I said. "I have to go. My dog is in trouble."

I don't know how I knew that, but I had to get home fast. When I pulled into the driveway, I heard Greta barking in the back yard. *I didn't leave her outside,* I thought. But she wasn't in the back yard. She had jumped out the window and was standing on the overhang to the garage. I ran upstairs and pulled her in through the torn screen.

"Thank God, you're all right," I said, holding onto my frightened dog. "Don't you ever do that again." I kept all the windows shut after that.

One hot morning, however, after returning from a quick trip to the grocery store, there was a knock at the door.

"Hi, John," I said to my neighbor. "What can I do for you?"

"I just wanted to let you know that my son saved your dog's life today."

"What do you mean? She's right here, and she's been in the house all morning."

"My son said she ripped the screen out of your upstairs window and tried to jump out."

"Oh, no," I said, realizing I had forgotten to close my office window. "How did he stop her?"

"He sat in his window and talked to her, trying to calm her down. When he told her to "stay," she sat down — and then she ran out of the room. I guess that's when you came home." Greta and I had worked every day on her commands. She had gotten really good at "stay," which had just saved her life since that window was three stories high.

I lived in a city, and everything about it terrified her. She panicked when she heard a noise she couldn't identify and I no longer knew how to help her. I just knew I had to get her out of the city — and fast.

"God, please help," I said. It was a prayer I often said for Greta.

A few days later, my friend Sue called. She sounded upset. "I tried to adopt a little dog yesterday, but the owner wouldn't let my kids have her."

"Why, did something happen?" I asked.

"She said they made her dog nervous."

"That's too bad. I didn't know you were thinking about adopting a dog. Does it have to be little?"

"That's the funny thing," she said. "Just this morning, I decided I wanted a big dog, and I have no idea why."

"Oh, I think I might know why. Would you be interested in meeting Greta?"

"Sure, I'd love to. You can bring her here anytime."

"Great, I'll see you tomorrow."

Sue and her daughters fell in love with Greta instantly and wanted to keep her. But being in a strange house with people she didn't know made Greta nervous. With three hopeful faces staring at me, I tried to do what was best for everyone. "Let me take her home, and I'll bring her back tomorrow. I'll keep bringing her back until everyone is comfortable with the transition."

The next day, Greta walked into the house like she owned it, ran upstairs to the girls' room and jumped on the bed. They played for hours. Afterward, they all nuzzled together and fell asleep. I left quietly and cried all the way home.

Saying goodbye to Greta wasn't easy. But I found comfort in knowing she was safe, and that her new family loved her as much as I did. With the unfamiliar noises of the city gone, she quickly overcame her fears and anxiety and stopped jumping out of open windows. And I get to visit her any time I want. When I do, she shows her love and gratitude by giving me lots of sloppy kisses.

— L.M. Lush —

Chapter 4

What a Character!

Ding Dong Doggy

*Accept the challenges so that you can feel the
exhilaration of victory.*
~George S. Patton

OVID-19 made "social distancing" the catchphrase for 2020 and forced us to adapt in new and often creative ways. My super-social teenage daughters adapted by meeting with their friends on video chat; school campuses closed but adapted with online classes; my husband's office closed, but he adapted with teleconferencing.

However, social distancing with my parents added an extra challenge. We'd recently moved them, at the venerable ages of eighty and eighty-one, into the house across the street from us. It was wonderful to have them so close, but once COVID-19 arrived, everything changed. My sister, who was a heroic nurse on the COVID-19 frontlines, gave us strict orders: Because we could be unknowing carriers of the virus, and my parents were in the high-risk age group, we should not get close to them… AT ALL!

How could we care for and interact with my parents but social distance at the same time? I could purchase their groceries, disinfect the packaging, and leave them on their doorstep — that would be easy. Meeting their social needs, which we felt was an equally important necessity, was another matter. They did not use computers or smartphones, so there had to be another way to connect. After much thought, my daughters decided we could reach out with beautiful cards, letters and pictures… and one of our dogs could deliver them!

We'd read in the news that although animals could be carriers of the virus, the likelihood was low, so we felt excited about the prospect of our new delivery method. The question was, which dog was best suited for the job? We considered each one carefully: Tootsie the Parson Russell Terrier, Stevie the tiny Poodle/Maltese mix, or Stuffy the mutt who more closely resembled a teddy bear.

We opted to give Tootsie the first shot at it. We looped a small package loosely over her head and sent her toward my parents' door. We watched with bated breath as she approached the house. Suddenly, she veered left! She made a beeline for a large dirt patch, shook the package from her neck, and proceeded to bury it, undeterred by our shouts of dismay.

Little Stevie was up next. He had more focus; surely he could do the job. With the package affixed to his back, we set him on course. Stevie looked strong going in. He proceeded toward the door and nearly made it, but then a lizard ran in front of him. Chasing lizards is Stevie's favorite pastime, so the moment we saw that little critter dart by, we knew all bets were off. Sure enough, Stevie chased that lizard all over the yard and then went running down the street. I watched with a sigh as my daughters disappeared after him.

Later (after finally catching Stevie), we were ready for a final go. We were left with Stuffy. The vet had recently told us that he needed to go on a diet — too many treats apparently. Not as spry as our other two, he was our last choice. But Stuffy loved to chase his ball, so maybe there was hope. We saddled him up with the package (which was looking a bit sorry by then) and walked him across the street. My daughter threw a ball toward my parents' front door, and Stuffy bounded up the path. My parents opened their door just as Stuffy reached the threshold, and they successfully removed the package from his back as we all cheered and jumped up and down for Stuffy. Mission accomplished!

Stuffy received treats (healthy carrots) and seemed truly proud of himself. He did so well and enjoyed it so much that he continued to deliver cards, pictures and little items to my parents every day.

We call him our Ding Dong Doggy, even though we have yet to teach him to ring the doorbell.

—Julie Theel—

35

Chicken Soup for the Soul

What's in the Bag?

Curiosity is one of the great secrets of happiness.
~Bryant H. McGill

E very year, my parents went on vacation to Longview, Washington, where my mother's uncle lived. Their purpose was to go salmon fishing, but one time, they returned with another animal — a live one. My father had fallen in love with a Cocker Spaniel puppy that we named Tammy.

This was our first dog, and Tammy and I became great friends. She also spent a lot of time with my mother, who would take her along when she went shopping.

One day, my mother returned to the car after grocery shopping. She put her grocery bags in the back seat of the car and proceeded to another store, leaving the dog in the car. Finally, when they arrived home, Mom opened the rear door of the car, and found all the bags torn to pieces. Her purchases were scattered all over the floor, mixed in with the shredded paper.

Mom came into the house, steaming. "Your stupid dog shredded all the grocery bags," she told Dad. "I'm sure she ruined all the meat packages."

I helped Mom bring her purchases into the house a few pieces at a time. With each trip out to the car, Mom scolded Tammy, who hung her head in shame. However, as we brought the things into the house, we noticed there wasn't even a tooth mark on a single item. Even the meat was untouched.

Tammy was not allowed to go shopping with Mom for a long time after that. When Mom finally relented Tammy shredded the bags again. Once again, Tammy hung her head in shame as Mom scolded her. Yet nothing was damaged.

After another break, Mom decided to give Tammy one more chance. But this time Mom handled it differently. When she returned to the car, Mom took each item out of the bag and showed it to Tammy. Then she put everything back in the bags and went to another store.

When Mom returned to the car, everything was just as she had left it. The bags were still sitting on the car seat, and none had the slightest tear. So, this became the rule with everyone in the family. If Tammy was along, we would always show her what we had bought. We never again had to clean up torn bags.

This was fifty years ago, and I thought Tammy was the only dog to have such a weird curiosity about what was purchased when we went shopping. But about ten years ago, my wife and I got a new dog, Smoky, a miniature American Eskimo.

We do quite a bit of shopping on the Internet, so we often have boxes delivered to our door. Whenever one arrives and we bring it inside, Smoky waits with anticipation for us to open it. Once she has seen what we received, she is satisfied and goes about her business. Her interest is not limited to the boxes delivered. She also wants to know what's in our grocery bags, too.

An old saying goes, "Curiosity killed the cat, but satisfaction brought him back." But I don't think curiosity is limited to a cat. And who would ever imagine that, in my lifetime, I would have two dogs who wanted to know, "What's in the bag?"

— Lee E. Pollock —

36

Fiber Diet

*A well-balanced person is one who finds
both sides of an issue laughable.*
~Herbert Procknow

When my daughter was five months old, I began to notice that her socks were losing their mates. At first, I thought it was my imagination, but it soon became clear that something else was to blame.

I would sit in the living room, folding clothes and pairing socks while my daughter played in her swing or on the floor. Our dog, Mojo, was never far from us. He loved the company, and at a robust eighty-five pounds, he was big even for a German Shepherd.

Mojo was red and black, with stunning features that were a trademark of his breed. Often, he stole apples for a snack, but he'd eat them one small bite at a time between his paws. In many ways, he was the most human-like dog I'd ever met.

In other ways, however, he was all canine, and his odd eating habits soon took an even more interesting turn.

One day, when my daughter started whining, I scooped her up and noted that it was time for a diaper change. As I went about the task of removing a smelly diaper and discarding it, something caught my eye.

From my periphery, I could see Mojo carefully stretching his neck toward the pile of laundry I'd left on the couch. I didn't think much of it, so I finished changing my daughter and set her down to play.

When I looked up, I saw Mojo licking his lips. Had he found a stray Cheerio?

Then I noticed him stretch his neck out again, open his mouth, and carefully pick a loose sock from the group of mismatches on the couch.

Gulp. Down it went.

"Mojo!" I said in disbelief.

After a quick call to the vet, they assured me that he would pass the sock soon and to call again if he acted strangely.

"Stranger than eating socks?" I asked.

Winter came and went in our little town, and the snow that had accumulated melted to reveal a back yard with grass that was ready for spring — and about two dozen socks that Mojo had "passed" throughout the winter.

— Eilley Cooke —

37

The Honey Trap

Anybody who doesn't know what soap tastes like
never washed a dog.
~Franklin P. Jones

It's midwinter, and my daughter Emma is hiding in the hallway wearing nothing but her swimsuit. I'm sitting in the living area, and George, Emma's two-year-old white Lab, is lying as close to the fire as he can get. I'm wondering how his ears don't catch on fire when I hear Emma's urgent whisper.

"Mum, act normal. Don't wake George!"

She's peeping around the doorway, tying her long blond hair into a messy topknot.

"What the…" I start, but Emma interrupts. She is on a mission, something that happens once a month. It requires a lot of planning and a bit of bribery.

"Talk like you're really happy, like nothing's wrong," she instructs, waving an arm in a loop. "I need the atmosphere full of good vibes."

I'm confused. Emma is my older daughter, the sensible, steadfast child not given to fancy flights of imagination.

I look over at George, who remains in a heat stupor. He's been fed and walked and probably has plans to spend the rest of the day right where he is.

"He hasn't heard a thing," I whisper back.

Emma has gone to find supplies. She comes back wearing a robe over her swimsuit. She juggles dog shampoo, several towels and a jar of dog treats.

"He hates this," she says. "I'm going to prep the bathroom."

Her planning is close to something military. The Bath War occurs once a month, and I happen to be visiting at the right time to help with the operation.

George was an unexpected gift from her husband Todd. Emma, a nurse, came home from work one day and was not impressed to find a tiny white puppy waiting for her. She already had a cat to manage, a moody ginger tom full of fluff and attitude.

But George was quick to steal her heart. This gentle soul loves everyone and everything, except the cat — and bath time.

Quietly, I get off the couch to see what's happening in the bathroom. Towels cover the floor, and Emma throws one at me.

"I suggest you put this around you," she says.

I take the towel and wrap it loosely around my shoulders. Emma raises her eyebrows.

"You're going to get very wet."

I scoff with the parental wisdom that I've earned. *Child, I've raised two girls — one of them you — from colicky infant years and toddler taming to teen sassiness and the hormonal ups and downs only mothers of girls will know. What trouble can this gentle giant of a dog be?*

"You've been warned," Emma says. With a practised flick of her wrist, a blob of honey attaches itself to the shower wall.

"Let's go," she says. "Remember, I need the air charged with positivity."

He's still blissfully unaware, and Emma pulls her robe tighter to hide her swimsuit because George will know what that means.

She rattles the jar of dog treats. There are two things George loves: Emma and food. His ears prick, and his head rouses. He spies Emma and food, and his tail thumps happily.

In a singsong voice, which George always falls for, she leads him one treat at a time through the living room and down the hall into the bathroom.

It's only as Emma shuts us all in the bathroom and takes off her robe that George realises he's been duped.

George's gentle nature, his desire to please and devotion to those who love him, mean that instead of aggression, he turns into a statue.

His way of disobeying is to freeze, drop like a rock and pretend he's not there.

George is a big Lab, and even heavier when pretending to be a stone. We deadweight lift him into the shower stall and close the door quickly, trapping him and Emma inside. Then it's my turn to soothe with singsong talk while Emma does the real work in tight confines.

"What's with the honey?" I ask.

"It's to distract him. He likes peanut butter better, but let's face it, he'll eat anything."

That's true, and I see George momentarily distracted from his terror to lick honey off the shower wall.

It's ironic that he adores swimming in the ocean and river but loathes baths and showers. We've unpacked and re-wrapped this concept many times. His anxiety is illogical, but to her credit, Emma doesn't give in to his whims. He needs a bath, and he will get it.

He is quick to recover. Out of the shower stall and three wild shakes later, George is a happy boy, and I am a soaked spectator.

— Jennifer Watts —

38

Hide and Seek

Animals can communicate quite well. And they do.
~Alice Walker

Not long after we rescued our one-and-a-half-year-old Bloodhound, Hunter, we discovered his aptitude for tracking. His favorite game became hide-and-seek. He obeyed when we told him to "sit" and "stay," and then we would hide an item for him to find and bring back.

We started out with his plush toys. We would show him a toy and let him sniff it, and then we would "hide" the toy while he watched. He caught on to that instantly, so we began making it a little more difficult each time, hiding the toy behind pillows on the couch or inside an open box. We continued to make it more challenging over time, hiding the toy in different rooms, in drawers or closed cabinets, and then in the back yard or our garage. We were amazed at how easily he found the toy each time, no matter which toy we hid. It became one of his favorite activities, and he would often drop a toy at our feet and then sit at the ready for us to hide it.

He was very obedient with the "stay" command. One day, he gave me a toy while I was carrying a load of laundry downstairs, but I forgot about the toy after I started the load of laundry and got distracted by another household chore. Thirty minutes later, I came back upstairs, and found him still sitting at attention, ready to search for his toy. I felt terrible, but he didn't seem to mind at all when I set him loose to find the toy I had "hidden" down in the laundry room.

My father was incredulous when he learned that Hunter would find the exact toy that we had hidden rather than just any toy around the house. To prove the incredible capabilities of our pup, we tried something new. We had Hunter "sit" and "stay" out of view, and then we hid his toy at the bottom of his very large toy bin, mixed in with all the other toys.

When I released Hunter to find his toy, he used his incredible snout to sniff around and follow the path I had taken arbitrarily throughout the house. Ultimately, his nose led him to his toy box. My father was amazed when Hunter began rifling through all his toys until he finally dislodged the majority from the bin itself. Then he pranced back to us, carrying the exact toy that we had hidden.

We continue to push his capabilities every day, giving him new challenges to use his incredible tracking abilities. And then, Hunter turned the tables on us.

One day, Hunter was outside playing while we did some yardwork. He kept bringing me one of his squeaky balls, but rather than dropping it for me to throw for him, he would run away with the ball and then come back without it. He would then sit directly in front of me, seeming to want something. He did this a few times, always returning without the squeaky ball.

"What are you doing, silly boy?" I asked.

He ran off once again to retrieve his squeaky ball. This time, when he brought the ball to me, he put a paw up on my leg to grab my attention when he showed me the ball. He then touched the ball to my leg and ran off. When he returned, he did the same thing he had done before and sat directly in front of me with a sense of expectation.

"What do you want me to do, buddy?" I inquired. "Do you want me to go find the ball?" I started walking in the direction from which he had returned. He got up and followed me as I walked toward where I had seen him set down his squeaky ball. I walked slowly and peered around here and there. He watched me attentively with his ears perked up as I meandered slightly off track at times. Once I retrieved the ball, Hunter danced around gleefully. Then he came and sat by my side, almost as if he were giving me praise for finding the ball.

Sure enough, when I handed him the ball he trotted over to my husband. He began the same behaviors that he had just demonstrated to me. He poked my husband's leg with the ball, making sure to have his full attention as he showed him the squeaky ball before running off.

"What, you don't want me to throw the ball, Hunter?" my husband asked.

"I think he wants you to search for the ball, just like we have him do," I explained to my husband. He tested it out, too. After Hunter came back and sat expectantly in front of him, he went to search for the ball. My husband ended up with the same reaction from our playful Bloodhound. Hunter had reversed our game of hide-and-seek.

To this day, Hunter loves to search for things, but being the full family member that he is, he makes sure that we humans share in the fun. And he has only improved with time. Hunter has quite large jowls, and sometimes we cannot quite see what he has before he runs off to hide an item for us to find. It becomes the mystery of the day when our silly pup returns from his secret hiding mission, and we have no clue what he has hidden. We have ended up with many temporarily misplaced work gloves, tape measures, and even nuts and bolts.

— Gwen Cooper —

39

A Pup with a Purpose

Dogs got personality. Personality goes a long way.
~Quentin Tarantino

t was our first evening dog-sitting while our teenage daughter was on vacation in Costa Rica for two weeks. Louie, aka Louis Vuitton, searched the entire house for his "mommy." Then, that disappointed but determined Miniature Dachshund formulated a plan.

While my husband Paul and I were watching TV, we heard a commotion on the stairs leading to Rochelle's bedroom on the third floor. Something heavy was being dragged down the stairs, causing a loud thumping sound. I peeked around the corner and saw this six-month-old puppy laboriously dragging his large, hard-sided Louis Vuitton carrier down the staircase.

He glanced at us, wagged his tail and scurried back up the stairs. "What do you think he is doing?" my husband asked.

We watched in amazement as Louie dragged his worldly possessions, one by one, down those stairs: first, his blankie, and then his bowl, bone, ball and sweater. He even made one last trip to get his leash.

This project took most of the evening, and Louie never tired. He was on a mission, but we were not certain what it was... yet.

What happened next made us realize that not only did this dog have a mission but he obviously put thought and reasoning into each move. He took each of the personal items he had lugged down the stairs and put them in the carrier. This was extremely difficult as the carrier had a lip that was considerably taller than he was.

After Louie finished packing his "suitcase," he attempted to jump inside. It took several tries, but he made it. But he wasn't done yet. Once inside, he got the zipper between his teeth and, with all the strength he could muster, he pulled the zipper closed. I envied his patience and tenacity. Then he lay down and went to sleep.

The message was abundantly clear. He wanted to go see his mommy. He had seen her pack her suitcase and go away. He must do the same so he could find her. He stayed in the carrier all night, and when I unzipped it in the morning, he was elated. Believing he had arrived, he jumped up — but his mommy was not there.

I started making notes about Louie's escapades to share with Rochelle. He surprised us with new undertakings every day.

When the telephone would ring, he would run to it, knock it off the hook and bark until we picked up the receiver and said, "Hello."

His absolute favorite activity was going for a car ride. The possibility of stopping at McDonald's for chicken nuggets was his inducement. But one day, my husband didn't stop at McDonald's and then left Louie in the car with the window cracked while he went off to do an errand.

That dog, with legs about two inches long, managed to jump out the window of Paul's truck and land without injury. He then walked two blocks in a busy urban area and found Paul in a hardware store. As Paul was paying for his purchase, he heard a man say, "Well, little fellow, where did you come from?"

Paul was shocked to look down and find Louie, who looked up at him as if to say, "Here I am. I found you all by myself. I waited at the streetlights with all the other people. Aren't you proud of me? Can we have chicken nuggets now?"

Indeed, they stopped for some nuggets on the way home.

One evening, when I put Louie outside to pee, I noticed a huge black bear in the driveway. I screamed at Louie to come back inside the house. Instead, he fearlessly charged the bear's back legs and nipped at them. The bear ran as fast as he could to get away from the little annoying dog. I was terrified yet laughing hysterically at Louie's bravado.

For Christmas that year, I turned Louie's daily journal into a hardbound book written from a dog's perspective. When Rochelle opened her gift, she laughed and cried at the same time. I will never forget her words: "Mom, *now* will you write your memoir?" She began a campaign, and no matter what excuse I gave her, she persisted until I finally said, "Yes!"

Writing Louie's story changed my life, and set me on the path to a new career as an author and radio talk-show host. Louie is an old, gray-haired dog now — just as cute, certainly as smart, and still up to his old, and new, tricks.

— Carol Graham —

40

Say Cheese!

Dogs act exactly the way we would act
if we had no shame.
~Cynthia Heimel

We chose Taffy, our English Sheepdog, from a litter in a suburb south of London. I was doing a tour in the military in continental Europe then. The breeder said she would be friendly, sociable, intelligent, and a pleasure to be around. She would travel well and rarely pose a problem around people or dogs. Taffy has been all that.

Recently, we took her with us on a holiday jaunt to a resort in the North Carolina mountains. Although I can hardly claim to be an unbiased observer, I must say that Taffy conducted herself with greater discretion and decorum than some of the other guests at the resort. If this sounds a little catty (I sought in vain for a substitute adjective but could discover no suitable canine equivalent), I can only say that the facts bear me out. It is embarrassing to acknowledge that our pets not infrequently seem better versed in etiquette than ourselves.

But, alas, Taffy has a few weaknesses, no less so than her human counterparts. With Taffy, it happens to be cheese, and the smellier the better. She has what can only be described as a *passion* for cheese. Somehow, her ancestors must have made a foray across the English Channel to France, where they were schooled in the wonders of cheese in the nation that understands it best.

I had the misfortune to walk Taffy past a retail outlet on the resort premises that offered an assortment of wines, smoked meats and, yes, cheeses. Cheese tends to boldly announce its presence by its fragrance, and Taffy was quick to detect and react to it. I only became aware of what was happening when the leash went taut in my hands. It was so taut, in fact, that I was jerked backward in mid-stride. Even if she had been a Pointer, Taffy could not have identified her quarry with greater precision or eagerness. She smelled cheese, and she wasn't about to go anywhere until she had partaken of some.

I tried reasoning with her. I tried cajolery. I tried to buy Taffy off with the promise of a treat when we got back to our room. None of it had any effect. Taffy wasn't budging. The aroma of cheese had flooded her senses and hypnotized her. I don't think she heard a single word I said.

People were forced to detour around us. At this point, it was obvious that I had lost control of the situation. Drastic action was required. I snagged a friendly-looking passerby and asked him to hold on to Taffy's leash while I ducked into the store.

Once inside, I found myself confronted by a bewildering assortment of cheeses: Gouda, Provolone, feta. I'm no authority when it comes to cheeses, but neither was Taffy. Pretty much anything would serve my purpose. I grabbed one of the most fragrant cheeses, paid for it, rushed back outside and retrieved Taffy. I let her inhale the strong, compelling scent of the cheese. Afterward, she was putty in my hands. I guided her back to our room so that we might both enjoy a taste of *la vie belle*.

From that day forward, I took to referring to Taffy as "Mademoiselle," a reference to her sophisticated French taste. "Would Mademoiselle kindly move so I can sit down?" I would address her. Or "It's a beautiful day for a walk, Mademoiselle, *n'est-ce pas?*" My wife disapproved of making fun of Taffy in this manner.

Taffy took it in stride — at first. But over time, she seemed to pick up on the sarcasm, and something very like resentment would kindle in her eyes. No matter. I have only to offer her a bit of cheese to restore her to an amiable frame of mind. Mademoiselle is quite unable to resist.

It's fair to say that such tactics very much resemble bribing a child with ice cream. But it's the perfect lever to employ to make certain that Taffy behaves herself. On the rare occasions when she acts out, I've never known it to fail. And I'm the first to admit that, if a passion for cheese is a vice, it's one that the two of us share. Few meals fail to benefit from a dusting of cheese — or even a bloody great chunk.

— Thomas Canfield —

41

Our Suspicious Shih Tzu

*I think we may safely trust a good deal
more than we do.*
~Henry David Thoreau

"Honey, can you fill the dog dishes, please?" my mom asked. I grabbed the dog bowls and headed to the pantry to fill them. I was thirteen years old, and our family had three dogs: a Sheltie named Andy, a Poodle mix named Brown Sugar, and a Shih Tzu named Blooper.

As soon as I opened the pantry doors, all three dogs came running. I scooped dry dog food into the bowls and set them down on the floor. Andy and Sugar ate their food standing in front of the dish — like normal dogs.

But Blooper had a different way of doing things. As soon as I filled his dish, he filled his mouth with as much food as he could carry, walked into the den, emptied his mouth onto the floor behind the door, and then ran back to the dish to get another mouthful of food. He made several trips, carrying his food into the den and setting it on the floor.

When he'd transported all of it, he'd lie on the floor next to the food. If either of the other dogs entered the den, he picked up as much food as he could with his mouth and held it there until the other dog walked away.

As a child, I could understand this habit. I was one of four kids, and sometimes I wanted to make sure I got the last cookie or slice of pizza. When Blooper laid claim to his food to ensure the other dogs didn't eat it, I sympathized.

What I couldn't understand was why Blooper did it with me, too.

Any time I went into the den, Blooper would hurry to scoop up his food into his mouth. Then he'd eye me warily.

"Why are you so suspicious of me?" I'd say. "I don't eat dog food."

He'd just stare at me, still holding the food in his mouth.

"You can put it down," I'd say. "I'm really not interested in it."

He'd continue to eye me.

I'd go back to the pantry and re-fill the dog dishes. Blooper would follow me. "See, there's lots of food," I'd tell him. "There's no reason to guard it."

He'd grab another mouthful, trot into the den and spit it out on the floor, adding it to his stash. But as soon as he'd spot me, he'd pick it up again and hide it in his mouth.

Even as a kid, I understood that some dogs who have been mistreated might hoard food. But we'd had Blooper since he was a puppy. He'd always had as much as he wanted to eat. There was no logical reason for him to do this. But he continued to guard his food from the other dogs — and me.

My parents and siblings could walk into the den and sit on the floor next to Blooper, and he'd wag his tail, leaving the food on the floor.

But the second he spotted me, he'd grab the food and hold onto it until I left, eyeing me suspiciously the entire time. Blooper wasn't afraid of me. He liked me. He let me pet him and pick him up. He just didn't trust me near his food.

More than once, I sat down in the den with a book, just to see how long Blooper would hold the food in his mouth.

I can't tell you how long he would have lasted. I always got bored and gave up before Blooper gave in and put down the food. But it was often a mushy mess from his saliva by that time.

That never bothered him. When he got hungry, he ate the food, even if it had spent half the day in his mouth. It was so gross that my mom had to lay down a puppy pad to save the carpet from Blooper's slimy food piles.

It never bothered Blooper, but it really bothered me. Why was he suspicious of me, but not of any other human in the family? Even guests could come into the den without triggering his food-hoarding reflex.

It was just me.

One day, when Blooper was guarding his food pile, I deliberately entered the den and sat down next to him. Of course, he scooped up a mouthful and eyed me.

I sighed and stroked his head. "I've told you a million times that I don't eat dog food," I said softly. I picked up a piece of food and put it up to his mouth. "See, I don't want it. It's all yours." To my surprise, he spit out the food in his mouth and ate the piece in my hand. I scanned the pile for another mostly dry piece, picked it up, and fed it to him. I hand-fed him the entire pile, even the super-soggy pieces.

It was beyond gross.

As soon as the food was gone, Blooper ran to the food dish and came back with another mouthful. He spit it out on the floor in front of me and then looked at me expectantly. I picked up a piece and fed it to him. He wagged his tail, so I fed him the rest.

He made several more trips from the food bowl to the den that day. I hand-fed him each piece until he finally laid his head down on my lap and fell asleep.

As he snored softly, I stroked his head. "I told you I don't eat dog food," I said. "Can we be done with this now, please?"

That day, Blooper finally decided that he could trust me with his food. He still carried his meal into the den each day, and he still scooped it into his mouth when the other dogs entered the room, but he left it on the floor when he saw me.

Finally, I had proven myself trustworthy in Blooper's eyes.

Being trusted by a dog is a huge compliment indeed.

—Diane Stark—

42

Floor Phobia

*Part of the journey in life is slipping and
falling along the way; in these times true friends
are the ones who pick you up and dust you off.*
~Ken Poirot

"**D**anny, come on," I pleaded as I tried unsuccessfully to tug the leash. Danny, a Labrador Retriever, responded with a whimper and continued to dig his feet into the rug, vigorously resisting my efforts. He was facing his greatest fear, and no encouragement was going to convince him to overcome it.

People moved around us, staring as they walked by. It wasn't every day they saw a dog in the mall, let alone one refusing stubbornly to move an inch. We stood at the entrance of the building, stuck on the large rug that lay just beyond the doors. We had barely moved a foot into the building before Danny stopped and refused to walk farther.

"I think he is just nervous. Once he gets used to the noise and all the people, I am sure he will be okay," a woman from our Seeing Eye club said reassuringly, her hand reaching down to pet Danny's head.

I nodded, hoping that she was right. But, realistically, I knew better. This wasn't the first time we had had this problem. We could have been in a completely empty mall and Danny would still have refused to move.

My adorable, seven-month-old Seeing Eye trainee had a deep phobia of certain surfaces. And the sleek, shiny tiled floors that characterize malls across the country are just that type of surface.

When I got Danny as a puppy, his fear wasn't readily apparent. Our home was mostly carpeted, and our wood floors were roughened with age. The first month I had Danny, I focused eagerly on house-breaking before moving on to basic commands like "sit" and "down." Danny was a smart dog and a quick learner. He was also sweet, calm, and obedient — surprisingly so compared to other rambunctious Lab puppies I've been around. I was convinced that he would make a perfect guide dog one day.

Raising a guide dog is the same as raising any dog, with a few added requirements. The organization I was raising Danny for required monthly meetings with other puppy raisers. Often, these meetings were at locations where someone might use a guide dog, like a shop or train station. This particular meeting consisted of all the puppy raisers and trainee puppies going on a walk around the mall.

But now it seemed clear that Danny and I would not be walking around the mall with the rest of the group.

"He will be okay soon enough. He just needs a few minutes," the woman murmured, as she continued to pet Danny.

"Unfortunately, I don't think so," I replied. "It's not the people; it's the floors. He refuses to walk on smooth surfaces like this. I have tried to convince him not to be afraid, but nothing seems to work."

I thought back to a few months earlier when I first realized that seemingly perfect Danny had a flaw. He stepped onto the tile in a friend's house and started to flail and whimper, refusing to walk despite encouragement or food bribery. I hoped it was just a puppy phase, but the problem persisted. I asked the Seeing Eye puppy-raiser group for advice, searched the Internet, and talked to guide-dog trainers about Danny's problem, but nothing seemed to work.

At the mall, the woman looked down at Danny thoughtfully. "Hmmm. Have you tried dog shoes? My son is very sensitive to touch. He can't stand his skin touching rough surfaces. Luckily, socks and gloves help him."

Dog shoes? I hadn't even known such a thing existed. It was worth a shot.

That night, after I returned home with Danny from our failed mall trip, I bought dog shoes — or booties, as they are often called — online as a last-ditch effort to help Danny overcome his walking troubles.

When the booties came in, Danny and I went to the friend's house with the sleek tiles to test them. I put the booties on Danny, and he seemed to have no problem with his new footwear. Gone was the stubborn dog who refused to set foot on a tile. Cheerily, Danny walked on the floor with no hesitation. It was as if a spell had been placed on him that took away all his anxiety and fears.

Of course, the discovery of booties didn't solve all our problems. For a pet, wearing booties outside the house wouldn't be much of an issue. But for a guide dog, this was impractical and would not be allowed. I continued to work with Danny to overcome his fears. With great reluctance, he was able to walk on smooth surfaces eventually. But when he was taken back to the Seeing Eye institute for training six months after the mall incident, he still had visible anxiety when he was encouraged to do so.

Just two days after I left Danny at the institute, I got a call saying he had failed the program. It was one of the fastest failings a dog has ever had. The reason? He freaked out at the kennel floors.

Danny came back to live with me and no longer had to deal with uncomfortable floors. I always brought dog booties whenever we left the house. It was no longer fair to put him through so much stress for the slim chance that he might fully overcome his floor phobia. I realized that not every dog is meant to be a guide dog. Some dogs are just meant to be pets, ones who bring their owners joy and wear booties whenever they leave the house.

— Rose Eaton —

43

A Ruff Game

All my dogs have been scamps and thieves and
troublemakers and I've adored them all.
~Helen Hayes

Because I am not playing with a full deck, I will never be a high roller in Atlantic City or Las Vegas. That was painfully obvious when I lost a blackjack tournament to my dog.

The low-stakes showdown was prompted by two news stories I read about man's supposedly best friend. In the first story, German researchers found a Border Collie named Rico who understands more than 200 words and can learn new ones as quickly as many children. That was good news for people who talk to their dogs. It proves that we are on the cutting edge, not just a bunch of eccentrics.

In the second story, the Sands casino and hotel in Atlantic City re-created artist C.M. Coolidge's famous painting "Dogs Playing Poker" by using five dogs to play in a blackjack tournament. Unfortunately, they were big risk takers, asking for another card when they were way too close to 21.

When I read these two stories, I knew that my dog, Lizzie, not only could beat Rico in an IQ test but could play cards better than those pooches in Atlantic City.

Lizzie is part Border Collie, part Terrier and part Italian. She is also very smart, with a vocabulary much larger than 200 words. I have to spell out some of them, such as C-A-R and W-A-L-K, because she would go crazy otherwise. I talk to Lizzie all the time because she is so smart, which makes me a cutting-edge communicator and not, as is widely believed, an eccentric.

One day, I bought a deck of cards. That evening, Lizzie and I played blackjack. The rules, as I explained to her, were these: The first one to win ten games is the champion. Anything over 21 is a bust. And no cheating by sniffing the players' cards.

As we sat on the floor in the living room (we don't have a card table), I shuffled the deck and asked Lizzie to cut the cards. She did so by using her paw to separate about a third of them from the rest of the deck.

Then I dealt Lizzie a jack and a 10. I dealt myself a jack and a 4. I said to Lizzie, "Hit?" She just looked at me. So, I said, "Stay?" She gave me her paw. She knows the word "stay," of course, but I didn't realize she knew what it meant in blackjack. I told you she's smart. She stayed with 20. I had 14, so I took another card. It was a 10. I busted. Lizzie won the first game.

"Beginner's luck," I told her.

"Ruff," she replied.

Lizzie's luck continued, and at one point she was leading, five games to two. But I caught up, and then went ahead, 8–7, only to see Lizzie rally and tie the tournament at 9–9.

One more game for the title. There was a lot of nervous panting. Lizzie was panting, too. I dealt her an 8 and a 7. "Hit?" I asked. She gave me her paw. I dealt her a 2. I asked Lizzie if she wanted another hit, but she played it safe and didn't respond. "Stay?" I asked. She gave me her paw. She was holding at 17.

I had a 5 and a jack. I had to take a hit. It was another jack. I busted. Lizzie won! I had been defeated by a dog.

When it comes to blackjack, I'm an L-O-S-E-R. Just ask Lizzie.

— Jerry Zezima —

Chapter 5

A Dog's Purpose

44

Officer Rambo

If there is a heaven, it's certain our animals are to be
there. Their lives become so interwoven with our own,
it would take more than an archangel
to detangle them.
~Pam Brown

Police dogs are part of the police force in every sense of the word. They serve the community with selfless loyalty, unhesitatingly answering the call of duty and putting their lives on the line every day. When my brother was a canine officer for our local police department, I got a rare opportunity to know some of these dogs and see their lives up close.

And, one day, one of these retired four-footed officers became my own.

I had always enjoyed the times that I guest-attended training sessions for these dogs and saw the drilling that made them a highly valued part of the force. The dogs were a revelation to me. I had always thought that police dogs would be German Shepherds — and there were indeed a few out at the training "ranch" — but most of the dogs I saw were enormous, intimidating Bouviers des Flandres.

These dogs looked like bears, covered in thick, curly black fur that was a perfect fit for their cold European homeland but seemed out of place in Southern California. But their fierce appearance was one of the qualities that made them good police dogs. Their temperament was also a plus, as they were calm, quiet animals... until they went into action.

I also learned that bonding between dog and officer was a crucial element. The dogs lived with the officers and forged a family connection, which was important when the dog needed to protect the officer on the job. After the dogs were retired, they remained with the officer as a much-loved and protective pet.

One of these retired dogs, named Rambo, became mine. My brother, no longer with the police force, was moving to a house that had a very small yard — and Rambo happened to be a very big dog. He needed space and someone with more time than my very-busy brother was able to give.

As it turned out, Rambo needed me... and I needed him.

I was still living at home, working part-time as an activity director at a skilled nursing facility while attending art school, so I had a fair amount of free time to get to know this gigantic bear of a dog. Rambo missed my brother greatly, but I did everything that he had done for him, such as his meticulous grooming routine — very necessary in the desert climate — and playing the games I knew he loved.

Rambo responded fairly well. I could tell that he grew to see me as an acceptable substitute for my brother, but there was still something missing. Rambo wasn't happy. As much as I tried to compensate for his previously busy life, it just wasn't enough. In fact, it seemed to me that this situation was similar to one I faced at the nursing facility: No activity could compensate for the previous lives of purpose the residents had enjoyed.

I pondered this during my working hours. At home, I was an incomplete replacement for my brother in Rambo's eyes. And at work, I couldn't fully replace what the elderly residents had lost either. While the residents were polite to me, it was obvious that I didn't bring them joy. I wanted things to be different. I wanted them to look forward to seeing me as much as I looked forward to seeing them.

And Rambo... Well, I felt like I was letting him down. This wasn't the life that he loved. He was no longer a part of the police force, taking down the "bad guys." He found himself no longer needed, and his depression was evident. I felt that, much like the residents I worked with, Rambo tolerated me, but he didn't enjoy our time together. After his years of dedicated service, Rambo deserved better. What, I wondered, could I do?

And then it hit me: Rambo could join me at work!

Bringing a dog into work was not anything novel. Dogs had visited before, but those were little dogs. Rambo, an enormous dog, was another matter. I counted on Rambo's excellent demeanor, always quiet, to help. And he was, after all, a highly trained professional. I knew all his commands, and he had gotten to the point where he obeyed me the same as he did my brother.

And so, with Rambo at my side, I strode into work one morning. To say that Rambo caused a sensation is an understatement. There were more than a few nervous glances as we entered the activity room where the residents had gathered for morning coffee. A few murmured comments let me know that Rambo had everyone's attention, but the cautious and wary glances made it obvious that this huge, hairy visitor was regarded with suspicion.

Taking a deep breath, I said, "Good morning, everyone! I've brought a visitor. His name is Rambo, and he is a Bouvier des Flandres." No one moved. Wide-eyed stares were the only reaction. I continued: "Rambo is actually Officer Rambo. He's a retired service dog for the police force. As I'm sure all of you can imagine, he has had a pretty busy life. But now that he is retired, he misses being a police dog, and I thought it would be good for him to make some new friends."

That did the trick. Suddenly, Rambo had something in common with the residents. Ida, a spry little lady of ninety-three, broke into a big grin and said, "Retired, huh? Well, he is in the right place then. We are retired too, you know." Everyone laughed. The ice now broken, they began to ask questions: "What did Rambo do when he was working for the police?" "How much does he eat?" "Does he obey commands?" And, best of all, "Is it okay if I pet him...?"

After that, Rambo frequently accompanied me to work. Now that he had a "job" again, he was supremely happy. The residents fell in love with him, complaining if I didn't show up with him by my side. But the nursing home wasn't the only place where Rambo joined me.

He even had a role in a play put on by the theater group I participated in. Like many retired individuals, Rambo needed a purpose, and this gentle, retired police dog thrived when he found one.

And the bond he forged with the residents was a miracle to behold. As he grew old, the big dog, now troubled with arthritis, was greeted as one of their own—a beloved member of the family. His pain was lessened because he had others to understand, ready to offer comfort. And that, after all, was always the plan. He deserved to spend his retirement surrounded by love. And he was.

—Jack Byron—

Certified Puppy Love

*Dogs don't make judgments about physical appearance
or abilities, they care about the quality
of your character and your capacity to love.*
~Elizabeth Eiler

I hear Katie laughing as Misha dashes across the room chasing a ball. What power that simple sound holds for me! There had been too many years when my daughter didn't laugh.

Misha, our gangly, forty-pound Labradoodle, came to us as a pup about a year ago, after a couple years' hiatus from pets. After our dog Cocoa died, I had decided I was too busy and traveled too much to take on another pet. But then Katie changed my mind. She has Down syndrome and still lives with us. She has been plagued by anxiety, anger, and pain for many years due to serious abuse deep in her past. That trauma made her unable to relax her guard and fully open her heart to anyone. Katie's counselor advised me that she would benefit from the help of a service dog.

I knew it was difficult to evaluate the temperament of a puppy when I went to the breeder's home to visit a litter that was only four weeks old. Most people look for the cutest pup or the sweetest personality, but I had a different agenda. My puppy had to be bold, but patient, tolerant of being handled roughly by my well-meaning daughter.

Of course, the puppies were all adorable. Some were all chocolate, some were all black, and some had those colors mixed with white. One stood out from the rest. He was a miniature mass of black curls with a tiny spot of white on his rear left foot, and he was bold. When he was placed on a hardwood floor for the first time in his life, he scrambled to investigate the shoes lined up against the wall. The other pups just stood, legs splayed, frozen in fright. This pup startled to noise but recovered quickly, and he accepted handling and snuggling like a pro.

What a sweet moment it was when, a few weeks later, Katie met Misha for the first time! Katie wasn't sure how to respond to the wriggling bundle of curls, but Misha knew what he was doing. He wormed his way into her lap and eventually into her heart.

Misha began his puppy training at twelve weeks and has continued training to this day. "Will work for food" is Misha's motto, so he quickly picked up many basic commands in exchange for tidbits of meat. Next in the training process was public access. In this phase we exposed him to numerous environments and people to acclimate him to handle any situation without much reaction. More training helped Misha learn impulse control. Toys, food, small children, other animals, flapping flags, noises and scents all tempt a young dog to break from service protocol. Misha is still working on these skills.

Learning service tasks is the final step of training. Any would-be service dog must learn specific tasks that are customized to a particular individual's needs. Misha learned many tasks quickly, such as retrieve, open, close, pull, and put things in place. But Katie's needs are more psychological than physical. Misha is learning to detect signs of anxiety and respond. He is trained to lie upon her lap and lick on command. He knows how to press in close to Katie's body, and he will use his large, moist nose to insistently interrupt self-harming behaviors.

Misha has that special something that is more instinctive than trained. He has an innate ability to sense Katie's emotional needs. To us, her needs are complex. But to him, they're simple. When she's in a funk, he brings his Kong toy to her and won't take no for an answer. Though much too big to truly be a lap dog, Misha sprawls across Katie, waiting patiently for her caress when she's talking to her therapist about tough memories. Every night at bedtime, Misha lies with Katie to say prayers and tuck her in. His puppy love is a powerful force.

Katie loves her Misha. We've had many pets over the years, but he is the first to capture her whole heart. She claims her status as his mother and calls me his grandmama. Besides being attentive to his need for food and water, she spends time every day "getting his ya-yas out," as she likes to say. Though she's usually quite a serious soul, Katie will engage in playful baby talk with Misha as she snuggles him and throws his ball. He springs faithfully off the floor on jackrabbit legs, twisting impossibly to catch it midair.

When I see her smile at him, my heart is touched. I'll gladly spend countless hours and too much money training and caring for Misha to hear my sweet girl's genuine laughter again. Nothing else had been able to release this unguarded, free side of Katie in many years.

Usually, it takes a couple of years of constant work before a dog becomes certified for service. Many don't make it. As it turns out, Misha's weakness is overreacting to canine friends. We're still training, but there are no guarantees.

Even if Misha never becomes a certified service dog, I won't be too disappointed. He is already 100-percent certified in our hearts.

— Elizabeth Gardner —

46

Good Listener

Today a reader, tomorrow a leader.
~Margaret Fuller

His name is Flanagan, and he is my four-legged best friend. At a mere sixteen pounds, his lineage hails from the Spaniel family. He is a precious combination of a Cavalier King Charles and a Cocker Spaniel.

He has floppy ears, a tail that never stops wagging, and a fluffy brown and white coat. His dark brown eyes reflect his sweet temperament. While his fine features are to be admired, his remarkable ability to change a child's life is what makes me most proud of him.

Some time ago, I enlisted Flanagan in a program to assist children who have difficulty reading aloud, especially in the classroom setting. The mission of the program is to improve a child's self-confidence when reading aloud, as well as cultivate and instill a passion for reading. Most of the children enrolled in the program perceive reading as a dreaded, stressful task, but reading aloud to someone who is not judgmental — a dog — changes everything for them.

When I announce, "It's time to go to the library," Flanagan conducts a search for his leash and his uniform: a neon orange vest bearing the message in bold black lettering: "Reading is FUNdamental." After I unroll Flanagan's paw-print rug in the children's section reading corner, Flanagan sits adjacent to a bright yellow bookcase neatly stacked with all types of inviting books for a child to explore. Perched on top of the bookcase is a globe and an adorable plush puppy with a striking resemblance to Flanagan.

When the first child arrives, Flanagan wags his tail in welcome and the reading session begins. Flanagan listens carefully as the child reads. Sometimes, he curls up next to the child, sits in her/his lap or rests his head on the child's knee.

Flanagan has heard stories about spaceships, castles, baseball players and princesses, as well as art, history and science. His attentiveness as each child reads aloud is amazing to observe. Every Thursday evening at six Flanagan makes a difference, changing a child's life story one word at a time.

— Patricia Ann Rossi —

47

Sadie by My Side

When I look into the eyes of an animal,
I do not see an animal. I see a living being.
I see a friend. I feel a soul.
~A.D. Williams

Standing in the checkout line at my local pharmacy, I clutched a bottle of hand sanitizer, Lysol, and a container of disinfecting wipes. While I was not yet overly concerned about the coronavirus, I wanted to be prepared. At the time, there were only 729 COVID-19 cases in New York State, but most were within fifty miles of my home. School closures, social distancing, and wearing facemasks had not yet gone into effect.

Someone in line began coughing uncontrollably. Everyone, including the employee at the register, froze in horror. I mustered up the courage to turn around, and saw the coughing man standing directly behind me. He was visibly ill. His hands were full with items to check out so he wasn't coughing into his elbow. His face was uncovered, and so was everyone else's. "Oh, no," I mumbled.

I was next in line and quickly moved forward to the register. "I don't know what to do," the young cashier said.

Everyone else in the line had scattered, leaving me, the ill man, and the terrified cashier. Shielding my nose and mouth with my hand, I said, "Cover your face with anything you have and check me out fast. When he leaves, go wash your hands."

After I paid, with my one free hand, I threw my items in my purse and walked briskly out the door to my car.

Sitting in the passenger seat was Sadie, my black Labrador Retriever. With her head cocked to one side, she looked at me, bewildered. "Get in the back seat," I said, sounding somewhat frantic. Instead, she leaned against my arm, put her head on my shoulder, and looked up into my eyes—her way of trying to comfort me.

At home, I removed my clothes quickly and stuffed them in a plastic bag. After a long, hot shower and a fresh change of clothes, I grabbed my computer and anything I might need to get through the next two weeks. To isolate myself from my ninety-one-year-old mother, who had multiple health issues, I moved into the basement. There was no door to prevent Sadie from coming downstairs. And wherever I went, she went. *Maybe it's for the best,* I thought. If I had been exposed to the coronavirus at the pharmacy and it could be passed on to dogs, Sadie would have been exposed to it in the car. I couldn't take the chance of her passing it on to my mother.

I found some old puzzles in the closet and used them to barricade the stairs, and then we hunkered down. Our long and difficult quarantine had begun.

Instinctively, Sadie knew something was wrong. She always did. Sensing my nervousness, she climbed into my lap and lay across me in protection mode. Eventually, she fell asleep. For the next several hours, I used her back as a computer desk. I worked and tried to keep my mind active.

By day three, I was bored to tears. With my work completed, I tried to stay busy by cleaning, talking to friends and family on the phone, watching way too much TV, and kibitzing on Facebook.

Sadie was bored, too. Fortunately, she had brought "Baby" downstairs with her—her favorite stuffed animal. For hours on end, we played tug of war with it. I walked Sadie early in the morning and late at night, trying to avoid people at all costs. There would be no running off-leash for a while, which I thought would be hard for Sadie. But she seemed content with our short walks. Surprised by the number of people who were out walking their dogs at 6 a.m., we took to walking in the cemetery. After that, running into people was no longer a problem.

On the fifth day of my self-isolation in the basement, shortly after having my dinner, it happened. I felt an odd shift — a "dis-ease" — and my body suddenly felt like it was on fire. Feeling weak and tired, I sat down and took my temperature. It was 100 degrees. Sadie put her head on my knee. With her ears pulled back and a sad look on her face, she began to whimper. "No, Sadie. Go lie down," I said. Three hours later, my temperature was back to normal. But I was not feeling well at all. *Here we go,* I thought.

I took Sadie for a walk and came home. I retrieved my end-of-life paperwork from the safe and rested it against the music rack on the piano for my mother to find "just in case." I pulled Sadie's bed up against the chair, which by now had become my office, dining room, living room, and bedroom.

The next morning, I awoke to a stabbing pain in my left lung and a burning sensation I had never felt before — not in my lung or anywhere else. And I was fully congested. Sadie was already at the door, crying to go out. I wondered how I was going to take her. I willed myself to get up, and then steadied myself and somehow managed to walk her to the woods across the street from my home. I stood there and waited.

Usually, Sadie required a long walk. She had never been trained to do her business on command. But, somehow, she knew exactly what I was waiting for her to do. Barely making it back home, I collapsed in the chair and fell asleep. When I awoke, Sadie was lying on the arm next to me, watching me intently. "Don't worry, Sadie," I whispered. "I'll be okay." She drew in a deep breath and let out a heavy sigh of relief.

During the second week, I was in constant pain and terribly sick to my stomach. I couldn't eat or get comfortable in any position. I tossed and turned, stood up and sat down — always changing positions. To keep up, Sadie darted this way and that, never taking her eyes off me. Then, suddenly, I crashed and burned.

The sicker I got, the more attentive Sadie became. Eventually, she took up residence in the recliner with me. By day, she lay by my side on the overstuffed arm. By night, she slept lying across the chair with her head resting on my arm. We took turns comforting each other.

When I couldn't breathe and sat up in the chair, Sadie got down, lay in her bed, and waited for me to tell her she could get back up in the chair. And on the days when I was just too ill to move but tried to get up and walk her, she wouldn't budge. I still don't know how she managed to hold it in for three days.

For nearly three weeks, I fought a hard battle. Sadie, my constant companion, was just the caregiver I needed. She got me up when I needed to move and let me rest when I couldn't breathe. True to her nature, she never let me down. She may have even saved my life.

—L.M. Lush—

48

Absolutely Worth It

Sadness flies on the wings of the morning
and out of the heart of darkness comes the light.
~Jean Giraudoux

Whenever my husband suggested we get a new dog, I steadfastly refused. I was still grieving the loss of our first dog, Sammy, to cancer. How could I risk falling in love with a new dog only to have my heart broken again when the time came to say goodbye?

After my husband recruited our seven-year-old son Erik to the We-Need-a-Dog Campaign, my resolve weakened. Yes, I agreed, the house did feel a little too quiet. Yes, Erik — an only child — needed a companion.

Soon, I found myself on a reservation list for a Goldendoodle puppy. We got to bring the roly-poly, cream-colored puppy home in July 2018. We named him Ole after my husband's Norwegian grandfather.

When I looked at my son's smile as he hugged that chunky, big-eared pup, I knew we had made the right choice. From the day we brought him home, Ole brightened our lives. He was a quick learner and always wanted to be near us. Even when one of us was taking a shower, the curious puppy would push the curtain aside and stick his head in as if to say, "Hey, what are you doing in there without me?"

Ole's loving temperament led us to get him certified as a therapy dog. After completing puppy kindergarten, we continued to invest time and treasure into weekly obedience classes. On March 11, 2019,

Ole made us proud by passing his Canine Good Citizen (CGC) Test, which is the first step in becoming a therapy dog. Unfortunately, just seven days after passing his CGC Test, we received devastating news.

During the development of Ole's adult teeth, we noticed a spot on his top gums where two teeth were missing. Our vet advised us to get this spot X-rayed. The X-rays revealed a bony growth just below the gum, blocking one adult tooth and a baby tooth. Our vet was concerned and consulted with a specialist. The specialist identified the growth as a complex odontoma, a tumor caused by malformed embryonic tissue originally destined to develop into teeth. We were told that a surgical removal of the odontoma needed to be performed as soon as possible. Without surgery, the tumor would continue to grow, eventually overtaking Ole's upper jaw and ultimately taking his life. The cost for this surgery could be as high as $4,000.

We were shocked by this serious medical issue so early in Ole's life, and the unexpected cost was overwhelming. Would this tumor kill our sweet puppy? What if we couldn't afford the surgery? Many tears were shed as we talked through this scary situation as a family. It felt like my worst fears were coming true.

Ole's CGC trainer recommended we set up a GoFundMe page to share Ole's story and ask for help in paying for this life-saving surgery. We did, and the support and generosity of others astounded us. We raised enough to cover the cost of Ole's surgery and his follow-up appointments. Days after the successful GoFundMe campaign, Ole had surgery at the Veterinary Medical Center at the University of Minnesota. To our great relief, the surgery went smoothly, and a biopsy revealed the tumor was benign. Six months after surgery, X-rays confirmed the tumor had been removed successfully, and the jaw was healing nicely. Ole was healthy and tumor-free!

With Ole back in good health, we resumed his therapy-dog training, which included a practice visit at a local nursing home. After checking in at the front desk, a slightly nervous me and a very happy Ole entered the first room. Inside, a white-haired woman sat in a recliner with a blanket over her lap. After she accepted my offer to meet my dog, I walked Ole to her side. Calmly, Ole rested his head on her lap.

"Oh, he's so soft!" she exclaimed, stroking Ole's curly blond head. Ole glanced back at me as if to say, "Mom, look at my new friend!" In the next room, Ole gave a woman resting in her bed a generous serving of doggy kisses.

"What a sweet boy! So many kisses!" she laughed.

"Wow, he really likes you!" I replied.

As the practice visit continued, we walked past the dining hall. A woman in a wheelchair leaned over, holding out a half-eaten sandwich, and said, "The doggie needs a treat!" I had learned the proper response in class, and I walked Ole away quickly, saying, "No thanks! Therapy dogs are not allowed to eat while working."

Next, we approached a gentleman sitting in his wheelchair in the hallway. As he petted Ole's back, he told me about the dogs he had on his farm during his childhood.

Another resident we met grew wistful talking about the dog she had to give away when she moved to the nursing home. "You're so lucky to have your dog," she told me.

After each encounter, I thanked the resident for petting my dog. "No, thank you for coming!" one resident replied. In fact, residents and staff thanked us for coming throughout the visit. It was touching to hear their gratitude. Near the end of the visit, I overheard the therapy-dog trainer say, "That Ole is a natural. He was born to do this." I felt so proud!

Two months after Ole turned one, we passed the final test. Ole became certified with Therapy Dogs International (TDI) with me as his proud handler. When the evaluator told us we had passed, my son — who attended many of Ole's training classes — jumped up and down, cheering. I couldn't stop smiling. A few weeks later, the big envelope arrived with Ole's official red TDI bandanna. When I tied the bandanna around Ole's neck, tears filled my eyes. I hugged Ole. "You're a real therapy dog now, Ole! What a good boy!" Ole seemed to smile back, his wagging tail thumping the ground.

Now Ole and I enjoy visiting nearby senior care facilities a couple of times a month. Ole interacts with each resident for only a few minutes, but it makes a big impact. These few minutes are an escape, an uncomplicated moment of unconditional love and acceptance. There's a special moment during our visits when the loneliness of the sterile nursing-home room fades away, and it's just my dog and his new human friend enjoying each other's company. It continues to be a humbling honor for me to take Ole on these visits.

My dear Ole is the pet who almost wasn't a part of my family. He's a special dog who many people helped support when a tumor threatened his young life. He's a survivor and friend. I am so glad I opened my heart to a new dog. Yes, there will be heartbreak when Ole's life ends. However, the love we have now and the joy he brings to all we meet in his work as a therapy dog make that distant reality absolutely worth it.

—Joan Oen—

49

LiLi's Story

*If having a soul means being able to feel love and
loyalty and gratitude, then animals are better off
than a lot of humans.*
~James Herriot

One year, when homeless dogs and puppy-mill take-downs were overwhelming animal shelters, I was called by a shelter to see if I would consider taking a black female Pekingese. She was tiny and sweet, but she had an obvious neurological condition that made her turn her head to one side all the time. My rescue vet recommended euthaniz-ing her, believing her to be unadoptable. Since she was in no distress, and seemed happy and otherwise healthy, I chose not to follow his recommendation. I took her home, expecting her to live out the rest of her life with my husband and me.

LiLi had been in our home for a few weeks when I received an adoption inquiry from an elderly woman in a town about two hours from us. She and her husband had been lifelong Peke owners and they loved the breed. She had attempted to adopt a dog from another rescue group but had been denied because of circumstances surrounding the death of their last Peke. Normally, when a dog escapes its fence and dies, a rescue group considers that an automatic denial. I was prepared to make that same decision until I heard the full story.

The adopter's husband was terminally ill with cancer, so they seldom left home. However, their children, who lived out of state, had come to visit. They all went out for a couple of hours to shop and eat dinner. While they were gone, a neighbor boy, intending to rob them, cut a hole in their fence, and their dog escaped through the hole. The dog was hit by a car and killed. When they returned home and found him, they were devastated. The story was confirmed by the daughter who had been with them when it happened. She had repaired the fence and assured me that it was secure.

The daughter also told me that her mother had to work, so her father was sitting at home alone, grieving for the dog. I thought of little LiLi and told the family about her. The father's condition was so fragile that he needed a quiet dog, and LiLi was a good match. They told me her tilted head only made them love her more. So, we agreed that little LiLi would go to live with them.

I met the adopter and her husband in a parking lot about an hour away from my home. They had driven halfway so we could meet. The husband sat in the front seat of the car, too weak to get out. His frail arms were covered in bruises from the blood thinners, which caused him to bleed under the skin. Gently, I placed LiLi in his lap and watched a smile spread across his face. He hugged her, and she began kissing his poor, fragile arms. The adopter said LiLi kissed his arms during their entire trip home. The sweet adopter and her husband lived on a limited budget, so I waived adoption fees. The woman touched my heart, however, when she handed me twenty-five dollars, a fortune on their budget. When she told me that she had picked up aluminum cans to recycle so she could make a donation to the rescue group, I nearly cried.

Later, I heard from the wife that LiLi had sat on her husband's lap and comforted him every day for the remaining three months of his life. The little dog that my vet thought should be put down had brought a dying man comfort and joy at a time when he needed it desperately. Her destiny complete, LiLi died less than a month later. Her adopter had her remains cremated and plans to have her ashes interred in her own coffin when she dies.

Although this seems like a sad story, it was a win-win. The little "unadoptable" dog happily lived out the rest of her natural life sitting in the lap of the man she was destined to love. He, in turn, lived out his remaining days loved by the little dog who never left his side.

—Judy Quan—

Sharing Barney

A kind gesture can reach a wound that only
compassion can heal.
~Steve Maraboli, Life, the Truth, and Being Free

I had been volunteering for hospice for a couple of months. When I learned the nearby rehabilitation center loved to have pets visit the residents, I invited my grandson Ernie and his dog Barney to accompany me.

My thirteen-year-old grandson had adopted his Beagle from a shelter several months earlier. He had been found abandoned and tied to a telephone pole. The workers at the shelter believed the dog had been severely abused, since he cringed whenever someone approached him.

However, contrary to his usual behavior, the dog seemed to take an immediate liking to Ernie. He jumped up and kissed him when they met. Needless to say, Ernie would have no other dog and took him home.

Soon, Ernie discovered that Barney, true to his nature, loved to chase squirrels and would immediately run away from Ernie if he had the opportunity. After spending a long time searching for the dog several times, Ernie's father got a GPS attached to Barney's collar with a corresponding tracking device attached to a mobile phone.

By now, Barney had become more acclimated to strangers, and we felt it would be a good test for him to visit the rehabilitation-center patients.

As we entered the facility, the administrator said, "Good morning,

Ray. And who do you have with you?"

"This is my grandson Ernie and his dog, Barney. We are here to visit your patients."

We visited several patients on the hospice list before entering Room 210 where we spied a teenage boy sitting in a wheelchair, looking out the window. He appeared to be just a little bit younger than Ernie.

"Excuse me, son," I said. "We're looking for Mr. Fox."

"Sir, he went home this morning. My name is Timmy Bower. I'm here for a couple of days to get my meds adjusted. I have cancer and need special treatments."

Timmy looked over and saw Ernie standing behind him with Barney at his feet.

"Say, can I hold your dog?" Timmy asked. "Does he bite?"

Ernie stepped forward, picked up Barney and placed him on Timmy's lap. "No, he's gentle. In fact, he is a little bit afraid of strangers, but he loves to be petted." Ernie noticed Timmy had no hair but said nothing about it.

As Timmy petted the dog, I leaned down and said to the boy, "The cancer seems to be taking a toll on you, son."

He replied, "Well, the chemo is a little rough, but it is supposed to kill the cancer cells. I go home tomorrow."

Then he looked up at Ernie. "Gee, I love your dog."

"Thanks. And you ought to see him swim," Ernie replied.

At that moment, a tall and slender young woman with long, blond hair entered the room. "This is my mom, Kim," Timmy said.

After I introduced Ernie and myself to her, she said, "Sorry, gentlemen, but you'll have to leave the room. The nurse is coming to give Timmy his meds."

"Okay Mom. Just let me hold Barney for a few minutes longer." As Timmy stroked him, the dog licked the boy's face. "See, Mom, Barney loves me. Can he come to my birthday party on Friday?"

"I don't see why not," Kim replied. She reached into her purse, pulled out a slip of paper and wrote on it. "Here's our address, Ray. Why don't you bring your grandson and the dog over about 2:00? I'm sure all the other children will enjoy meeting them."

The following Friday, as Ernie, Barney and I were headed up the walk to Timmy's house, Ernie stopped suddenly in his tracks. "I know we brought a game along for Timmy's birthday present, but I have something else I would like to give him."

"What's that, Ernie?"

"He loves Barney so much, and Barney seems to really like him. I want to give Barney to Timmy to help him with his sickness."

I was astonished. "Your dog, Ernie? You love this dog. That's really some sacrifice."

I didn't know until later that Ernie had brought along a bag with Barney's food and water dishes in it.

When we entered the house, we were surprised to see only one boy and one girl there. Wearing a stocking cap, Timmy explained, "I guess the other kids were busy today. You and Barney can stay, can't you?"

My voice choked as I replied, "Yes, of course."

Needless to say, Timmy and the other two children were delighted with Barney's presence. Timmy and his parents were totally surprised when Ernie stated he wanted to give a second present to Timmy — his dog, Barney. "Take good care of him, Timmy," Ernie said, his voice just a little bit weepy.

Timmy cried as he nuzzled his face into Barney's neck. "Gee, Dad, now I've got the dog I always wanted."

"That you have, son. And a mighty fine one, too," his father replied.

For the next several weeks, Ernie and Timmy kept in touch over the phone and exchanged information about how Barney and Timmy were doing.

I could see that although Ernie was happy that he had given his dog to Timmy, he still missed Barney terribly. All his friends asked where Barney was. And when Ernie told them what he had done, they said, "Gee, I could never give up my dog."

Gradually, Timmy got better. In fact, his cancer was in remission, his mother, Kim, said when I called her to invite Timmy and her to the last baseball game of Ernie's Little League season.

We were delighted when Kim, Timmy, and Barney showed up at the game. Barney got really excited when Ernie walked up and talked to him before the game.

Ernie had been a terrific pitcher throughout the season. That day, he needed only one more strike to win. With all his might and strength, Ernie threw the ball as fast as he could. The umpire called "Strike!" and the game was over. Ernie's team had won. His teammates put Ernie on their shoulders and carried him around the field. When the parade was over, Ernie walked back over to Timmy and Barney.

"I'm glad you brought Barney to see me pitch," he said to Timmy.

"No, I didn't bring him to see you pitch. We brought him so you can take him home with you. He's your dog, Ernie. Even though he was good to me and stayed with me through all the chemo treatments, I could see he really missed you. My dad is going to get me a puppy. And Barney belongs with you."

Ernie picked Barney up in his arms, and the dog gave my grandson numerous kisses and even licked Ernie's nose in delight.

Tears started to flow down Ernie's face. "Thanks, Timmy. I really did miss Barney."

Timmy smiled bravely as he also started to cry. "Thank you for sharing Barney with me, Ernie. The doctors say I'm in remission. Maybe next year, I can join a baseball team, and you can show me how to pitch."

"That's a promise. Right, Barney?" Ernie gave his dog a big hug.

— Ray Weaver —

51

The Nanny Has Paws

For me, a house or an apartment becomes a home
when you add one set of four legs, a happy tail, and
that indescribable measure of love that we call a dog.
~Roger Caras

When I was growing up, my family joked that we had a dog for a nanny, just like Wendy, John, and Michael Darling in *Peter Pan*. Wherever my brother and I went, our huge Newfoundland/black Lab mix wasn't far behind. She was a gentle giant who let us dress her up in hats and blankets, use her broad side as a pillow while we watched television, and sneak her the food we didn't want off our plates.

My parents said that they could tell which neighborhood friend's house we were visiting because the dog was always sitting in their front yard. Having walked us there, she waited patiently to walk us home. Such large dogs often don't live past ten years or so, but she was with us for sixteen years. She passed away a week after my little brother graduated from high school, having hung on through years of declining health until both of her children were grown.

I suppose it's natural for parents to want to give our children the best of what we remember from our own childhoods. I longed to give my daughter the experience of having a dog for a nanny, but I didn't think I would have that chance. Lina, the high-energy Sheltie mix my husband and I had adopted four years before our daughter was born, didn't seem to have a maternal bone in her body. Clearly, she preferred being the family's baby to having one, and I wasn't sure how she would react when we brought an infant home.

At first, it was a bit of a struggle. She looked, sniffed and ignored. Then she conned her human grandparents into giving her more treats and playtime so she wouldn't feel neglected. She ended up with an upset tummy and a temporary limp from playing too hard and long. When our daughter became a toddler, we were vigilant. Lina, a rescue, startled easily at loud noises and unexpected stomps, and the fluffiness of her tail meant it was easy to accidentally tread on a long piece of fur. We kept dog and child separated, and I sighed, regretful that it didn't seem my dog daughter and my human daughter would have a close relationship.

But it turned out I wasn't the only one worried about keeping my daughter safe. Like many dogs, Lina is terrified of the vacuum cleaner. One day, I was cleaning up a spill and looked up to see her standing between the loud, vibrating machine and the small human who was ignoring it. Lina was trembling with fear, but she wasn't going to let that monster near her kid.

It wasn't long before I learned that my human child felt the same way about my canine child. We were talking about family relationships, and I named people who were brothers and sisters. I paused, and my only child said with complete confidence, "And Lina is my sister."

As my human daughter grew from a baby into a kid, Lina's muzzle grew white, and her high energy waned. In the evenings, we often take a family walk around the circular road our house is on. Now when people ask my daughter what kind of dog she has, she answers, "A one-loop dog," because Lina has made it quite clear she only wants to do one loop.

It seems that Lina always had a bit of "nanny dog" in her, but she specializes in slightly older children. My daughter has always had trouble napping, but she still needs rest, so we instituted a quiet time after school. Both she and Lina are happy as long as the door is open and they are together. Lina serves as a quiet audience and compliant playmate, the living animal among all the stuffed ones.

Lina has also taken over bedtime. At night, she accompanies me upstairs and lies on the floor while I read bedtime stories. As I leave, I crack the door to let in the light and let out the dog (when she's ready). Then Lina waits patiently until my daughter falls asleep. Every night, about a half-hour after I leave the room, we know our daughter is safely sleeping when we hear the click of the nanny's claws coming down the stairs.

— Courtney McKinney-Whitaker —

52

FaceTiming with the Dog

*I have caught more ills from people sneezing over me
and giving me virus infections than from kissing dogs.*
~Barbara Woodhouse

Our black Lab/Dachshund/Boxer mix, a rescue from a Georgia shelter, has been mourning his daily leash-free romps at the nearby wooded, dog-friendly park. Two things make Noah truly happy: those walks, and visits from my newly engaged daughter, currently isolated in her small Manhattan apartment.

Unfortunately, we live in the epicenter of COVID-19 in south-western Connecticut. Early in this plague, our underutilized park had to be closed because of the many people crowding the grand lawn, the children's playground, and even the deep woods trails.

In the few days before the mayor's stay-at-home order was made official, Noah and I watched the number of people walking their dogs at the park catapult from an average of perhaps three dogs walking their one "person" to five or six people trailing one dog. Once, we counted a family of eight, ranging in age from maybe five to ninety years old, with one tiny Pekingese. Maintaining social distance from them on the narrow trail forced Noah and me to hack our way through a muddy byway, leaving him confused by the change in our routine.

Later, we approached the field designated for dogs, where Noah usually sprinted ahead of me, eager to engage in glorious friend sniffing, friend chasing, and stick tugging with his buddies. To my amazement and Noah's ears-down disappointment, the field was crowded not with dogs, but with boys playing soccer, children having play dates, and families walking around as if it were just a lovely March Sunday afternoon and not a virus-ridden Thursday when everyone was supposed to be isolating at home.

Noah seemed to understand why we left so quickly. He didn't resist when I put him on a leash to thread our way through the crowd to the safety of our car.

That was our last walk-in-the-park day.

Since then, I have taken him for an occasional walk around the block on a leash, which makes him happy enough. His tail wags, and he finds a few sprouts of onion grass on a neighbor's lawn to sniff at and then add his scent to. But, most of the time, he is relegated to the back yard and chasing the squirrels raiding the bird feeders.

There's more disappointment for a dog during these COVID times. Every night at bedtime, before following me to our bedroom, he trots over to my daughter's room, sniffing hopefully to see if she has come home yet.

Of course, she can't come home. If she could, we would still be planning her large wedding. Sadly, Noah wouldn't be there. He would stay with a dog sitter for the weekend, and we would be at a hotel near the venue.

It was going to be at a beautiful location, with live music and a catered dinner. Family was coming from all over the world. But COVID-19 came first, and that ended the big wedding.

The night that we decided for sure that the wedding was off was an exciting night for Noah. As we discussed switching to an intimate Zoom wedding in our back yard with only the bride, the groom, an officiant, and the parents, Noah licked away my tears of disappointment. We agreed that we would try to have a large, festive party on the first anniversary, one we hope everyone can attend.

Before we hung up our FaceTime call, my daughter asked me to turn the phone screen so she could see Noah.

"Nooo-ah," she called, as she always did when she entered the house. "Hello, baby! How's my sweet Noo-ah doing?"

Noah sprang to his full height. Ears erect, he walked up to the screen. Then he looked behind it. He returned to the front and cocked his head. He seemed to think about licking the screen but decided just to stare. I heard my daughter laughing for the first time that sad night and asked what was funny.

"I just realized it's going to be okay, Mom," she said. "You know those silver linings? I just found one."

I was stumped and told her so.

"Don't you see? Now Noah doesn't have to go to a dog sitter. In fact, he can be our ring bearer!"

I turned the screen toward the dog again, and my daughter crooned, "Would you like that? Would you like to be at my wedding? Will you be my ring bearer?"

At that, Noah's tail wagged so hard that I thought it would come off.

I guess that meant "yes."

— Marla Sterling —

53

Unemployed

Every puppy should have a boy.
~Erma Bombeck

My family began raising dogs for the Seeing Eye organization when I was eleven years old. A seven-week-old German Shepherd named Igor became ours for a year. It was a whirlwind year of housebreaking, training, socializing, being pulled down the street by a dog trained to pull, going to community events, and meeting other working dogs. My siblings and I fell in love with Igor the way children do — completely, irresponsibly, head-over-heels in love.

And then Igor went back to Seeing Eye. As puppy raisers, we only get to keep the dogs until they're fourteen to sixteen months old, at which point they return to Seeing Eye to continue their formal training. If they pass, we see the dog only one more time at their graduation "town walk" where they show off their new skills, like crossing the street and avoiding tree branches.

By the time we attended Igor's town walk, we were already on our second Seeing Eye puppy, an affable Labrador named Charlie who was doomed to fail because of his tendency to walk and pee. (Charlie went on to a successful career as a drug-sniffing dog.) And then there was a third… and a fourth….

Long story short, my family is currently raising our thirteenth dog for Seeing Eye.

We have six dogs currently guiding throughout the United States and Canada. If a Seeing Eye dog fails out of the program, the puppy-raising family has the option to adopt it. Sometimes, we say no, and a dog like Charlie might be placed with another agency. Sometimes, though, we adopt the dog. My brother has the only Golden Retriever we raised, a sweetheart named Kramer. And I adopted one of our many German Shepherds, this one named Wolcott.

Wolcott would have been a great working dog. He was tolerant, patient and confident. We were sure he would be a great success when he went back to Seeing Eye for his formal training. And he was! We were invited to watch his "town walk," proud of him as he circumvented obstacles like potholes with ease.

Three months later, Wolcott was removed from the program due to his gastro-intestinal problems. He was a fully trained guide dog without anyone to guide.

As happy as I am to have Wolcott as my constant companion, I still mourn the life that could have been. Once home, his GI issues cleared up quickly. He was a healthy but unemployed working dog.

So, I set out to find Wolcott a job.

Wolcott was trained to be a service dog, but in the absence of someone to serve, perhaps he could change careers. I'd seen therapy dogs in libraries and hospitals. A calm, gentle nature seemed to be all that was needed, and Wolcott had that in spades.

So, last summer, I began to expand my definition of working dogs.

The therapy-dog world differs in many ways from my experience raising puppies. I found it to be a very solo experience. Most facilities, like hospitals or schools, only have room for a puppy or two. I no longer had a group of fellow raisers to rely on. When I responded to a request for a therapy dog, I was often responding alone.

Or... almost alone. After all, people were excited to see Wolcott. I tend to blend into the background. That's partly because anyone can get lost behind a seventy-five-pound Shepherd, but mostly it's the magic of dogs. They render all else invisible, even dreary hospitals, schools, or pain. A dog brightens any setting.

Becoming a certified therapy dog is only half the battle, though. You still have to find a place for your dog to work.

Our match happened almost immediately at a school down the street for children with multiple disabilities. Most students were on the autism spectrum. Some were unable to move or speak, communicating through iPads or gestures. All were under the age of twelve. The school leaders wanted to try animal-assisted therapy. Would Wolcott be a good fit?

Before our first day at the learning center, Wolcott had never seen a wheelchair, been poked in the eye by an overexcited child, or been sat on by a meaty eight-year-old. All those things happened within the first hour of our first visit.

Yet Wolcott is always calm in the center of the storm at this school. Upon entering a classroom, he lies down, sometimes on his side, sometimes with his head in a child's lap. He licks their hands. He lets them poke and prod. He knows that they need to explore him.

I follow Wolcott from classroom to classroom. Some kids are in walkers and enjoy having Wolcott as company while they practice walking the long hallways. Some don't walk at all, leaning their weight against Wolcott's furry back.

Wolcott licks the students and aides who are having rough days, spending two hours a week in the center being pulled into therapy sessions and classrooms. We are welcomed everywhere.

Dogs are better than magic words at opening doors.

By our fourth visit, we had a long list of friends, but no one needs Wolcott like Stephen. He is a nonverbal eight-year-old on the autism spectrum who spends most of the day trying to talk through an iPad. I was told this by an aide because, whenever I see Stephen, he is fully engaged with Wolcott. The iPad never makes an appearance.

"He's a different boy," the aide whispers as we watch Stephen use Wolcott's belly as a pillow. He lifts his hand to Wolcott's face. Stephen loves Wolcott's "kisses." He smiles at the sensation, burying his head deeper in Wolcott's fur.

It's hard for Stephen to be this still. His brain doesn't process things the way most people's do. He has no sense of boundaries. He fixates. He is often anxious.

Yet with Wolcott, he can be motionless. He can be gentle. He lets

Wolcott lick his fingers. With Wolcott, Stephen can exist in the present moment. He can answer questions. He half-signs, half-grunts what he wants. Today, he wants the dog. To sit next to the dog. To pet the dog.

"Show me the dog's feet," the aide urges.

Stephen points to the feet. Then, when asked, he points to the eyes, the ears, the tail. Processing these questions is a visible challenge, but he keeps his hand near Wolcott's face, waiting for the lick.

"Do you love Wolcott?" the aide asks. "Pet Wolcott gently if you love him."

Stephen presses his forehead to Wolcott's. He rubs Wolcott's ears gently. So gently.

Sitting on the floor with Stephen, I think that Wolcott would have been an amazing working dog. And then I realize that, in all the ways that matter, he is one.

— Katie Avagliano —

Chapter
6

What I Learned from the Dog

54

Transforming Hami

We could have bought a small yacht with
what we spent on our dog and all the things he
destroyed. Then again, how many yachts
wait by the door all day for your return?
~John Grogan

Hamilton von Watts was the last dog I would have adopted. When we first saw him, the big German Shorthaired Pointer/black Lab mix lay abjectly in his cage. A yellow identification tag noted his name.

But I wasn't going to have much say in the adoption matter. This was going to be our thirteen-year-old son's dog, and he was doing the selecting. I groaned when Cory asked the shelter employee to let Hamilton out of the cage to visit with him.

The seventeen-month-old mutt looked worse on inspection — filthy, with open wounds and a battalion of ticks. Touching his punctured ear elicited a sharp whine; patting him produced a dust cloud. His puffed right eye oozed, and he emitted an odious scent. But I could see the love pass between Cory and Hamilton when their eyes locked.

And then Hami plucked our heartstrings by flashing a toothy smile, a grin he produced by wrinkling up his nose, and baring his brilliant white teeth and chomping them together several times. An energetic snort punctuated each chomp. He even mustered enough pizzazz to happily paw the air. I could almost hear him cry out, "Please give me a chance!"

An hour later, after Cory and my husband, Chris, filled out the paperwork and plunked down the money for him, Hami bounded around the back of our Suburban. He seemed so grateful. I, however, remained dubious.

Hami's introduction to our home was rough. He charged our cat, Tibbs, who attempted a warm nose-to-nose welcome. Our Queensland Heeler, Sydney, gave us an alarmed, now-you've-ruined-the-neighborhood look.

And while he clearly adored Cory, he cowered and scampered away from our eighteen-year-old son Parker and his buddies and acted anxious around Chris. When Chris removed his belt while undressing, Hami bolted from him. When friends visited, the sixty-five-pound dog growled and hid behind my legs or beneath my skirt. His legs quivered as he peered out at intruders. When frightened, which happened often, he urinated on the floor.

Hami was also undisciplined. He ignored commands and boundaries and led us on lengthy hunting expeditions for him through our hilly, cactus-filled neighborhood. A frequent refrain around our house was "Cory, come get your dog!"

I felt guilty about my uncharitable feelings, but Hami aggravated me. It wasn't that I didn't like dogs. Chris and I had cared for six of them so far during our marriage. And Chris said he knew I was "the one" because I was the only female his Border Collie, Felina, had ever liked.

But I liked high-IQ, compliant dogs. Classy dogs with manners and respect for my personal space. Not unruly dogs who barreled into rooms, knocking things — and me — over.

I tried to avoid him, but as much as I tried, he insisted on following me around like a sheep to a shepherd. He got underfoot when I worked in the kitchen. When he'd had enough roughhousing with Chris and the boys, he'd scurry away from them and lean against me for protection. I'd shoo the guys away and tell them sternly that the dog had had enough.

He seemed so grateful for everything I did for him, no matter how small it was — stroke his back, acknowledge his presence, or feed him. He'd give me that big, chompy smile and slurpy kiss and then tap dance in front of me.

I think Hami knew his perseverance would wear me down eventually. His smile, gratitude and amusing antics chipped away at my defenses. I couldn't keep my heart from surrendering to this hurt dog. But my rigid brain needed coaxing to follow suit. I wrestled against frustration and expectations, prayed for divine patience, and changed my behavior.

Instead of avoiding Hami, I gritted my teeth and embarked on a mission to uncover his potential. I knew it had to be there under all that fear and pain. But could the trauma be undone?

I instructed Chris and the boys to top his kibble with nutrient-packed chicken and duck eggs. Cory spent hundreds of dollars of his own money to heal Hami's wounds and eradicate his external and internal vermin. We lavished love and attention on him and made sure we avoided his anxiety triggers. When I sat on the floor next to him and massaged the right hip that caused him to limp and whine so much, he'd heave exaggerated sighs and lick my face. It took weeks of scrubbing ground-in grime from his broken body to uncover his sleek, dark chocolate coat.

And with all that love and attention, a miracle occurred. As the grime washed away, and his body and heart healed, Hami transformed. His formerly ragged coat glistened in the sunshine. He started trusting and obeying. His once fearful eyes emitted security. And he gained confidence in himself.

He started doing surveillance patrols around the house. He learned his boundaries and responded to commands. He became comfortable with our friends and made the rounds among them for fanny scratches and ear rubs. Every morning, primed to enjoy another day, he smiled and tap danced. In fact, he smiled all the time — when he went outside and when he was invited back in; when he was fed; and when he got leashed up for a walk. The refrain around our house became "Everyone should be as happy as Hami." Even Sydney started to pal around with him.

In the process, I realized I was learning from Hami.

He taught me to be eternally grateful for everything, even the small things. Especially the small things. And to lighten up. He'd wheedled the dormant Type B personality out of me, the one I had long ago discarded. In the chaotic swirl of wifedom, motherhood and work, I'd become uptight, rigid, and preoccupied by trivial things. Hami re-directed my attention and taught me to smile at each new day.

And I'm still learning.

The ravages of time and a neurological disease wasting his hind leg muscles have taken their toll. But thirteen-year-old Hami is teaching me how to decline physically and age gracefully. I'm taking notes:

- If you feel inclined, sleep a little more, and make the most out of what you can do when the body parts are limbered up and operating properly, which may take a while after a nap.
- Don't be too proud to let someone help you stand upright to get moving. Hobble outside to do your business, bark at the Amazon Prime guy, and soak up the sunshine. Life is good.
- If you forget the rules and do something wrong, give your person a brilliant smile and bury your head in their lap. It works every time.
- Never let your infirmities steal your gratefulness.

Not long ago, I gazed into Hami's clouded eyes, cupped his gray muzzle in my hands, and thanked him for what he'd done and for being patient with me. He heaved a sigh, plopped onto the floor next to me and fell asleep, seemingly satisfied that I'd understood his purpose.

Cory's selection had been divinely directed.

Love and patience had transformed Hami — and me.

— Andrea Arthur Owan —

Lilly

There is nothing truer in the world
than the love of a good dog.
~Author Unknown

hen I was eight and ruffling our German Shepherd's fur on the family-room carpet, he lunged at me suddenly with open jaws and bared teeth. My older brother arrived just in time to push Jagger off before he bit my face. That experience traumatized me, and after Jagger died four years later from old age, I wanted nothing to do with a dog as a pet. I even hated watching movies with dogs in them.

That's why I argued desperately with my mother when she planned on getting a Yorkshire Terrier. I had no idea what a Yorkshire Terrier looked like or how it behaved, but because it was a dog, I knew I didn't want it in our house or around me. I remembered Jagger's teeth, menacing growl, and dark eyes. "No way," I told my mother at the dinner table. "Not another dog!"

I was older (seventeen) and a little embarrassed to be so wimpy, but dogs were unpredictable. Right? My older brother was gone, living pet-less on his own. Who would defend me from this new dog?

"I'm getting us a Yorkie," my mother insisted. "I've already made arrangements with the breeder."

I slumped in my chair and ignored the rest of my meatloaf and mashed potatoes. I was doomed.

The next day, Mom showed me pictures of cute Yorkshire Terriers and assured me they were gentle. But even with her assurances, I wasn't comfortable with getting another dog, even if it was small. Nevertheless, two days later, Mom returned home in the afternoon with a four-pound Terrier. She named it Lilly. Gently, she cradled the little bundle of brown-and-tan fur in her arms and smiled. Then she dropped a bombshell.

"Keith, you're going to train Lilly."

"What?" Had I heard her right? She wanted me to train this dog? Didn't she remember that I hated dogs?

"You will feed her before you go to school and again at dinner."

I glanced at Lilly, whose eyes darted around our family room as if looking for a place to settle in. "But I want nothing to…"

She raised a hand, stopping me. "Plus, you will potty-train her and teach her to behave."

"Me?" I still could not believe this was happening. "How am I supposed to know what to do?"

Mom smiled and walked away. "You're an A student, aren't you?" she said over her shoulder. "Do your research."

So, I did. Over the next week, I researched Yorkshire Terriers online. I talked to friends at school who were experienced dog owners about the methods they used to train their dogs.

At first, Lilly tried to behave like an alpha dog, nudging me to pet her, barking to be fed, or pulling on her leash when I walked her. Yorkies can be demanding, and Lilly was no exception. She had small-dog syndrome, and I learned from Sharon Maguire on the Dog Breed Info Center website that dogs like Yorkies should not be viewed as cute and cuddly just because they're small. They must know their limits. If Lilly barked at friends, I put her in the bathroom and closed the door. If she barked at other dogs outside, I yelled "No" and made her sit until the other dog passed. A dog's size, I learned, does not matter regarding its behavior.

Lilly would run and jump when I came home from school, which I interpreted — incorrectly — to mean she was excited to see me. What she needed was exercise, so I took her for long walks to tire her out. If she pulled on the leash, I stopped until I decided we would continue so she knew I was walking her, not her walking me. I let Lilly sit in my lap when I wanted her to and sleep in my bed if she behaved, but only at my feet.

It took five months, but the training paid off, and Lilly became an obedient and friendly dog, although she still barked at strangers, especially the pizza-delivery guy. I had overcome my fear of dogs and felt more confident about my ability to train one and control its behavior.

When Lilly passed fourteen years later, I grieved for those times when she licked my face and cuddled with me on the couch. I missed our long walks together and even her yapping at strangers. I especially missed her friendship and loyalty, which, surprisingly, had turned me into a dog lover.

— Keith Manos —

56

The Greatest Lesson Learned

My therapist has a wagging tail.
~Author Unknown

Bringing home a dog was the furthest thing from my mind. My previous dog was a gentle Doberman named Calhoun, who I had for ten years. When he died of cancer, I had no interest in replacing him.

My daughter Emily had other plans, however, and that girl — who was only seven at the time — could be very persuasive. So it was that, on a hot August day, when I still maintained I had no desire to bring home a dog, I found myself with Emily and my wife Betsy driving to the animal shelter an hour away to look at puppies.

Betsy and Emily picked her out: a small, shy white Lab/Greyhound mix with large brown eyes and droopy ears. We named her Sophia, but she preferred "Sophie the Dog" when called, or just "Dog."

Emily gave us the speech every parent has heard concerning a dog: "I'll keep it in my room and take care of it and walk it every day." But since I worked from home mornings and taught classes only in the afternoons, that turned out to be my job from the first day. I slept downstairs on the couch the first night, and many nights afterward, with Sophie nearby in her crate. She was scared, and I took the soft, shaking pup out and let her sleep with me or put my finger through the crate's grill to pet her until she slept.

I was a goner by the end of her first night with us. Soon, it seemed she had always been a part of our family. I realized I hadn't replaced Calhoun. I'd honored his memory by giving a good home to another dog who needed one.

But that wasn't the last or largest lesson I learned from Sophie the Dog.

Two months after she came to live with us, my mother was killed in a car accident. Ma and I were very close, and I felt shattered by her death. In the mornings, after Betsy and Emily had left for work and school, instead of getting to my writing, all I could do was stare into space. I felt stunned by Ma's death, and that feeling seemed as though it was going to last the rest of my life.

Sophie, however, was not interested in watching me stare into space. She would nudge me to take her out. Once we were at the park, she would annoy me until I played with her. I'd trained her to walk off-leash, and she'd run in circles around me, pick up a stick and drop it at my feet. When I'd throw it for her to catch, she'd leap high in the air, snatch it and run back to smack me in the leg with the stick before running off again so I'd chase her.

She led me down forest paths I'd never explored and took me to ruins of old estates and silos in the woods I never knew were there. Some days, we'd spend two hours out roaming and exploring the hiking trails around the village. When we came home, she'd sit by my chair and put her head on my foot or rest it against my leg. It was so reassuring to feel her there, to be able to reach down and pet her soft head, and to see her look up at me with her dark, kind eyes. I learned from her that life goes on, no matter what kind of tragedy knocks you down, and that it can be good again even if it can never be the same.

I learned that lesson multiple times through many different events: when Betsy's breast cancer returned, when Emily suddenly grew up overnight, and when any other sorrow or uncertainty came my way. Sophie the Dog was always there with her bright eyes, wagging her tail and telling me it was time to get up, go out and see what life had to offer. And so we did; we played so much over the years, the four of us. Emily grew up with Sophie, and so did Betsy and I in our own way.

When Emily was twenty and about to leave home, she decided she wanted a dog to take with her who would be as close a companion as Sophie had been. She went to the shelter and came home with a Miniature Pinscher named Monty whom Sophie took to almost immediately. I'd been worried that maybe Sophie the Dog would feel she was being replaced and be resentful, but I should have known better. Sophie always welcomed anyone we welcomed to the house. When Monty arrived, he was a little unsure of the situation. He wouldn't bark and didn't want to eat much, but it wasn't long before Sophie had shown him that everything was all right, and he could feel at home and relax.

Monty was with us for four months before the time came for Emily to head out on her own; they moved to Georgia. It was another difficult time as Betsy and I experienced empty-nest syndrome, but Sophie was there for us just as she'd always been. She was older now, thirteen, and not as keen on racing around with a stick or leading me on adventures through the woods or old ruins. But she was there with all her grace, warmth, charm and love. It was impossible to remain depressed with Sophie around and hard to think about how sad it would be someday when she was gone.

And when she left us finally, it was difficult, but I could only be grateful for the many years we'd had together. Sophie had come into our lives unexpectedly and filled them with light, love and laughter. All along, I knew that it wouldn't last, and I needed to be thankful for the time we had and the adventures we shared. After a few months, I went back to the shelter and got another little puppy we named Sammie, a soft brown Beagle/Feist mix, and she lit up our home with her antics just as Sophie had done sixteen years earlier.

Life is perpetual change, and we all hate losing what we love. But I learned from Sophie that life goes on. No matter what knocks you down, you need to get back up, knowing that it can be good and beautiful again, even if it can never be the same.

—Joshua J. Mark—

57

Walking Bug

*Ever wonder where you'd end up if you took your dog
for a walk and never once pulled back on the leash?*
~Robert Brault

My nine-year-old granddaughter giggled as the tiny Boston Terrier crawled up her chest to lick her neck and face. "Ladybug," she said. "You should name her Ladybug."

"It's a good name," I said.

A week later, Audrey changed her mind. "Grandma, we need to call her Bug."

"Why's that?" I asked.

"Because she's no lady!"

And she wasn't. Bug was all energy and no finesse. We loved her that way.

She added healthy exercise to my schedule as a new retiree. In an empty field next to my house, she was my zigzag racer, able to run circles around me without getting to the end of her retractable leash. She knew just how far to go, just like she knew when I needed an extra cuddle.

Every morning at ten, Bug let me know it was time for her walk. She loved everyone in our Lawrenceville, New Jersey neighborhood. She'd jump with joy and lower herself on her front paws to encourage people to play with her. Many bent down to accept her adulation and laugh at her happy dance. Her whole body vibrated whenever anyone reached down to pet her.

The COVID-19 quarantine changed but did not eliminate our walks. I kept Bug close to my side and maintained more than the six feet of recommended separation from other people. Bug didn't understand the change. When she couldn't run freely, she'd stand on her hind legs and prance for attention. She got it. People talked to her but kept their distance. Those in cars, yards, or on the street waved and talked.

A man walked by and said, "She reminds me of my sons."

"Why's that?" I asked.

"They're ten and twelve and have no idea what a historic event they're experiencing."

"They will," I replied.

"You're right, but for now they just want to play games and talk to their friends."

Bug pulled to the left, and we walked past the elementary school. "Lawrence Strong" was written in paper cups inserted into the chain-link fence. We passed a field where I loosened the leash and let Bug run.

"May I take a video of your dog?" asked a policeman who watched from his car on the side of the road.

"Yes," I said.

"I want to send it to my son. He's ten. This will make him smile. We have a Boston Terrier."

Bug jumped into the air and ran in circles as if she knew her antics mattered.

My dog encouraged me to keep walking in new directions where I fed my spirit with the sights we saw. Painted rocks along the path of an old trolley line read: "Smile," "Be happy," and "We're with you." Handmade shamrocks were displayed on doors and windows for a neighborhood scavenger hunt. They were replaced with Easter eggs and then rainbows. Notes of encouragement and hearts made with tape and chalk appeared on driveways.

I exchanged hellos with a woman we passed on the street around the corner from my house. After she walked on for several feet, she stopped and said, "What's your name?"

"I'm Judy," I said.

"I'm Linda," she said. "And I'm sorry."

I tilted my head and raised my eyebrows.

"I've lived here for seventeen years and have seen you many times. This is the first time we've spoken, and I'm really sorry."

I smiled at her. "I'm glad we're speaking now." I knew we'd speak again and maybe even become close friends.

Bug and I obey the six-feet-of-separation rule with members of our community, but in many ways it's like we're not separated at all.

—Judy Salcewicz—

58

Focus, Calm, and Discipline

Why does watching a dog be a dog
fill one with happiness?
~Jonathan Safran Foer

hen I was seven, I imagined growing up on a farm. I pictured myself milking the cows and growing my own corn. In the late afternoons, I daydreamed about cattle dogs rounding up the sheep to lead them back home.

But despite my active imagination, I was a city girl, raised in Cleveland. It wasn't until I grew up and had a family of my own that I could realize my dreams. I was thrilled when we found a home in the middle of the city of Bellevue, resting comfortably near the border of Kelsey Creek Farm.

Kelsey Creek Farm had a fair in the fall, and one year my husband Steve and I went with our five-year-old twins to watch the sheep shearing, go on a hayride, and then treat the kids to cotton candy and kettle corn.

The highlight of the day would be the sheep-herding demonstration, so we got our places along the fence early. Near where we stood, a woman had opened her canvas folding chair inside a large, metal pen. At her feet were five dogs. Four of them were strongly built, princely-looking Australian Shepherds, and the fifth appeared to be some kind of Cattle Dog or Blue Heeler mix. Lying beside the other dogs, she looked like the runt, and her odd overbite made her a misfit among them.

"That's Lucy," the owner said as we stared at her. "And I'm Martha," she said, standing to shake my hand.

The kids were still in that stage when they would say whatever came into their minds. "Why does she look like that?" Helen asked.

"Well," the woman answered, "she has two different colored eyes. Isn't it interesting?"

My son was not about to let it go. "But what's wrong with her mouth?"

"Oh. She has an overbite, and it makes her look a little different. Nobody would adopt her from the shelter, but we love her! Wait 'til you see her go. She's probably the best herding dog here today!"

The demonstration began, and the kids stood on tiptoe to watch one very well-trained Australian Shepherd herd a pack of twelve not-so-well-trained sheep out of a holding pen. The dog maneuvered them around the cones and small children who had volunteered to be placed as markers. (To my children's great dismay, they were not chosen for this honor.) Then the dog chased the sheep back into the enclosure.

As a mom of twins, some days I feel like it's hard to simply manage my own two children, but we watched with interest as one dog was able to manage a whole herd of sheep! The discipline, focus and composure of these dogs made me realize I still had a lot to learn.

But after about twenty minutes, it did not appear that Martha's dogs were headed into the demonstration any time soon, and the kids were still sulking about not getting picked to be posts. So, as my five-year-olds' attention spans dictated, we started toward the parking lot.

Suddenly, chaos erupted beside us! The sheep broke out of the makeshift enclosure and burst through the ribbons separating them from the throngs of families. The sheep scattered, stood dumbstruck, bucked, spun and ran amok. Families pulled their small ones aside, while others raced to touch the sheep. One sheep snapped at some eager fingers trying to pet his wooly pelt. Another meandered lazily in the direction of the ticket booth, probably wondering who had herded all the humans into a line. I felt catapulted into a Looney Toons episode and thoroughly expected Wile E. Coyote to appear, followed by a flying sheep with a stick of dynamite in his mouth. Some folks screamed; others laughed.

But the dogs knew just what to do.

With a signal from Martha, her waiting dogs bounded out of her enclosure and began circling the sheep, keeping a wide berth. Each dog's focused stare shouted, "This is our chance! Now we get to show 'em all what we can do!"

As a team, they crouched, stood at attention, and side-stepped. Magnificently and stealthily, they fanned out around the park, trolling for stragglers. Silently coordinating their movements, they moved the sheep into a tight bunch, heightened their control with each step, and herded the wayward sheep back to safety.

But my eyes were on Lucy, who had spotted a sheep that had made it surprisingly far. The wayward sheep was nose-to-belly with a small boy whose face was scrunched in fear. Lucy kept her distance, but her presence alone was enough to get the sheep's attention, and she pulled the sheep back into the flock with her tenacity and skill.

I was impressed with the drive and discipline of the dogs. They didn't need to shout or bark, yip or snap. Their instincts showed them how to maintain order, restore calm and protect their charges. As a mom, I sometimes find it hard to keep my frustrations in check, yet I know how important it is to define the boundaries and stick with a discipline that will keep my kids feeling safe. Instead of barking or yipping at my twins, I'll work on channeling those dogs the next time I feel like I'm herding sheep!

— Ilana Long —

59

Unleashed

*The most important thing in communication
is to hear what isn't being said.*
~Peter F. Drucker

Our grandson changed trucking companies and was no longer able to bring his dog along. I took some time weighing the pros and cons before inviting his feisty, little Cairn Terrier, reminiscent of Toto in *The Wizard of Oz*, to come and live with me and my mother.

The biggest obstacle to having Ralph the dog join our family was our hoity-toity, arrogant feline, Pumpkin. It was no secret that she is queen of the house, and she was adamant that no dogs were allowed. But, I thought, given time, she might warm up to Ralph.

Another concern was that a dog might be hazardous to my mother's fragile health. She was ninety-eight, and we worried that an affectionate dog might jump on her or trip her while she was using her walker.

I believed we could keep a keen eye on both of them — elderly woman and little dog. And on the plus side, our many grandchildren and great-grandchildren spent a great deal of time at the house. They would play with Ralph and run with him on our farmland.

Ralph was taken aback when he first approached Pumpkin. He'd never met a cat or dog that he didn't befriend instinctively, so Pumpkin's rude hiss stopped him in his tracks. Only one thing frightened Ralph more than Pumpkin's hiss — loud thunderstorms!

I learned this rather abruptly one night when I was awakened from a wonderfully sweet and perfect dream by a trembling ball of fur sprinting back and forth beneath my covers. After rescuing the terrified pooch from the tangled bedding, I swaddled him in the comfort of my arms until dawn.

By the end of Ralph's first year with us, Pumpkin had softened her demeanor toward him. She no longer hunched and hissed when he approached, and sometimes even appeared to be a bit friendly. This, of course, didn't mean by any stretch of the imagination that she had any intention of stepping down from her position of royalty.

Ralph had become a good playmate for the grandkids; he especially loved walking to the school bus stop in the early morning with six-year-old Maze. The two loved chasing after birds, squirrels, or rabbits along the way.

By now, Mom was ninety-nine and had grown increasingly more fragile, physically and emotionally. She seldom communicated and spent a great deal of time sitting or napping in her recliner. Her eyesight and hearing were poor, making it more difficult for her to interact with the young kids, which she had once enjoyed immensely. As a result, they didn't relate to her the way they had in the past.

We no longer allowed Pumpkin to leap onto her lap, but that didn't stop the spoiled feline from napping on the back of her comfy recliner during the day. At night, the cat slept devotedly on her bed atop the soft, fluffy comforter.

Ralph never tried to jump onto Mom's chair; however, he did like to lie protectively at her feet whenever Pumpkin allowed him to do so.

On a stormy Saturday evening many months after undergoing that first thunderstorm with Ralph, we were sitting in the living room watching a movie when one of the grandchildren shouted, "Look at the lightning!"

We watched as bolts of lightning tore across the sky followed by loud booms of thunder rolling overhead. I was so engrossed in watching the kids' reactions to this amazing force of nature that I completely forgot about Ralph, who must have been hiding somewhere, trembling with fear.

But what I found was so much better than what I had expected.

My mother was sitting in her recliner with her arm firmly around the little dog. Apparently, with the rest of us out of sight, Ralph had sought comfort from her, even though he knew that she lived in her own little world now and hardly interacted with the family.

The sight of the two of them calming each other filled my heart with joy. I stood there for a bit taking in the beauty of the moment before calling in the rest of the family to witness the priceless scene.

Ralph's behavior that night reminded me that no one should be deprived of the opportunity to feel needed. I had been so caught up in caring for my partly deaf and blind mother that I'd lost sight of the fact that she still longed to care for others. All she needed was to be presented with the opportunity.

Because of a little, loving canine, Mom's ability to express empathy was unleashed, and she was once again able to reach out and offer comfort and compassion to those around her.

— Connie Kaseweter Pullen —

60

You Can't Hide Your Heart from a Dog

*It is amazing how much love and laughter they bring
into our lives and even how much closer we become
with each other because of them.*
~John Grogan

When I met the man who later became my husband, he came with one big, old, worn-out dog named Chip. I walked into his house, which smelled like dog, and saw little wisps of dog fur all over the floor. I thought, *Uh-oh, he's a dog man, and I'm a cat woman. There's no future here!*

I had never owned a dog. I had cats most of my life, as well as hamsters, birds, fish and even a spider monkey when I was a child. Dogs were a mystery to me.

Recently divorced, I thought that men were mysteries, too.

I got to know my first dog at the same time I was getting to know my future husband, Tom. In many ways, the dog was easier to get to know.

Tom, too, had just ended a marriage. But his had been a much longer marriage, and the divorce had been very painful for him. He was withdrawn and quiet and didn't seem very anxious to open his heart to another woman who might end up hurting him.

Tom was a good man who worked hard, but he wasn't very expressive with his feelings, so I learned much about him by the way he treated his dog.

When I met him, Chip was a thirteen-year-old black Lab that was a bit past his prime.

Tom had gotten him as a puppy, and I saw many photos of them running, playing and swimming together. They were constant companions.

But the extra years had taken their toll on Chip. And as our relationship progressed, Chip became frailer.

Every night, when Tom came home from work, Chip's tail would start wagging furiously as he struggled to his feet. Many times, Tom would have to help him up. And then they would take their slow, limping amble of a walk up and down the driveway. It always looked like it was painful for Chip, but he still wanted to go, and Tom was always willing to take him.

At night, Tom would lift Chip up to share his bed, and he would lift him back down in the morning.

I felt almost jealous sometimes. Tom always seemed to greet the dog before me. He even seemed to talk to the dog more than he talked to me. No matter what was happening between us, Chip could always seem to distract Tom with a simple "woof" or wag of his tail.

Tom took Chip to the vet on a regular basis and even gave him medication for his arthritis. Eventually, it got to the point where Chip could hardly stand. Often, when he had to go to the bathroom, he couldn't get up in time. For the longest time, Tom just kept cleaning up after Chip. He knew the alternative, and he didn't seem able to face it.

Finally, Tom realized that Chip would be better off if we had him put to sleep, so we made an appointment with Chip's vet.

On the day of the appointment, Tom was silent all morning — to me, anyway. He kept up an almost constant chatter to Chip.

When we drove Chip to the vet, the doctor was nice enough to come out to the van and administer the shot so we could hold Chip in our arms in private. Our tears started then, and we drove home sobbing quietly.

We had decided to bury Chip on the piece of property that we had purchased to build our dream home. We pulled up on the property, and Tom got out and started digging a hole, crying softly the whole time. Then he lifted Chip out of the truck gently, wrapped him in his favorite blanket and placed him lovingly in the hole. Almost as an afterthought, he slipped Chip's collar off his neck and placed it in his pocket.

When we finished burying our dog, Tom fell into my arms, and I held him as we both cried what seemed like an endless sea of tears. It was the first death we shared together, the first time we shared tears, and they seemed to seep into our hearts and break something free inside. There had been a wall around our hearts before that moment — a fear, perhaps, of letting ourselves get too close to each other, of loving each other all the way.

But when we laid Chip to rest, we realized that as painful as parting can be, it is still well worth the love that comes before it. In that respect, Chip's death was not an ending for us but a new beginning.

— Betsy S. Franz —

61

A Higher Purpose

When you are sorrowful look again in your heart,
and you shall see that in truth you are weeping
for that which has been your delight.
~Kahlil Gibran

I t was love at first sight when I picked up Robbie from Freedom Guide Dogs in Cassville, New York. There was just one teensy problem, which I was trying to ignore: Robbie was not mine to keep. I would be fostering him for about a year and a half and then he would become a guide dog for a blind person. I called him my "puppy with a purpose." It was my responsibility to provide basic obedience training and ample socialization opportunities. My house in Vermont was the perfect location, with a big fenced-in yard and built-in playmates.

Fostering a guide-dog puppy sounded like a noble thing to do, so important and fun. I would be making a difference in someone's life. So, I launched full throttle into the project while falling more in love with Robbie every day.

In his cute red "Puppy in Training" vest, we had access to all public places. I strolled proudly into the likes of Walmart and Price Chopper, museums, libraries, office buildings, restaurants, even Boston's Logan Airport—where at six months Robbie lay calmly at my feet as we waited in a crowded, noisy line to board an airplane. Robbie came to work with me at the nursing home where I was the activity director and to the local university where I taught writing intensive classes.

He was the perfect dog in every way — behavior, temperament, and cuteness. He had a special gift, a unique energy, and a kind, gentle spirit. He even converted one student who was terrified of dogs into his number-one fan. Vanessa was a bright, articulate young woman from Nigeria. Whether she or anyone in the class was terrified of dogs hadn't come up in the course of our discussions during English Comp. Shortly after acquiring Robbie, I brought him to class with me, not even considering that his presence wouldn't be embraced by all my students. When I walked into the room with Robbie, Vanessa leaped out of her seat and jumped up on her chair, quivering in fear as he waddled over to her, a wiggly bundle of love.

Over the semester, Robbie managed to earn his way into Vanessa's heart. On the last day of class, when we went around the room with the obligatory "what is your take-away from the semester," Vanessa's take-away had nothing to do with any of my brilliant writing instruction. The highlight of the semester for her: "Robbie taught me not to be afraid of dogs."

Mission accomplished.

At the nursing home, the seniors were comforted by Robbie's presence. They stroked his head while they told stories about their own dogs from years past; Robbie sat patiently and listened. He was therapeutic for the staff as well. "Can I borrow Robbie for a few minutes?" was a frequent request from someone having a stressful day. Robbie was a therapy dog long before he officially became a service dog.

But alas, Robbie was also still a puppy. He chewed through two TV remotes and two pair of prescription eyeglasses — not the cheap dollar-store readers, mind you, but the expensive prescription ones. Countless shoes, slippers, socks, and toys met their demise thanks to The Robster. The couch was, however, his most memorable conquest.

Okay, so it was the kind of couch that most people have given up after their starving college-student years. The neighbor offered it to me with this announcement: "If you don't take it, it's going to the dump." Still, Robbie managed to dig a crater in it and pull the stuffing out so that all that was left of the couch was a gargantuan pile of fluffy cotton.

Robbie was about a year old when another neighbor approached me one day and said, "Robbie sure likes swimming with my grandkids." Seriously? Unbeknownst to me, on days when he didn't go to work or school with me, the little bugger would dig out of my yard and trot next door to the neighbor's large, above ground swimming pool, climb the ladder, and jump into the water with the kids. After his dip, he trotted back home, slipped under the fence, and later greeted me innocently.

These events only added to my ongoing hope — actually, it was more delusional thinking — that Robbie would flunk out of training. I just couldn't face the prospect of losing him. If he failed the training, I could get him back.

Fail, Robbie, fail, I prayed selfishly.

Robbie was a year and a half when I got the dreaded e-mail from the puppy-raiser supervisor. "It's time to bring Robbie back."

One of the hardest things I have ever had to do was to turn over Robbie and watch him disappear into a kennel where he would spend the next four months in intensive training. The kennel door closed behind him, and this lovable, gentle, fun-loving dog who had been my constant companion for the past sixteen months — who had run with me every morning, slept at my feet at night, and been a focal point of my life — was gone.

I cried for days. I couldn't say his name without bursting into tears. It was small consolation that he would soon be with someone who really needed him. Months later, I got a picture of Robbie leading his new handler, Frank, through the streets of Manhattan. This Vermont puppy was now officially a working city guide dog.

A few months later, at Christmastime, I sent Frank and Robbie a Christmas present through Freedom Guide Dogs. I didn't want to invade Frank's privacy; I just wanted to try and connect with him and Robbie in some way. Frank called to thank me, which began a wonderful friendship where I get frequent texts from Frank bragging about Robbie's amazing skills as a very competent guide dog in a crowded and potentially dangerous city.

Best of all, thanks to Frank and his wife Sue's generosity, Robbie walked me down the aisle when my husband Joe and I got married! He refused to leave my side and planted himself between Joe and me during the entire ceremony. There was not a dry eye in the place!

Robbie has taught me a valuable but painful life lesson. Sometimes, it's not enough to love. Sometimes, we must be willing to love and let go.

— Candy Fox —

62

Sun Dog

Let sleeping dogs lie.
~American Proverb

Mozzie is a black Lab who knows the value of a sunbeam. Even as a puppy, he sought any stray ray of sun through a storm door or window, constantly adjusting his napping position as it crept across the floor or even up the stairs. Jokingly, I referred to him as my Sun Dog, until the day I discovered the benefits of a sunny nap for myself.

It was 4:00 on a July afternoon in Kansas. I had been awake for a full twelve hours since I had been called to work as a Spanish interpreter extra early that morning at a plant in a nearby town. From my chair in my home office, I heard Mozzie snore from his sunlit spot on the rug at the front door. I saw his paws twitch as he chased the squirrels of dreamland, his ears flicking as he barked, closed-mouthed, in his sleep.

"Must be nice to take a little nap in the sun," I said, yawning and struggling to stay awake after my early start to the day. I glanced over at his bed in my office; it was no accident that his fluffy pillow was right up against the low, west-facing window. I stared at the warm pool of prismatic light cast upon the floor by the suncatcher, and a thought began to form. I glanced back at Mozzie, who continued the twitchy run of his dreams by the front door.

"I mean, if you're not going to use it…" I said, slipping to the floor and into the unoccupied sunbeam there. I stretched out, head on Mozzie's bed, and was soon fast asleep.

I'm not sure how long I slept before something began to jiggle my subconscious. Something or someone was close to me, but not close enough to bring me fully awake. Suddenly, a big, furry paw flopped across my arm. I pried one eye open and studied it.

"Moz?" I said sleepily.

Then I felt a cold nose upon my neck and realized what was happening: Mozzie was spooning me. I lay there immobile for a minute, wondering what to do. Finally, my better judgment won out. Who was I to waste a perfectly good sunbeam? I burrowed my head back into Mozzie's bed, and he snuggled closer, relieved I had learned my lesson about the value of a sunny nap.

—Julie A. Sellers—

Melting Hearts

63

A Diplomatic Dog in Paris

A dog can express more with his tail in seconds
than his owner can express with his tongue in hours.
~Author Unknown

I cannot think of Bucky without remembering Paris, and I cannot remember Paris without thinking of Bucky. Many years ago, when my husband and I were assigned as diplomats to the American Embassy in Paris, we worried about whether our shy, seventy-pound Golden Retriever Bucky could transition from his quiet suburban back yard to the hubbub of a big city. Bucky did fine, however. More than fine. Back then, dogs were considered royalty in Paris.

Bucky easily ensconced himself in our home in Neuilly, a tree-lined hamlet on the western edge of Paris. The Embassy provided the house, which came with Asunción, a housekeeper from Barcelona who spoke French with a Spanish accent, and her mature female cat Mignon. Bucky had no French and zero experience with cats. But he rubbed noses with Mignon, and they became fast friends. Asunción taught him dog French: *assis* = sit, *couche* = down, *viens* = come. In return, Bucky gave Asunción a "new leash on life," an excuse to promenade outdoors with the denizens of Neuilly. (Previously, she had tried to walk Mignon on a leash, but the feline refused to be tethered.)

In those days, the Labrador Retriever reigned in France. It was said the French President's black Lab Baltique drank only mineral water in the Élysée Palace. Since Golden Retrievers were a rarity, Bucky became the subject of neighborhood inquiry and admiration.

"What breed of dog?" neighbors asked Asunción.

"A Golden Retriever."

"A Labrador?"

"No, a Golden Retriever, not a Labrador!"

"But Labradors can be gold," they challenged, thinking Asunción had it wrong.

"No, a Golden, from England, though Bucky comes from America!"

Given the back and forth, one would think Asunción was explaining the Iranian nuclear program. Soon, Bucky was known as the *chien Américain diplomatique* — the American diplomatic dog. He greeted passersby with tail wagging and tongue licking, breaking through French reticence as they hailed him, *"Bonjour, Bucky! Ça va?"*

Bucky adapted to city life faster than most humans. He became an urban explorer and discovered fountains to wade in and a riot of scents to titillate his nostrils: freshly baked croissants in *boulangeries*, aromatic *pain au chocolats* in *patisseries*, fragrant *cafés au lait* in brasseries and pungent raw meat hanging outside *boucheries*. Not to mention doggie "calling cards" deposited on the sidewalks. Olfactory heaven!

Bucky caroused with other dogs and played Frisbee in the Bois de Boulogne, the Central Park of Paris near our house. He drew crowds murmuring *"oh la la"* as he leaped into the air to snag a flying disc. Frisbees were rare in Paris at the time. Occasionally, a French dog seized with Frisbee envy would race Bucky to catch one, only to jump into the air a moment too late. A Boxer named Edouard really wanted the Frisbee one day, so Bucky dropped it at his competitor's paws, gifting it to him. Edouard grabbed it eagerly.

"Ici, le Frisbee!" Edouard's owner said abashedly, handing the Frisbee back to us.

"Keep it!" we said.

"But how do you get him to catch it?" he asked in accented English. We shrugged. He just did.

While normally law-abiding, Bucky loved plunging into the ponds of the Bois, ignoring the signs "*Baignade Interdite*" (swimming prohibited) and pretending not to hear us begging him to come out. The French dogs never followed him in but stood at the water's edge, barking furiously, or perhaps enviously, while their owners were scandalized by the impropriety. "*Lunatique!*" they hissed. He always climbed out before the park police arrived. We assumed Bucky shared our diplomatic immunity but did not want to test the theory before a magistrate.

Dogs were allowed to go everywhere in France back then, so Bucky accompanied us on our "familiarization" trips and vacations around France. The housekeepers at ski resorts allowed him to roam the premises while we skied. He'd scrounge for edibles or chewables — such as smelly ski socks — and check out the guests who were checking in. Inside, he lolled in front of the fireplace, a real-life Norman Rockwell scene. Outside, he would glide downhill on his back, legs bicycling in the air with the biggest grin on his face. He didn't need skis!

After skiing, we'd find him playing hide-and-seek with little boys, their shouts and laughter echoing through the hotel. No language barrier there. One day, he stuck with a young girl with a hurt knee, keeping her company by the fire. He was so popular with the guests that the management gave us a free dinner and placed a bowl of meat morsels under our table for him.

Once in Saint-Malo on the Brittany coast, we entered the lobby of a small hotel where a baby wailed in a bassinet on the floor. Approaching the screaming tot, Bucky licked her toes and her crying turned to giggling. The dog and the baby locked eyes in unspoken communication. "*C'est magnifique!*" the parents said, asking if Bucky could babysit. Our furry Frisbee virtuoso-cum-diplomat had the magic touch.

Bucky only embarrassed us once. In the garden of an exquisite outdoor restaurant, he decided to dig a hole under our table and sent clods of earth flying into the faces of nearby diners. Oops! Even the dog-loving French drew the line when dirt showered onto their meals!

Though we worked long hours at the Embassy, Bucky never missed us. He was busy on the home front, winning over hearts and minds, and an occasional cat. He was the perfect "ambassadog." In the end, he introduced us to French people in the streets, parks, beaches, restaurants, hotels or wherever we went. He knew more people than we did and probably garnered more goodwill.

Sadly, dogs are less free in France today. Many parks do not allow them off-leash or even to enter. Signs are everywhere: "*Tenez Votre Chien en Laisse!*" (Keep Your Dog on Leash) and "*Inderdit aux Chiens*" (Dogs Forbidden). Bucky was lucky. He had the best of it, and so did we. After we returned from Paris, life was not as glamorous, day-to-day existence not so fun, shopping and dining lacking that *je ne sais pas quoi* (certain something).

Our three years in Paris showed us that the canine is the natural, universal diplomat — capable of engendering good feelings, transcending language barriers, developing strong relationships and enjoying fine dining. Even more, we realized that the dog is family, and for us, life without one unimaginable. We relive in thought our days in France when the entire family, including our dog, could travel, ski and dine out together.

A trip to Paris is long overdue, but we hesitate. Is it because of other destinations still on our bucket list… or knowing it will not be the same? We will never live again in Neuilly, ski in the Alps, or throw a Frisbee for Bucky in the Bois.

Writing about Bucky brings him back to life, the memory of him and Paris becoming more real. Bucky was lucky to be with us for those three exciting years in Paris, and we were even more lucky to have him, the best liaison officer a diplomat could ever want when starting out with a new assignment.

— Anne Gruner —

For Now and Forever

If there are no dogs in Heaven, then when I die
I want to go where they went.
~Will Rogers

When news of the impending COVID-19 quarantine hit, I'd called the founder of the animal rescue I work with to discuss what this meant for our local animals. Apparently, Las Vegans had already begun dumping their pets at the local shelter in absurdly high numbers, either out of fear of catching the virus from them or because of job loss and looming financial insecurity.

Our rescue, Hearts Alive Village, had jumped into action. Our first step was to clear out our adoption center, placing all our available dogs into foster homes so we could open up space for the animals being newly surrendered. I had told our founder, Christy, that while I never foster due to my hectic schedule, I'd be happy to take in a pup during quarantine (assuming it got along with my dog Akasha).

"That would be great. Let's see where we are in a day or two," she said.

I called her again the next day. "Hey, Christy, don't forget I can take in a pup to foster."

"Yep. We've got some people coming in tomorrow. Let me see who they want to take first."

But on the third day, the conversation was different. "Christy, I need to foster. For me. I'm already losing my mind."

You see, I've had Akasha for fourteen years now. She's been with me through two cross-country moves, divorce, enough ex-boyfriends to fill the Island of Misfit Boys, a concussion, bankruptcy, and clinical depression. She's my best friend, cuddle buddy, and therapist. More times than I'd like to admit, I've cried into her fur. At fifteen years old, she's still in good shape, but she's cranky and over being my emotional support system. She rarely stays on the same floor as me and is totally done with cuddling. The moment I start to cry, she hightails it out of the room. Sometimes, I think I should send her for a spa day once a month so she can have some time away from me.

Mind you, I'll love Akasha until the day I die and do everything I can to give her the best rest of her life possible. But when it comes to the unconditional love and attention I'm looking for from a dog... yeah, she's not bringing it. Add that to being single at the moment and living alone.

I needed some company.

When I stopped into our adoption center later that afternoon, my friend suggested I take Butters, a Chihuahua/Corgi mix. "He'll do great with Akasha," she assured me.

This wasn't my first time meeting this fur ball. Two months earlier, I'd brought him on a local news show to help get him adopted. I remembered how polite he'd been in my car, tossing a paw up on the center console. If I stopped petting him, he'd glance up once in a while with his big chocolate-colored eyes as if to say, "Excuse me, ma'am. I'd like more." A lap-sized brown pup, his tail curls over your hand when you scratch his butt, and the tallness of his ears makes up for the shortness of his legs.

When I brought Butters home, I leashed up Akasha, and the three of us went for a walk. They sniffed and pooped together, and Akasha didn't seem to care very much. I accepted her apathy as her blessing to give this little guy a safe place to ride out the craziness.

Butters spent the first week attached to my hip (and then to my back). Where I went, he went. We took daily walks and then did some "social-distance hiking" with friends. I have to give him credit. It was a 5.5-mile hike. He walked 4.5 miles of it. That last mile? Well, let's just say he enjoyed the view from my backpack.

I put a blanket on my desk, and he spent the days sleeping next to me while I worked. I'd never had a small dog. That's what they're supposed to do, right? He never made a peep while I was on a Zoom call — except when he started to snore.

Friends joked that I wasn't letting him go, but I laughed it off. This was just temporary.

Until the e-mail came.

It was Christy. We had a potential forever family for Butters, and she wanted me to screen them and do a meet-and-greet.

My throat tightened, and I found myself blinking back tears as I imagined the thought of Butters waving a single paw as he drove away in his new human's car.

I couldn't do it. Butters had officially nosed his way into my heart.

Akasha and I sat down to discuss it. Was she okay with adopting a brother? While she didn't say anything, her eyes told me she was happy I had someone to snuggle.

We FaceTimed Christy. She teared up when she realized that Butters would be staying with me permanently.

We visited my parents that evening, facemasks on as we sat the obligatory six feet apart from one another in their back yard.

"You're keeping him, aren't you?" my stepmom asked after I plopped Butters in her lap.

"Yep. Say hello to your new grand-dog."

There was just one problem… I didn't like the name Butters for him.

I considered naming him Hendrix due to his "foxy" ears, but the sound was too far from his current name, and I didn't think it would be fair to do that to an eight-year-old. Instead, I jumped online and looked for boy names that started with a "B." That's when I discovered Bodhi, Sanskrit for "enlightenment." I'd named Akasha (in a fit of goth-ness) after Anne Rice's mother of all vampires, but later I found out that her name was Sanskrit for "soul space."

Bodhi couldn't be more perfect — the name or the dog. As I write this, he's sleeping soundly next to my desk. We take at least one but often two walks a day as a family. I feel like a momma elephant with Akasha leading the way and Bodhi bringing up the rear.

We've discussed the pup's responsibilities in the home and decided that Akasha will continue her role as the hiking buddy (with Bodhi holding down the fort at home). Bodhi is the chief cuddler, giving Akasha the alone time she prefers.

Quarantine has been stressful, with a roller coaster of emotions. But thankfully, with Bodhi glued to my side, I know that everything is going to be okay. In rescue, we always like to ask, "Who rescued whom?" In Bodhi's case, I think we all know the answer.

— Sheryl Green —

Raising a Family

Whoever said you can't buy happiness
forgot little puppies.
~Gene Hill

Her labor pains began at 3 a.m. She paced back and forth. Occasionally, she stopped to take a cool drink of water before pain wracked her body again. She lay down, twisting and turning to find a comfortable position. Her breath came in short bursts.

Suddenly, a little head appeared. A new life took in a bit of air. I heard a tiny squeak. One. Momma squeezed her eyes tight. A groan escaped from her mouth. Now there were two. She didn't have a chance to take a breath or a sip of water, or even cuddle the first two before I witnessed the birth of number three. By 4 a.m., there were seven! I watched numbers eight, nine, and ten emerge. Taffy, our beautiful Golden Retriever, finally relaxed and took note of what she had accomplished.

The puppies were all light gold in color, just like her. The last one born, the runt, seemed to be having a hard time. It was a little girl, and she fought for a teat. She struggled to wiggle her way past the nine stronger puppies. I reached down, gently picked up the nursing firstborn pup, and moved him aside to give the tiny runt a chance. Her little mouth grabbed on like a magnet.

During the next few days, I devoted hours to arranging puppies for feedings since mom's eight feeding stations couldn't handle them all at once. I encouraged an exhausted Taffy to stay in her whelping box to nurture her squirming sausages.

In just a few weeks, the puppies wobbled on shaky legs to stand. The runt continued to be a fighter. She proved that she was a force to be reckoned with. She opened her eyes first, and I think she must have then assessed her need to survive ahead of the others. Her high-pitched squeal when the others pushed her aside gave me the cue to run to her aid and place her near the milk supply.

Taffy let us know her brood was just too big for her to handle. She started hiding, and I had to carry her to the box for feedings. A trip to the vet confirmed she was ill and couldn't care for her puppies. Her mammary glands were infected.

The first item on the agenda was milk for these starving beauties. I drove forty miles on a dirt road to get goats' milk, which our vet suggested is best for puppies' little tummies. Every few hours, I listened to them cry and took turns feeding all ten of them, rotating them according to their demands at each nursing.

Next on the agenda, I had to secure a place for ten fast-growing, now fast-moving balls of fur. Did I mention I lived in northeastern Arizona at 7,500-feet elevation, and it was the dead of winter with snowdrifts four feet high? I turned the mudroom into a nursery, with a baby gate holding back the forces.

It wasn't long before the puppies developed the strength to wiggle out of the whelping box and meander everywhere. Need I tell you they were not potty-trained? I stepped over the gate fifty times a day to change the newspaper that absorbed potty messes. I picked up spilled water bowls and puppy-chow dishes filled with dried gruel that I had crushed in my blender. Can you imagine ten puppies running through puppy-chow gruel and then jumping on the walls and each other? The runt, now one of the fattest, took up residence in the chow bowl in order to lick the sides clean.

Ten growing puppies needed to be taken outside in an effort to potty-train them. I realized newspapers weren't hacking it any longer for their growing deposits. These adorable bundles needed to go out into the cruel world, but it was cold outside.

I armed myself with a shovel and cleared an area I thought might be big enough for the ten darlings to romp in. I went to our local feed store and bought a bale of straw I planned to put down for warmth. By the time I returned, I couldn't find the area I had cleared because the snow fell harder while I was gone! Finally, I accomplished my goal and returned to the mudroom to transport five puppies at a time to their new playpen.

Running, nipping, and growling puppies tromped everywhere. I watched in disbelief as the puppies plowed through the snowdrifts like snowmobiles. They had much more fun doing this than staying on the warmth of my carefully laid-out straw bed. The runt disappeared into one of the deepest snowdrifts, only to peek out and yip at the others as if calling them to follow her. I couldn't help myself. I stood in the snow and laughed until tears ran down my face.

Ten weeks passed, and I realized how hard it was going to be to let any of my brood go to new homes. Despite having to retile the mudroom, paint the walls, and replace chewed carpet and baseboards, I was in love with my golden balls of energy.

When the time came, I handpicked each of the new owners. Later, I organized a first-year birthday party for the puppies. The new owners came with presents and special cakes made of quality dog food and vegetables. We all became close friends.

That summer, our vet spayed Taffy. She seemed perfectly happy to have us devote all our time to her. And I realized I'm just not up to raising big families, especially the kind with four legs.

—Alice Klies—

Bear Paw

*At the height of laughter, the universe is flung
into a kaleidoscope of new possibilities.*
~Jean Houston

The sun was starting to poke through the clouds as we began our morning hike to Crystal Lake. Despite the warm sun, there were still mounds of snow strewn about the trail on this early spring day in Colorado.

My husband and I were setting off on a five-mile hike with our beloved Bloodhound, Hunter. We were spending the weekend in the mountains, carrying in everything we would need. Even Hunter dutifully wore his own puppy backpack with his water and food. He always got excited when he saw us get out his backpack, knowing that we'd be spending some serious quality time out in nature with him.

We went most of the morning without seeing other hikers, but more and more crossed our path as the day progressed. People always stop to admire Hunter, as he is quite the charmer, but his size is also hard to miss. When he stands on his hind legs and puts his paws up on my shoulders, his head is even with mine at just slightly over five feet. People are always drawn in and marvel at our gentle, cartoon-like giant of a dog.

We had met a couple on the trail that day with whom we continually crossed paths throughout the duration of our hike. They would take a drink break and a minute to rest, and we would end up passing them. Then we would take a little water break, and they would pass us while we were making sure Hunter was watered and in good shape. So, we shared their company throughout the day, chatting each time we passed one another and teasing back and forth that we were going to make it to the lake first.

On one of the last stretches, just before we would reach the lake, there was a lengthy, open incline covered with snow. It was warm and sunny, so the snow was soft. The other couple was just a short distance behind us when we heard the man call out, "Babe! Whoa! Come over here. You gotta see this!"

He was hunched over something in the snow.

"What is it?" The woman glanced around the snow, a little confused.

"Look! Bear paw!" he exclaimed excitedly. "How cool is this? Do you think we might see a bear today? It looks fresh." He grabbed his cell phone out of his pack to take a photo, clearly amazed and astonished at what he was seeing.

We had paused at this point and looked on curiously to see how this would play out. The woman remained quiet as she astutely observed the paw print in the snow, watching her companion take photo after photo with palpable excitement and anticipation.

"That's definitely a big paw print," she noted.

"I wonder where it leads." He placed his hand to his chin, looking around animatedly as he observed the vast, snowy hill around him.

"Whoa! I can't believe we found a bear paw!" the woman said. I saw a smile spread across her face as she glanced in our direction. We smiled back, stifling our giggles as we continued to watch the scene below us.

"Or…" she began, "it could be from that giant dog up there that we have been following all day."

Realization hit her companion's face. Obvious disappointment set in, and his entire demeanor shrank momentarily. It was followed quickly by him dropping his chin to his chest as he began laughing at his earnest mistake. We all joined in and had quite the laughing session. Our laughter could be heard ringing throughout the mountain that morning, and we were too doubled over to explain the hilarious scenario that had just played out to newcomers passing by.

Of course, we had to give the poor guy some well-intended grief, joking good-naturedly about bears the remainder of our interactions throughout the day. He took it like a champ, and I am sure he will never quite live it down.

We still joke about it to this day. Anytime we see muddy paw prints in the house from Hunter or his paw prints outside in the snow or on hiking trails, we always point and exclaim, "Bear paw!" Then we enjoy a good laugh as we recall this momentous hiking expedition.

— Gwen Cooper —

Letters from Akua

*No one is useless in this world who lightens
the burdens of another.*
~Charles Dickens

ooking at the writing on the page, I could feel the lump in my throat. The writing was shaky, nothing like the crisp, neat letters of a few years earlier. I knew this would be the last letter I received from the little Pug with enormous brown eyes. With this thought in my mind, the memories welled up inside me.

In reality, the little Pug never wrote me a letter. Akua belonged to a couple in the fancy neighborhood where I had lived previously. One of his owners was very ill with AIDS, and it had reached the point where he could no longer take the little dog for his daily walks. I didn't know the couple well, but I volunteered to take Akua on his walks in place of Chris, his owner.

And with that, little Akua and "his" letters became part of my life.

I only managed to live in such a wealthy neighborhood through the generosity of a relative who owned a home there, and from whom I rented a guesthouse. I was sort of an anomaly in the neighborhood because I wasn't wealthy. I was the poor relation, the somewhat bohemian member of my family who had attended art school instead of pursuing a higher-paying career.

The neighborhood had a large number of gay residents, and being gay myself, I socialized with them occasionally. Some of them generously bought some of the art I had in the local gallery. But I cannot say that I was truly close to any of them. I always got a polite, but reserved, feeling from them.

But then came the day when I knocked on the door of the house belonging to Rick and Chris, offering to walk Akua. Frail and gracious, Chris was quiet for a minute. I noticed a smile, however, as he said, "I will have to check with Akua, but I think he would like that very much." Returning the smile, I said that I looked forward to hearing from Akua.

That afternoon, a letter from "Akua" was passed through the mail slot. I looked at the stationery that featured a picture of the little Pug at the top. The letter said that he very much would enjoy accompanying me on a morning walk and hoped he would see me the next morning. Akua informed me that his daddy had helped him write the letter, which he appreciated. After all, he was just a little doggie, and pen and paper were difficult for him to handle.

The next morning, as I took the leash from Chris, I bent down and petted Akua and told him how happy I was to have received his letter. Akua smiled up at me with his big brown eyes and wagged his little curl of a tail furiously. I couldn't help but notice that Chris was beaming, too. For just a few moments, he looked as though he hadn't a care in the world.

And so began my walks with Akua and the occasional letters I received from him — written with the help of his daddy, of course. But I saw Chris less frequently over time. It wasn't long before Akua was brought to the front door by Rick; Chris began spending most of his time in bed. The letters still arrived, however, including one asking a further favor from me:

> *Hello, Jack!*
>
> *This is little Akua writing you, and I hope you can help me with something. Every day when I come home, my daddy asks me what I have seen on our walks, but I have a hard time remembering. If it wasn't so hard for me to handle a pen and paper, I would write it all down for him, but I am just a little doggie. If*

I tell you what to write, will you write it all down and bring it by the next day for my daddy to read? I would really appreciate it!

Tail-wagging love,
Akua

The next morning, in addition to being handed the leash with Akua, Rick gave me a supply of Akua's stationery. I told Rick that I would bring Akua's letters about the previous day's walks when I came to get Akua every morning. Normally, Rick was very reserved, but this morning he nodded and thanked me, his words choked with emotion. Akua's large brown eyes looked up at us solemnly, deep with concern.

On that morning's walk, I paid extra attention to everything, marking it in my memory to be recorded onto the Pug stationery later. The first of "Akua's" letters about our walks told about the roses in the park he had seen; the butterfly that had fluttered around his face and startled him, prompting excited little barks and furious tail wagging; and the very large dog that Akua had protected me from by wisely advising me to pick him up and head rapidly in the opposite direction....

I received a letter from Akua in return, telling me how much his daddy had enjoyed reading his letter, and how he looked forward to future ones. And, of course, Akua thanked me for helping him write it, since he was, after all, only a very little doggie. As usual, the letter closed with his tail-wagging love.

And so our days went, with walks and letters and roses and adventures with butterflies and neighborhood dogs, and friends seen and reported on along the way. One of Akua's letters asked me to check up on Mrs. Patterson, so her home was added to our route, and the joy of the elderly woman at seeing Akua was duly recounted. Her kindly, wrinkled face, under her enormous floppy hat, featured in several letters. One of the most difficult letters I "helped" Akua write reported that Mrs. Patterson's daughter informed us that she had slipped away peacefully during the night.

Two years passed, and I faithfully walked Akua and "helped" him write his letters to his daddy, although I received fewer letters in return. Finally, there came the day when I had to say goodbye to Akua. My relative was selling his home, and I was moving to another city. The last time I returned Akua to his home, I was greeted by Chris, whom I hadn't seen in a long time. He hugged me fiercely and whispered goodbye.

A few months later, after I had moved, I received a final letter from Akua. He told me that his daddy would soon be in heaven, and he was trying not to be sad. But he wanted to thank me for all the fun he had on our walks and for helping him write his letters to his daddy. He hoped that I could visit sometime, that he would like that.

I did visit a few weeks later, the soonest I could, but Chris had passed away, and Rick and Akua were gone. An agent was handling the sale of the now-empty house. I hoped I might track them down, but the neighbors said that Rick, distraught at losing Chris, had left the state and was considering moving to Germany, where he had relatives.

It has been over fifteen years since that last letter. I have moved yet again in the intervening years, but Akua remains in my heart. The little Pug with the enormous brown eyes became an important part of many lives, the connection between people who seemingly didn't have much in common. Akua and his letters touched my heart… and doubtless the hearts of a few other people.

— Jack Byron —

The Power of Love

*It is astonishing how little one feels alone
when one loves.
~John Bulwer*

The thought of facing winter with a puppy concerned me. My dog-loving husband, Gary, let every dog sleep in our room, although not on the bed.

"Honey, think about it. You don't want to housebreak a puppy in winter."

And Gary agreed.

Six days later, Gary answered the phone. I couldn't hear the other person, but the grin on Gary's face said a dog would live at our house, winter or not.

In the car, Gary said, "A woman brought in a dog to have her put down."

At the clinic, the veterinarian said, "I'd say she's five months old. A local farmer raises cattle dogs. When they don't herd well, they get rid of them. The woman who brought in the pup said this one ran wild in the woods. It appears to me she has bruised ribs. I'm not sure what else the dog has lived through."

He motioned for us to follow him to the back room.

A small black pup looked lost in the corner of a full-sized cage. Gary crawled to the back of the cage and picked her up.

"Yes, I'll take her," he said.

Before we left, the vet told us she'd had her shots, and he gave us a bag of dog food. Gary tried to pay the vet, but he refused the money.

"She needs a good home," he said. "I know how bad you felt when your old dog died a few weeks back. Remember, if for any reason this doesn't work out, you can bring this puppy back."

I drove home while Gary cuddled his Australian Shepherd puppy.

At the house, the skinny black pup with brown eyebrows ran to the first corner she could find. Gary found a blanket and pillow and lay on the floor next to the dog. He sang to her for an hour.

"What will we name you, sweetie?" I heard him whisper to her. He sang another song.

"Your dinner is ready," I said.

"Can you fix me a plate? I'll eat down here."

Before bed, Gary put layers of newspaper all over our bedroom carpet.

"I'm not getting up in the night," I said and turned off the light.

The puppy cried. Gary sang. I moaned.

About midnight, Gary sang "Waltzing Matilda." The pup quieted and slept.

"That's her name," Gary whispered. "Good Aussie name, Matilda. We'll call her Tilly."

Twice during the night, man and dog visited the outdoors. I cuddled under the covers.

The next morning, Tilly ran for the far corner of the dining room. Once more, Gary created a bed on the floor. He took his studies to the corner, sang and ate his meals beside his shaking Tilly. That night, he carried Tilly to the family room. Man and dog watched football.

The fourth morning, I rushed into the kitchen. Tilly snarled and bared her fangs. Scared, I backed up slowly.

"What if I take Tilly to the church study with me? I'll make her a bed close to my desk," my preacher husband said.

"What about people visiting you? If she growls and snaps at them, they won't be happy."

"She'll be fine."

For the next week, I stayed away from Tilly. Toward the end of the second week, I carried a dish from the kitchen to the dining-room table. Tilly ran at me. She barked, jumped, and snarled.

I screamed.

Gary grabbed Tilly.

"Hon, I'm sorry, but you've got to take her back," I said. "I can't live scared in my own home."

Tilly hid in the corner.

"You call the vet," Gary said.

I dialed. The second I handed the phone to Gary, Tilly scooted to where I sat. She set her chin on my knee and looked up at me with her brown eyebrows twitching up and down.

If dogs could talk, I'm sure she'd have said, "You aren't going to let him take me back, are you?"

The vet knew a dog trainer, a woman who specialized in abused animals. Gary called her. While the trainer and Gary talked, Tilly let me pet her for the first time. The trainer gave Gary several tips, one being to run the anxiety out of her.

Early each morning, the three of us walked to the football field. I stood at one end and Gary at the other. He threw me the Frisbee, and Tilly raced to me. We introduced commands to her in the field, too.

"Stay, Tilly," Gary would call out midway.

Soon, Tilly played dead, rolled over, and said her prayers. She was still territorial in the church study or our house, so we kept Tilly away from guests.

Every day, Gary took Tilly in the car with him. Before they came home, he bought her an ice-cream cone at the drive-through.

One morning, I needed to run an errand before Gary left the house.

"Tilly, you want ice cream?" She looked from me to Gary and back again. She jumped into the car. I bought her ice cream, and we cemented our relationship for a lifetime.

"What will we do about girls' camp this year?" I asked Gary one night. "We can't leave her with anyone."

"We'll take her with us, keep her on a leash, and share her story with the girls."

"But, hon, is that wise?"

"It'll be fine." I looked at the man, certain his love for Tilly had clouded his better judgment.

Being the camp chaplain, I wove Tilly's story of abuse into spiritual lessons and asked the girls to treat her with love and respect. Some girls lived Tilly's story, and they opened up to a counselor about their own situations.

The third day at camp, I sat at the top of a bank above a lake to watch the girls build sandcastles or play in the water. Gary sat beside me with Tilly between us.

Before we could grab her leash, Tilly took off down the bank, ran through a sandcastle, splashed into the water, back through the sandcastle and up the bank.

The wet dog, her coat covered in sand, made her way between us again. Tilly sat with her tongue hanging out and her eyes sparkling. I'm sure I heard her laugh.

The girls squealed, laughed and built another sandcastle. Before they were done, Tilly took off down the hill, raced through the castle, sand flying everywhere, then into the water, back between the squealing girls and up the hill.

The girls swarmed around "that silly dog" after she crashed through their sandcastles over and over again. They loved her, and she loved the attention.

I was amazed at the change in Tilly. Gary smiled at me and said, "The power of love can heal anyone."

Magically, the puppy I didn't want helped heal the lives of several young girls. And because of the love the girls showered on Tilly, we returned home with a changed dog. She lost her fear of others and loved everyone who came into our home for the remaining ten years of her life.

— Kat Crawford —

69

Darkest Before the Dawn

Until one has loved an animal, a part of one's soul
remains unawakened.
~Anatole France

When the lady next door had been taken into the hospital suddenly, a district nurse had knocked on my door asking if I would be willing to take in her dog while she recovered. I must have appeared hesitant at first, partly because I had taken such great care to avoid all my neighbours and not become involved in any pleasantries. I had previous experience of how reliant people become and how hard it can be to live a life in full view of a nosy street.

Still, after learning there was no family member or next of kin, I mumbled a sound of agreement. Two hours later, Sunny arrived, along with a bag of dog food. Arriving wet and covered in mud, she did not seem to live up to her happy name. Under her matted fur was the thin frame of an old dog, and I was already regretting my offer of help.

In truth, I had never understood dogs and why people chose them as pets. They were needy and completely dependent on someone else; those were not qualities I liked, probably because they reminded me too much of myself in the past. When my partner had left three years earlier, I had resolved never to need or love anyone again.

The reality was harder than I had anticipated. Trying to re-mortgage a house while out of work after an ulcerative colitis flare, I could hardly look after myself. Yet, looking at the pitiful animal before me, I figured I couldn't do any harm.

The first night was a rude awakening. She howled, clicked her paws on the floor, and scratched at the door. Neither of us got any sleep. Then I got a message; my neighbour had passed away in the night. The voice on the other end was sympathetic and left a number for the local dog shelter that might take Sunny.

I wasn't so sure of her chances there, though. She was an older dog, not as attractive as a puppy. Plus, if anyone took her home and had the same first-night experience that I had they'd probably bring her right back. Still, I thought I would call and speak to someone.

As I dialed the number, Sunny watched me with big, soulful brown eyes that had seen a lifetime of experiences. I wondered what her best memories were. She had lived most of her life on this little street. Her previous owner was just one of the people she had likely seen come and go. I wondered if she would remember me after I took her to the shelter.

My thoughts were interrupted when the call connected to an automated message, friendly but firm: "No rehoming is going ahead, and no animals will be collected due to the COVID-19 outbreak." My heart sank a little. I knew there was an outbreak, had heard there was a pandemic, but had figured it was mostly exaggerated. That afternoon, receiving my official letter labelling me a vulnerable person who had to shield for twelve weeks, brought home the stark realisation that it was serious.

Here I was, out of work, forced to "shield" during an unprecedented global pandemic in a home that was already starting to fall apart, with an uninvited house guest. This was a cosmic prank of the greatest proportion. Unable to appreciate the comedy, tired and frustrated, I was thankful for the tiny patch of a garden I had. It would be the only escape for Sunny and me.

Sitting in the afternoon air, I started to recognise Sunny's peculiar little traits. She would chase birds but run from flies, walk around flowers but wade knee-deep in puddles. Her failing eyesight didn't seem to hinder her. In fact, she was less clumsy than me. I dropped plant pots and tripped on watering cans as I tried in vain to find my ex-husband's gardening equipment. By the time the sun was dipping in the sky, I had found only six pots and two packets of seeds. Sunny watched intently, brown eyes encouraging me, almost smiling when I triumphantly set those six pots in a row with a wish that something would grow.

The following nights became easier as we got into a routine, with Sunny on a blanket by the bed and me watching documentaries until we were both tired enough to sleep until morning. We learned about primates in Africa, creatures under the ocean, and the busiest cities in the world. Sunny's ears twitched to the animal calls and strange sounds.

Three weeks later, we had become so used to our routine that it was easy to notice when Sunny seemed slower and confused. Worried, I called a vet for advice. Even though I was short on cash, I drove for an emergency appointment. The vet office was covered in signs about social distancing and COVID-19. Although I couldn't go in with her, Sunny reappeared a short time later. The vet described the symptoms as effects of age. Although nothing was critical at this stage, Sunny was old, and her health would continue to decline. My eyes pricked, and I shed a few tears on the drive home.

I'm not sure how long we have left together, and for now we remain on lockdown. Sunny and I continue our daily routine of watching documentaries and checking our plants. I learn from her and grow in confidence when her big brown eyes tell me I'm doing a good job, or when she licks my hand, appreciative of my efforts. I already know I will miss her when she is gone, but I will always have the memory of how it took a global pandemic and a little dog to open my heart to needing love again.

— Melissa Richards —

70

Best in Show

There is no psychiatrist in the world like a puppy
licking your face.
~Ben Williams

"**T**his beautiful puppy isn't for me, is it?" I asked as I picked her up.

"Yes, she certainly is," said my husband. It was my birthday. Knowing my love for dogs and my special affinity toward Cocker Spaniels, George had surprised me with her when she was about five months old.

Princess was a purebred Cocker Spaniel who George had rescued from the animal shelter. Although she was registered with the American Kennel Club, she couldn't be a show dog. Caramel in color with a long, sparse coat, her frame was quite small. This darling dog was probably the runt of the litter. Her tail was not docked as they do with Cockers that are intended for show.

Nine years later, my husband was paralyzed as a result of an injury. George was brought to the rehabilitation wing of the hospital four weeks after his injury. He shared a room with Bob. Next to each hospital bed was a visitor's chair, a rolling nightstand with several drawers, and a tray that rolled over the bed for mealtime use. Two televisions hung high on the plain white wall, one pointed at each bed. It was a typical dismal hospital room.

Princess hadn't seen George since he was injured and she was mourning him. So one day, I asked Bob, "Is it okay if I bring our dog in tomorrow for a visit?"

He exclaimed, "Of course! I wish I could see my dog, too."

In those days, there were classifications for specially trained guide dogs and search-and-rescue dogs who were used to do things like sniff out drugs, bombs and people buried in rubble. They were certified for their specific purpose. There were no certified therapy dogs yet. Dogs were not allowed in hospitals.

The next morning, I stuffed Princess's twenty-five-pound body into a large tote bag, leaving her head hanging over the top edge of the bag. I hung the tote on my shoulder, rested her chin on my bent arm, and covered her head with a light jacket so she was totally hidden. Taking a deep breath, I walked confidently into the rehab department of the hospital. After passing the nurses' station and greeting the staff with my usual "Good morning," I went directly to my husband's room.

So far, so good, I thought.

I closed the door immediately to eliminate any attention. I knew Princess wouldn't run away or bark, but I didn't want anyone to see her.

Already aware of George's presence, she got so excited that she nearly jumped out of the bag without my help. I held her up to George's face (the only place he had feeling), and she went wild licking his face. Then I placed her on the bed aligned close to his body. She continued to lick him as he cried happy tears. Bob was also happy to see a furry friend and wagging tail. It was a wonderful distraction from that dreary place for all of us.

Suddenly, the door flipped open, and a wave of panic came over me. A rehab nurse walked in. I knew we were caught red-handed, and there was no turning back. So, quickly and with confidence, I said, "Please shut the door." Right away, the RN spotted Princess, and instead of calling me out, she went crazy with excitement.

"Oh, how cute! Is this your dog?" she asked.

I nodded, and she rushed out to the hallway to share this new visitor with the rest of the medical staff. They all came flooding in.

All along, I was afraid they would kick us out, or worse, I'd be in big trouble. Instead, they welcomed the delight a dog brings. Princess was pampered and adored. Immediately, she became part of the "rehab family."

What had I been worried about? Dogs have a way of calming and transforming people in an instant. This precious animal transformed the entire rehab family: nurses, doctors and patients alike. She may not have been the perfect purebred Cocker Spaniel, but she brought enjoyment and peace to my husband and all who saw her. That little rescue dog was part of our family for fourteen and a half years, and she was nothing if not Best in Show for us — a true champion.

— Anita Lear Gonzales —

The Smartest Dog Ever

Everyone thinks they have the best dog.
And none of them are wrong.
~W.R. Pursche, The Canine Commandments

We had only been married a few months and were living in our first home when a friend of mine asked if I could help her find a temporary home for a puppy she'd just found. She and her husband lived in an apartment and couldn't have pets. I offered our house as a temporary place and silently hoped my husband, Steve, wouldn't object.

I called him and explained the terrible situation. My friend had been taking out the office trash when she heard a puppy whining behind the Dumpster gate. When she opened it, she found a tiny puppy in there. She concluded that someone had attempted to "throw away" the puppy.

I told my husband we weren't offering to adopt the puppy, just temporarily house her while our friends found her a permanent home. He wasn't convinced, and with good reason. We already had two cats, strays who had found me.

We arrived home about the same time, just moments before our friends arrived. Sue carried a large bag filled with everything a new puppy owner could want. Rich held the end of a pink leash. On the other end of the pink leash was the fluffiest, cutest Golden Retriever puppy. She had a large white streak on her nose, and white socks. She was adorable with her big brown eyes and her tongue hanging out. The puppy came right over to me. It was like she knew I was "her" human. I picked her up and rubbed my nose against her nose, and she licked my face. I breathed in her puppy breath and felt her soft fur. She nuzzled my neck and wrapped her tiny paws around it.

I fell in love instantly.

Steve was not as easy a sell as I was. I put her down, and he called her over. "Dog!" he said loudly. "Come here!"

I started to protest. "She's just a puppy. She doesn't …" As the words left my lips, the puppy cocked her head at him and then came over to him shyly. She lay down at his feet and rolled over for a belly rub, her happy smile showing with her tongue hanging out.

He picked her up, and she wiggled to try to reach his face with her tongue. He held her at arm's length and examined her, as if she were a piece of meat he intended to cook later. "Well, she's clean. And doesn't smell. She seems smart," he mused aloud. He put her down and, looking in the bag, found a tennis ball. "Let's see how smart she really is," he said, looking directly at the puppy.

He walked to the back door and went outside. Turning around, he looked at her again and said loudly, "Dog!" After a moment, she got up and walked over to him. He was quite serious and, somehow, the importance of this moment got through to her. Her goofy puppy self had morphed in front of our eyes. She was now a trained, mature dog. She followed him to the yard and sat down at his feet, staring intently at his face. He held up the ball and, waving it in front of her, said, "This is a ball. I am going to throw the ball into the yard. You will run and get the ball and bring it back to me."

My friends and I protested. "Really! She's just a puppy! She doesn't understand a word you're saying!"

"I doubt she's had any training at all. You have to train a dog to do that."

"You can't just expect her to know what you want. She just met you today."

Our protests fell on deaf ears. With a dismissive wave of his hand, Steve continued to talk to the puppy. She sat still and listened.

After several minutes, he threw the ball across the yard and yelled, "Fetch!" She took off. Our grass was a little long since we hadn't yet started the spring mowing. She ran to where the ball was last seen bouncing. She sniffed and ran in circles. He encouraged her with cries of "You can do it!" and "Come on, girl! Find the ball!"

After what seemed like forever, she found the ball. She gave an excited yip, picked it up, and ran proudly back to my husband. She dropped it at his feet and sat back, staring at him. He praised her, petted her and, picking up the ball, turned to us non-believers (with our mouths hanging open) on the deck and said, "See? I told you! If she wasn't already a smart dog, she couldn't have done that!"

We decided that we needed to give her an elegant name. Many names were suggested, but we all finally agreed on Sophia because the black fur around her eyes made her look a little like Sophia Loren.

We went back into the house, and she followed Steve. When he sat down in the living room, she lay down by his feet. During dinner, our friends and I would call her away from his side so we could pet her and praise her. But as soon as we stopped or returned to our conversation, she would go back to Steve's chair and try to get his attention.

Clearly, she adored him. Our friends left, confident that they had found Sophia a home. As we prepared a bed space for her from old blankets on his side of the bed, she kept coming back to Steve. He'd pet her and then settle her in again with her stuffed bear.

The next morning, he got up with Sophia and took her outside for potty. On his way out, he grabbed the ball. As I was brushing my teeth, I heard his voice in the yard, gradually getting louder and louder. I hurried outside to find out what was wrong.

I found him standing in the yard, pointing across the yard at the ball. "Sophia! Get the ball!" he commanded. She glanced at him, and then continued to roam around, sniffing the grass. He turned to look at me. "I don't get it! Yesterday, she did it. Today, nothing! What is wrong with her? Why is she so dumb now?" He tried for hours and then days before finally admitting defeat.

After many years with Sophia, we finally decided that she was the smartest dog ever. She knew she had to get that ball in order to stay with us, so she did. But for the rest of her fourteen years with us, she never fetched a single thing.

— Ruth Penderghast —

Converting Shaggy

Perseverance is not a long race;
it is many short races one after another.
~Walter Elliott

"H e will not be placed in a home with young children," warned the pet-adoption website. How could a cute little ball of white fluff be unfriendly? He looked like such a sweet puppy.

But as our daughter the counseling major says, "Everybody has issues." I suppose this even applies to little dogs if they've gone through a rough time.

Shaggy, all eleven pounds of him, ended up in foster care with a woman who rescued Bassets and Bloodhounds. Her local animal-shelter staff couldn't bear the thought of euthanizing him when he hadn't been adopted within their time limit, so they contacted this kind woman. She took him temporarily and he adjusted well to her family and menagerie. Now he needed a permanent home where life was calmer and he could be the center of attention.

What little we learned of his history from the foster mom was sad. He belonged to the husband of a couple who divorced, and when he left, he abandoned his dog. Apparently, Shaggy spent most of his time in the back yard, ignored and tethered to a pole on a long lead. Some of his bottom teeth were broken, presumably from abuse or neglect. Eventually, the wife just dropped him off at the shelter. When he arrived, it was clear he had been ignored. His hair was matted, dirty, and overgrown. And he was terrified.

The day we brought Shaggy home, he sat quivering in our teenage daughter's arms in the back seat of the car. The first night at our house, he was so upset that my husband slept in the easy chair, holding him on his lap until morning. Even though he was two years old, he didn't know how to walk on a leash. Those first few weeks of coaxing, tugging, and pulling to get him to go on short walks made us feel like we were torturing him. He would look at us with a pathetic expression, as if to say, "Why are you dragging me down the street?"

Happily, one day something finally clicked, and he began to trot along the curb, stopping to sniff and explore as far as the leash would reach. He wormed his way into our hearts, and we got to know him, issues and all. We saw him flinch and cower when we reached to pet him, and we learned to squat down and let him come to us. We learned he was a social eater and would completely ignore his food until we were eating, cooking, or sitting nearby. We learned the fastest way to send him into orbit was to ring the doorbell. We learned having company caused anxiety, and he expressed that by feverishly licking people's legs. And we learned he truly disliked small children.

That was a problem, not because we had any, but because he was so stinking cute. A small Bichon Frise with a cropped tail, he looked like a puppy and always would. Walking a dog in our neighborhood was a social experience, especially when the weather was mild. Passersby in cars waved; people on their porches and stoops said hello; small children ran to the end of their driveways and asked, "Can I pet your puppy?" We couldn't picture ourselves saying, "Well, he is not really a puppy. He is a cranky, middle-aged dog who doesn't like children," without sounding like cranky, middle-aged people who did not like children either.

One friendly toddler up the street loved Shaggy from the first moment he laid eyes on him. It was almost magnetic, the way he was drawn to our moody pet. Any time we walked past his house and he was outside, he would come bounding to the end of his driveway and ask to pet Shaggy. These encounters were most unpleasant for our little dog, but we would gently hold his snout so he couldn't snap at little Hayden.

Hayden would pet Shaggy tentatively and comment about his soft hair. When we continued our walks, he would say, "Bye, Shaggy. Bye, Miss Capi. Bye, Mr. Bob." Over time, our visits with Hayden, and eventually his little brother, became longer and more relaxed. Hayden would show us his toy or tell us about what he had done that day or what he was going to do tomorrow, all while petting Shaggy, who was no longer growling and did not need to have his snout held.

Gradually, we began to see Shaggy calmly interacting with the little girl who lived across the street from Hayden and with the twins who lived next door to us. It was almost as if his personality had changed. It never occurred to me to give credit where credit was due until I noticed something strange one day.

Shaggy and I were taking our afternoon stroll through the subdivision. When we got to Hayden's house, Shaggy turned and headed up the driveway toward the closed garage door. After a few steps, he paused, looked around, waited for a moment, and then retreated and came back to the curb to continue his walk with me. Suddenly, I realized he missed his friend, the one child in the world who made him feel safe and loved. Shaggy was looking for Hayden, the persistent little boy, who unknowingly, with several years of kind words and gentle pats, had converted him. He had a completely new perspective about children and had overcome his biggest issue.

Now we just need to conquer that leg-licking thing.

— Capi Cloud Cohen —

How I Fell in Love
with a Pit Bull

Properly trained, a man can be a dog's best friend.
~Corey Ford

My wife and I had been mourning our dog, Buddy, for nearly three months when she decided that it would be therapeutic to foster a dog for a local animal shelter. The house was eerily quiet and sadly empty without the companionship and pitter-patter of a dog.

So, my wife signed up to be a foster parent, and Partners for Pets called and asked her to come see a dog who needed a foster home. She was introduced to a small Chihuahua named Sparkle who was scheduled to be spayed and had a touch of kennel cough. Sparkle was a scared little creature, growling at everyone who approached her. My wife sat on the floor next to her, and Sparkle crawled carefully into her lap. After that, she had to bring Sparkle home.

We nursed that little dog through being spayed, having a hernia repaired and kennel cough. After about three weeks, a family applied to adopt her and we reluctantly relinquished Sparkle to her new family, our work as foster parents completed.

A few weeks later we were asked to foster another dog, a Malamute who had been returned to the shelter because he didn't get along with other dogs. When my wife showed up to meet him, they surprised her with a different dog, one that needed even help more. That's when

Melting Hearts | 243

she met Gypsy.

Gypsy had become increasingly aggressive with the other shelter dogs after she had problems in the play yard. Since she had become such a problem, she was only allowed in the play yard by herself to avoid altercations. When she was introduced to my wife, she came galloping toward her and jumped up, chest high, greeting her rowdily. The shelter staff explained that her behavior was deteriorating. Gypsy had been there for about two-and-a-half years, dropped off when she was eleven months old. My wife likes a challenge, so she brought Gypsy home.

I was shocked when I met this seventy-pound, fierce-looking Pit Bull wearing a choke collar. To say her appearance was intimidating and ferocious was an understatement. I had heard all the negative opinions of Pit Bulls and I couldn't believe my wife had brought one into our home.

That first evening, I moped around the house, eyeing Gypsy warily and trying to avoid having contact with her. I was disgruntled, to say the least. Meanwhile, my wife set about putting together her crate, getting her food and water bowl situated, and playing with her throughout the house and the back yard. Clearly sensing my opposition, my wife explained that I didn't have to come home for lunch and let Gypsy out because she was crate-trained from being at the shelter and should be able to hold her business throughout the day. (My wife's place of work was too far away for her to come home for lunch.)

I knew in my heart that I would come home for lunch and at least let the dog out in the back yard to run around and relieve herself. After all, that's what I did for our previous dogs and the recently fostered Sparkle. And after watching my wife play with her, and even discipline her, I was a little less intimidated. I was in awe that my wife was fearless while handling her, but I still respected that this was a powerful animal that could attack one of us at a moment's notice.

The first day I came home for lunch, I found Gypsy curled up in a ball, sleeping soundly in her crate. When I unlatched the door, she stretched out lazily, seemingly unfazed by having to be in there. She exposed her underside to me in a manner that said, "Please rub my belly." So, instinctively or reflexively, but certainly without thinking, I did. And she didn't bite me. Then she stretched out some more, tail batting heavily against the floor of the crate, appearing quite comfortable with this arrangement.

I continued to pet her and she continued happily batting her tail against the floor. I had to encourage her to get up so we could go outside. She needed to do her business because I only had so long for lunch. Eventually, she got to her paws, tail wagging furiously, and followed me through the house and into the fenced-in back yard. Once outside, she was doubly good. I praised her for expediting her business, and we went inside while I prepared something to eat for myself.

As I sat at the kitchen table, she came over to my side and sniffed vigorously at what was on my plate, but she didn't jump up on the table or try to bully me out of my food. When I instructed her firmly to "go on," she turned away and sat down, watched me for a moment, and then lay down and closed her eyes. When I finished eating, she got up and I took her outside again. Then I guided her back into her crate with a treat and latched the door. She eyed me curiously but didn't bark, growl, whine or fuss in any way. *That wasn't so bad,* I thought.

At work, I complained to my co-workers about what my wife had done and how this beast was living in our house, and what a burden it was to go home and let her out, etc. But the more I groused about Gypsy, the more my co-workers predicted we would end up keeping her.

Once my wife got home from work, it was time for Gypsy's daily walk. I decided I should tag along because I still wasn't sure that my wife could handle her if something unexpected should arise. If I said Gypsy was great with other dogs on the walking trails and didn't pull or tug against the leash, I'd be a liar. When other dogs were in the vicinity, she'd go on high alert and lunge toward any other dog that was within her reach. And then it was a struggle to restrain her until the danger passed.

My wife decided that we needed to learn more about this unique breed, so she checked out some books from the library and consulted professional trainers. If we were ever going to get anyone interested in adopting her, we had to nip some behaviors in the bud. Gypsy already had two strikes against her being adopted: a) She was dark tan/black, and statistically these dogs are adopted less frequently than light-colored dogs, and b) she was a Pit Bull.

One of my friends who owns two Pit Bull mixes came over to meet Gypsy and shared her knowledge and love of Pits with us. She thought Gypsy was adorable, and my wife later disclosed to me that it wasn't until this friend pointed out some of her features — her sweet face, expressive eyes, silky-soft muzzle, and smooth coat of hair — that she began to see Gypsy's actual beauty. It took me a bit longer.

We ended up talking with two trainers who had slightly different advice for us. One trainer informed us that Pit Bulls were bred to be animal-aggressive and people-protective, so the aggressive behaviors Gypsy was displaying toward other dogs were more or less innate. We had to be diligent about keeping her on a leash and careful around other dogs.

The other trainer showed us how to train Gypsy to be much better on a leash with a few simple changes — a snug-fitting collar and, surprisingly, a longer leash. She explained that by giving Gypsy some slack in the leash, she would be calmer. Keeping the leash taut just made her feel threatened. Much to my surprise, this technique worked very well! I can't say that Gypsy quit lunging at other dogs altogether or was perfectly behaved on her walks, but her behavior improved dramatically.

Through discussions with our friends, library books and trainers, I learned a lot about this unique breed, officially known as the American Pit Bull Terrier. Where I first saw an intimidating creature, I began to see a magnificent animal — heavily muscled, athletic, and seemingly in perfect health. I even started to see Gypsy's beauty.

Since we were officially foster parents for Partners for Pets, we were obligated to take Gypsy to local adoption events. These always went poorly. Gypsy didn't respond well around other dogs, and to have her locked in a crate as other dogs passed by simply set her off barking and snarling. It was painful to watch. On the few occasions we left her there, we came back to find that people had set up partitions between her and the other dogs being showcased, which only made her look more ferocious and unmanageable.

Since Gypsy didn't do well at those official adoption events, we made flyers with pictures of Gypsy and a short bio. We posted them around town, and some of my friends circulated them on social media.

One weekend, we received a call from Partners for Pets that someone had filled out the adoption paperwork for Gypsy. We had been fostering her for about two months by this time and had become accustomed to her. Nevertheless, we knew it was our responsibility to relinquish her. So, we reluctantly packed up her toys, food, snacks, dog bed, and blanket and dropped her off.

A few hours later, we received a phone call informing us that the person who had applied to adopt Gypsy did not show up or return phone calls. Did we want to pick her up? My heart raced furiously. Of course, we wanted to get her!

Gypsy seemed thrilled to see us when we picked her up. And that was it, the moment I knew we were going to keep her. She had gone too long without a permanent home. We had been searching for the ideal family — one with a fenced-in yard, the time to give her affection, discipline, and enough exercise, and the patience to deal with her sometimes manic behaviors and special needs. It dawned on me that there was no better place for her than with us.

Gypsy continues to improve every day and now tolerates dogs walking by. Sometimes, she even sits to watch them pass. At our home, she has her bed and a personal spot on the living-room couch. She can choose to sleep there or with us every night. In the back yard, she takes the time to smell the roses, teaching us about living in the moment. I also discovered there's always a little more room for love in a heart that seemed too full from the love of our previous dogs. Strangely, I no longer see the beast in her, only her magnificence and beauty. I can't imagine life without her.

— Scott Elliff —

Chapter
8

Who Rescued Who?

74

Bake Bubba Happy

Grandmas never run out of hugs or cookies.
~Author Unknown

My husband was racing down the highway, trying to make it through the border before it closed completely due to the COVID-19 crisis. He had just picked up his mother, who lived alone in France, a short twenty-five-mile journey from the German border. He was bringing her back to our house near the NATO base in Ramstein, Germany.

He had taken much more time than he had planned to load her things into the van because she had insisted on taking her whole pantry of food supplies along with her. I rolled my eyes when he told me about it over the phone. She is strong-willed and not always the easiest person to get along with, so there was no sense in arguing with her about it. We would have to grin and bear it over the next few months that we planned to live together.

My mother-in-law is a pack rat who has always kept a vast supply of non-perishable food items in her house, along with vegetables that would last for a long time. A cellar full of potatoes had saved her family from starvation in France during the Second World War, a lesson she never forgot. The COVID-19 epidemic brought back the desperation of the war years, so she doesn't take food storage lightly. When my husband went to pick her up, she insisted on taking all the goods with her. Now it was questionable whether they'd make it through the border before the total lockdown.

Biting my nails, I finally received a text from my husband saying they had made it through just as the guards were shutting down the border. I was relieved that they would be able to make it back to our house and had managed to load up all of Denise's stuff. We kept a reasonably well-stocked pantry at home, but it paled in comparison to hers. All the extra foodstuffs would come in handy during a long isolation period.

Our black Labrador, Bubba, would be thrilled when Denise arrived. He considered her his grandma and was always spoiled with treats and snuggles during her stays with us. He had been less than pleased with us lately since we were already rationing the treats for ourselves and all our pets during the lockdown. He could also sense our high level of anxiety.

As soon as Grandma Denise arrived, Bubba ran to greet her and jumped for joy, almost knocking her to the ground with his enthusiasm. His tail was wagging so hard that half his body jerked back and forth. She was his person. She hugged his scruffy neck and tossed him a couple of snacks, which he scarfed in the air before they hit the ground. Then they walked inside together like two old buddies, while my husband and I stood there watching before lugging in box after box of groceries.

The next morning, we awoke to a wonderful aroma wafting from the kitchen. Pancakes! Throwing on our robes, we made haste to the kitchen to get them while they were hot off the griddle. We needn't have hurried. Bubba was already there in the kitchen, leaning his head on Grandma's leg as she flipped his special doggie gluten-free buckwheat pancakes. She had even made him a tasty peanut-butter sauce as a topping. Bubba's tail was beating the kitchen cupboards like a drum. In this new age of social distancing, it was delightful to see them snuggling. We would just have to wait for our favorite pancakes to be made afterwards, but it would be worth it. We had to admit that Denise was an excellent cook, certainly better than we were. Bubba was bringing out the best in her.

As many people learned during the coronavirus shutdown, it's tempting to eat extra snacks when hanging around the house more than usual. While working from home wearing gym clothes, it's easy to miss any weight gain. Putting on the Coronavirus Fifteen had already become a thing, so we had made a point of not stocking up on many extra snacks. We had already been regretting that decision, so the sweet aroma of cookies coming from the kitchen later that day had us moaning in anticipation and soon scooting in that direction. We arrived in time to see Denise sitting with Bubba's head in her lap, with our other rescue dogs lying at her feet, all patiently waiting for her homemade doggie biscuits to bake. It looked like she was baking enough to last through the whole pandemic. Happily, a couple of trays of cookies for humans were on the kitchen counter, waiting for their turn in the oven. We were beginning to see who had priority here, though we were happy to wait for our share.

We always had a ragtag mix of stray cats around that called our place home. Bubba was a friendly giant who loved all other creatures and tried to befriend them. But the cats were generally wary of our dogs and stayed aloof. Now, however, they were curious about the wonderful aromas from the kitchen and the special relationship Bubba had with Grandma, the source of all the delicious goodies. Soon, they were circling around her legs as well as Bubba's as she continued to bake goodies for everyone in our place while he stuck to her like glue.

Bubba couldn't have been happier. His humans were all in one place and always home now, including his favorite person on the planet. The other dogs looked up to him because he had such a special relationship with the person who baked the treats. And he was now finally befriended by the elusive cats for the same reason. His exuberant disposition had managed to unite us all.

We were happy again, too. The lockdown gave us a break from our hectic lives, while working from home allowed us to become reacquainted with each other. Our relationship with my mother-in-law was improving quickly as well because we had finally slowed down enough to appreciate her again. We also saw the wisdom of her planning and forethought when it came to keeping supplies, not to mention the enjoyment we derived from the fantastic meals she put together. Not only had she baked Bubba happy, but she had melted all our hearts in a kitchen filled with love.

—Donna L. Roberts—

75

A Rescue Tale

We can judge the heart of a man
by his treatment of animals.
~Immanuel Kant

I live on a farm where dogs are part of the landscape. Yet the dog I spotted, as I steered down my driveway that chilly late February day, didn't quite fit in. At first glance I thought it was my brother's Chihuahua. But a second glance raised doubts. For I knew my brother's little housedog was no candidate for a swift run across a yard. So, I figured this unknown dog would soon find its way home, and I had errands to run.

A few days later, while walking past the door to my deck, I saw the deck swing move. Clearly, someone or something had set that swing in motion. Being home and alone that evening, the thought of an unknown presence lurking about set me on edge.

I was compelled to investigate. Reluctantly, I willed my hand to grasp the doorknob. Nervously opening the door just enough to stick my head through, I surveyed the deck. Seeing nothing that could be causing the swing's movement, I slipped back inside and locked the door hastily.

What I saw the next morning, though, gave me a start. Standing squarely in my front yard, nibbling on sprigs of grass, was that scamp of a dog I had spotted earlier. I summoned my husband to take a look. But when the dog heard the front door open, she bolted for the safety of the nearby woods.

It was just a matter of time before the elements or the coyotes would be the demise of such a small, defenseless dog. We realized the poor thing must have been lurking around our house for weeks. My husband and I formulated a rescue plan. We placed food and water near the deck swing. The next morning, the food and water had been consumed, so we put out more. It took several days of putting out food and water before we caught the dog in the act, and another two weeks after that before the dog felt comfortable enough to approach one of us.

One afternoon, I came home and found my husband holding out his hand while leaning forward in the deck swing. I witnessed a happy wee dog, tail wagging furiously, eating hot-dog pieces from my husband's hand. The stage was set for the final part of our plan: to coax the dog inside.

A few nights afterward, when it was pouring, I opened the front door and looked for the dog. And there it was, curled up in a lawn chair on our front porch! I startled her, though, and she leaped from the chair and vanished into the pouring rain.

I consoled myself with the hope that the storm would persuade our little friend to return to the porch. I propped open the storm door and raced to the refrigerator for more hot dogs. I cut them up and made a trail of hot-dog pieces from the front porch into the living room. My husband's recliner was at the end of the trail. He sat in wait, with more hot-dog pieces in his hand.

Moments later, my husband announced, "The dog is back."

Quietly, I inched my way through the living room, into the kitchen, and then into the dining room, closing the doors behind me. Hidden from our unsuspecting guest, I stood ready to close the door as soon as she entered the living room.

The little dog warily ate her way to my husband's outstretched hand. When she reached him I shut the door. She panicked and raced around looking for a way out. Then, she tired and we witnessed an astonishing transformation. She stopped, fixed her eyes on my husband, and then turned her gaze toward me. No trembling. My husband spoke softly as she allowed him to lift her gingerly to his lap. Her fear was gone. If a wagging tail is any indicator, the rescue was complete.

— Janet Warren Lane —

Just in Time

*Love — that which biologists, nervous about being
misunderstood, call "attachment" — fuels the bond
between dog and master or mistress.*
~John Bradshaw

There was a dog-shaped hole in our hearts and in our
home. My husband Nigel and I had lost our beloved rescue Terrier to kidney failure. After a suitable period of
mourning, we decided we couldn't live without another
dog. We began researching rescue centers.

At the same time, we were vaguely aware of something going on
in the world. As far as we were concerned, it was just some people
in China who had caught the flu — no big deal. The media must be
fresh out of news.

We didn't have any fixed ideas on what sort of dog we wanted:
sex, age or color. The one certainty was that he or she must be gentle.
Our dear deceased dog Cleo had been more like a baby dragon who
wanted to kill anything that moved. Come to think of it, even static
objects weren't too safe when she was around. Don't get me wrong,
we worshiped the ground her little paws walked on, but boy was she
hard work!

We heard of a dog rescue center a half-hour's drive from our
home. As I looked at the center's website, I was drawn to a dog with a
calm expression and slightly unkempt blue-gray fur. There were other
attractive and deserving dogs offered for adoption, but I kept coming

back to six-year-old Kamu, a male crossbreed. We decided to play it safe by having a short list of those we had seen online. At the earliest opportunity, Nigel and I went to visit the center with a view to finding the one dog who was meant to live with us.

Meanwhile, what we had been ready to dismiss as the "Chinese flu" revealed itself to be the deadly and infectious COVID-19. There was talk of a possible lockdown to prevent further spread of the disease, which was extending its tentacles worldwide and had even found its way to our home county of Lincolnshire, England.

When we arrived at the center, precautions against COVID-19 were already in place, with sanitizing sprays for staff, volunteers and visitors and antiseptic wipes for the door handles. The staff directed us to the long corridors of kennels where we could walk around and view the death-row dogs—mostly street dogs shipped in from a life of hell in Romania. There were "oohs" and "aahs" in abundance as we looked at all the hopefuls waiting for their forever home.

As we turned a corner, Nigel stopped and gasped. "Oh, he's gorgeous!" It was Kamu. His photo on the website hadn't done him justice. It was just as well, or someone might have beaten us to him. We knew immediately that Kamu must come home with us. We didn't even look at the rest of the dogs. Instead, we hurried back to the reception area where we could spend time with him and bond with him further. As he had kennel cough, we couldn't walk him. Instead, we spent nearly an hour gazing at him and stroking his incredibly soft fur.

After that, it was a race against time as the British government was to impose a lockdown the following week as protection against COVID-19. But there were formalities to be completed: a home visit by a volunteer to ensure our home was safe and secure for a rescue dog, a contract to be drawn up and signed, and a compulsory lecture on dog behavior.

It was most important that our yard be safe for a dog, but with high walls on either side and a double-bolted back gate, we passed with flying colors. Plying the volunteer who came to inspect us with coffee and homemade scones might have helped, too.

The fateful day arrived, and Nigel and I sat impatiently through the dog-behavior lecture given at the center by a volunteer who called herself a "dog listener." I can't say we did much listening. We were going to look after our dog our way, with love and kindness.

At last, we left with Kamu and the three lots of medication he was on. I suspect that under normal circumstances, he wouldn't have been released while still being treated. It was a matter of urgency to rehome as many dogs as possible before the lockdown. Our departure was perfectly stage-managed as staff led the adopted dogs out one at a time for a photo shoot with their adoptive "parents."

Kamu settled immediately into our home, and now his life is governed by the three Cs: comfort, couches and cuddles. There's a fourth C in our lives: COVID-19. It may be a horribly cruel disease, but it has its positive side. It sent Kamu into our arms at top speed so that we could ride out the lockdown in our own happy bubble. We may have had to spring him from kennels, but he has rescued us from a sad, dog-free existence.

— Mary Cook —

77

Afraid

*If you have been brutally broken, but still have the
courage to be gentle to others, then you deserve a love
deeper than the ocean itself.*
~Nikita Gill

K ody came into my life at a difficult time. When we found
each other, I was still grieving over the loss of Lucy, my
twelve-year-old Cairn Terrier who had passed away suddenly from a lung infection. Heartbroken, I was overwhelmed with emotions. Soon, sorrow turned to anger. I was mad
at the world. Although I wouldn't admit it at the time, I was also
terrified of facing the cruel void that the death of Lucy left behind.
My days were busy because of a hectic work schedule, but my nights
were filled with silent sadness. Coming home to a quiet house, the
stillness always surprised me, and the realization of just how much
energy and love a dog brought to my life was constant.

Kody and I found each other by chance. I happened to be in a
local pet store looking for a specific toy for my new cat, a rescued
stray. As luck would have it, a local shelter was there for an adoption
event. I passed by the kennel that Kody was in, and the connection
was instant. Looking up at me was the freckled face of a short-haired
Brittany Spaniel with hope in his sweet but lonely eyes. The volunteer
from the shelter explained that Kody had been with them since he
was born. He was almost two and had never had a home. That was
all I needed to hear. While filling out the official adoption papers, the

volunteer let me know that Kody was quite timid.

In the first few weeks, I realized my new dog was not only timid but petrified of everything. This included the doorbell, fireworks, thunder, and even the back yard. Similarly, I found myself retreating from my own life to be alone with my grief. Like Kody, I was afraid the world would see my sadness, and I would feel all the worse for it. Kody and I became couch potatoes, comforted by the fact that we only left the house when necessary. We were partners in our shared dislike of the outside world, preferring our solitude to the company of others.

Once my grief started to subside, I knew I needed to get Kody acquainted with life beyond our neighborhood. It was one thing for me to be a temporary recluse, but I didn't want the same for him. Our first trip to a local dog park was a disaster. Unleashed and free to roam and socialize with other dogs, Kody stuck to my side and trembled. I set up a play date with a friend of mine and his dog. Kody spent the entire time at the back door begging to be let back in. A few days later, a series of electrical storms nearly drove him over the edge. Observing his behavior, my friend commented, "He's afraid of everything."

Yes, I thought, *we both are.*

Yet, I knew Kody was much more than a scared dog. He was a kind, loyal, sensitive friend with a big heart and a lot of love to give. As I didn't want the death of Lucy to define my future, I wanted Kody to have his fair shot at a happier, more active life. Realizing that my own choice to disconnect was not healthy, I also knew I needed to get Kody some help. I did some research. I talked to fellow dog owners. I consulted with the vet. From each, I gathered great advice, resources, and some tactics worth trying.

We went back to the dog park a second time. Still, the fear was there. On our third visit, I saw progress. It was minor, but there was hope. By our seventh visit, I was an afterthought while Kody raced around the park, catching up with his new canine friends. At the same time, our walks became longer, and our couch time became shorter.

Soon, Kody wanted to explore the world. He waited anxiously at the door, ready for our next adventure. No longer the nervous backseat passenger, he now enjoyed our car rides with the windows rolled down.

While the thunder still left him rattled, he was no longer retreating to his kennel to wait out the storm. At the same time, I started to emerge from my self-imposed exile. Together, he and I braved our fears and joined the world around us.

Last week, we went to the dog park as usual. At once, Kody joined the other dogs. His tail wagged, and his eyes were filled with joy. He'd become a different dog, now embracing each new element he encountered. A fellow dog owner noticed. "Your dog... He's so outgoing and friendly," he said. I nodded and smiled, realizing that both of us had discovered a new form of fearless freedom.

—David-Matthew Barnes—

78

A Pitiful Scrap of Life

My little dog — a heartbeat at my feet.
~Edith Wharton

I was sitting on my front porch, enjoying my second cup of coffee and watching the hummingbirds buzzing around the two feeders hanging from the eave between the geraniums. It was my favorite time of morning, and the hummingbirds were so used to seeing me that they would let me fill their feeders while they fluttered around me inches from my face.

Sputtering as if it wouldn't make it another mile, Nancy's old white van pulled into my driveway. Sighing, I knew my morning respite was over. Nancy and I had been best friends since high school, but she never seemed to remember how much I cherished my early morning solitude. I wasn't ready for her cheerfulness and endless energy.

I watched her climb out of the van, carrying a basket with soft pink swaddling. I knew that some unfortunate creature lay in there because Nancy has been rescuing animals all her life. She would keep them all if she could, but at some point between puberty and adulthood, she realized it was impossible. Instead she finds homes for them.

I narrowed my eyes as she approached, holding the basket protectively. Nancy used to pester me endlessly about how much more enriched my life would be if I had a pet. Someone to love. Someone to love me back. Someone to entertain me. Someone to end my loneliness after my husband died. Someone to share my days after I retired. At some point, she finally quit trying to convince me that a pet was exactly what was missing from my life. I sighed. I could tell that Nancy was going to try one more time.

She sat beside me on the porch, and we made small talk for a few minutes while I pretended to ignore the basket. Then we heard a weak, plaintive cry coming from whatever unfortunate animal was in there.

Nancy's eyes met mine. "I need your help, Ann." Tears made her eyes shimmer in the morning light. Gently, she pulled back the thin pink blanket.

I gasped. "What a pitiful scrap of life!" I cried out. "What happened to the poor thing?"

"She was tortured and left for dead," Nancy said. "She was starved and beaten and, worst of all, set on fire and then abandoned to die in agony. She was found near death in a ditch by a man working for the power company. She was taken to the vet that I use, and he did what he could for her. But she needs constant care. She needs her bandages changed and her wounds dressed twice a day. She needs her cuts cleaned and dressed every day. She needs to wear doggie diapers because she is too weak to be house-trained. Most of all, she needs to be held and cuddled a lot. She had been abused and neglected, and she is afraid of humans. She needs to be loved."

Nancy reached over and took my hand. "You were a nurse. You have the skills to nurse her back to health."

I looked down at the tiny dog. She stared up at me with huge eyes that were filled with fear. Her little body was shaking. I reached my hand out to her, and she drew back and whimpered. My heart broke for her. "I can take care of her medical needs," I said. "But the rest…"

"The rest will take care of itself," Nancy said with a knowing grin.

That evening, I gingerly took the puppy out of her basket and awkwardly tried to cuddle her. She was so tiny that I didn't know what to do with her. After trying out several positions, I laid her upon my shoulder. I have shoulder-length hair, and she scooted underneath my hair, settled down and went to sleep immediately. That became her favorite place to nap.

She slept in her basket on my bedside table because she was very fragile. I wanted to make sure that I would awaken if she needed me. One night, I was wakened by sharp yelps. She was having a nightmare, crying and kicking in her sleep. I picked her up gently and lay back on my pillows, placing her on my shoulder. She scurried beneath my hair and fell asleep. I was touched by how quickly she felt safe being close to me.

Nancy called me one evening after I had been taking care of the puppy for a few weeks. "How is your little patient doing?" she asked.

"She's doing well," I said. "She's healing and getting stronger. She's following me around the house now." I chuckled. "She can crawl out of her basket by herself."

Nancy laughed. "You've done a good job. She must be about ready for me to find her a forever home."

"What?" I said. "No. I mean, she's not ready. Not yet. Not now. I'm in the middle of training her to potty on the pads you gave me. We can't stop in the middle of that."

"Tell you what," Nancy said. "Just call me when she's ready."

That was five years ago. That pitiful scrap of life still sleeps on my shoulder every night. And she is now beautiful, scrappy, and full of life. And Nancy was right. She has enriched my life.

— Elizabeth Atwater —

79

When Bo Saved His New Family

The poor dog, in life the firmest friend.
The first to welcome, foremost to defend.
~Lord Byron

We weren't looking for a dog when we found Bo. A friend of mine had shared his story on Facebook, and it tugged at my heart strings. Bo's owner had been murdered (in a tragedy that he witnessed), and he had flunked out of several attempts to rehome him.

When I went to visit him, he was running about energetically, but he came over to say hello. He laid his head on my leg and gazed up at me with deep brown eyes. He was calm and silent for a moment, beseeching, and it felt like a plea. I had to bring him home to our little farm nestled in the Blue Ridge Mountains where he could roam and have adventures with three little boys.

Bo was the goofiest of dogs, chasing butterflies and leaves, leaping through fields, trying to jump on the school bus daily, and opening any unlocked door in our house. He had a hard time focusing. It took me five months to teach him how to sit. But he was sweet with my boys and affectionate when he wasn't obsessed with birds.

About three months after we brought Bo into our family, my husband Paul went out of town for work. I took one of our boys to lacrosse practice, and we got home around 7:40 p.m. The boys and

I rushed in the house to begin the business of getting ready for bed. A strange sound rumbled from the back porch. *What was that? Was that Bo? Growling?* Surely, it couldn't be. I had never really heard him growl before. I wanted to investigate, but with bedtime looming and the business of brushing teeth and getting into PJs, I became distracted.

A bit later, the boys were all tucked in, and I went up to my room to do some reading. It was a mild night for October, so I opened the window to let in the balmy breeze. I had just settled into the pillows with our two cats and a book when Bo started barking like crazy. Sometimes, he barked at deer, so I didn't think too much about it at first. But then I heard yelling in the woods on the mountainous piece of property behind our house. I turned off all the interior lights, checking all the door locks along the way. Then I turned on all the exterior spotlights. Bo was barking on the back side of the house, so I went back upstairs and watched Bo from my viewpoint, listening carefully between his barks. He sat in the driveway curve, alert, barking and barking. I had never seen him do this before, so I peered out in the darkness, watching him quietly.

Imagine my alarm when, in the grainy darkness, I witnessed Bo jump up and start chasing a pair of running legs down the driveway. Immediately, I contemplated my options. I knew it would take the sheriff a good fifteen to twenty minutes to arrive, and then he wouldn't necessarily be willing to go traipsing along our land in the dark. Instead, I texted a neighbor who is a federal park ranger to see if he was home. He called me right away and said he'd come over to check things out.

Over the next hour, Bo continued to pace and bark, but the yelling and voices stopped. I got a text around ten from my neighbor. It was a long story, he said, but he had taken care of the situation. It wasn't until the next evening when my husband returned home that we got the full story. I think our neighbor didn't want me to be scared all night.

It didn't matter, though. I couldn't sleep that night and was up every hour to check on things. Know who else didn't sleep? Bo. Every hour I got up, Bo was sitting at the top of the driveway, quietly keeping watch over the horse pasture. He didn't go to his snug bed on the porch once. He didn't let down his guard once. Every time I peeked out, he was rigid, sitting tall and staring silently into the darkness. Even at 6:30 the next morning, he was still carefully keeping watch. It gave me such reassurance to know that he was monitoring for any potential danger and would let me know if I needed to be concerned about anything.

Our neighbor told us the next day that he had snuck up on our land from the back side. Even though he had encountered numerous dangerous situations in his job on the Blue Ridge Parkway, even he was taken aback when he saw the man in our horse pasture. Missing clothes, covered in blood (like something out of a horror movie, according to the neighbor), intoxicated and delusional, this is the man our dear dog chased away. Our neighbor detained him until the police and an ambulance arrived to take him away.

It takes my breath away to think of how our sweet, affectionate Bo protected his family that night, and then sat up all night making sure the threat didn't return. Some people may think that Bo was lucky to join our family after he failed so many adoption attempts. But the truth is that we were the lucky ones to get him.

Had it not been for him and our neighbor, things might have turned out very differently. Not even a high-tech alarm system could have handled the situation like Bo did. So, guess who got a big batch of home-cooked bacon and a good dose of hugs the next day? We made sure to show Bo how thankful we were for his protection and how welcome he was in his new family.

— Lisa Workman —

Three Pounds of Love

I'm convinced that petting a puppy is good luck.
~Meg Donohue, *Dog Crazy*

I was born into a cat family, and from an early age, I harbored an intrinsic fear of dogs. If someone invited me over to her house, and had a dog, I simply wouldn't go.

No one understood my fear. The number-one question I would get was, "Were you ever bitten by a dog?" They'd be puzzled by my answer, "No, I was never bitten." Why did I need to have been bitten? Most people haven't been bitten by a shark, but we're all terrified of them.

Without an explanation for my fear, I was branded as the girl who simply didn't like dogs. I'd be out with friends when we'd happen upon a waddling Pug. My friends would be beside themselves, barraging its owner with a flurry of questions: "What's her name? How old is she? How long have you had her? What's her favorite color? Did she like the new season of *Stranger Things*?" I watched from afar, trying to seem distracted by a billboard in the distance. "Chase, isn't she so cute?" they'd ask. "I just want to hug her forev… Oh, right, I forgot, you don't like dogs." Again, it's not that I didn't *like* dogs; I was *afraid* of them.

It wasn't until a crisp fall day in September 2016 that everything changed. "Come over," my mom texted me. She had agreed to foster a Chihuahua her yoga teacher had rescued from a local shelter and she wanted me to meet the dog.

I drove over, mostly just to see the spectacle of a dog in a formerly cat-only household. My sister and brother were perched on the couch when I arrived. I scanned the room for a dog but saw nothing. I listened for a bark from a different part of the house but heard not a peep. "Where is she?" I asked.

My sister opened her oversized cardigan to reveal the face of a caramel-colored, three-pound, full-grown Chihuahua. Our eyes met. Her name was Helena. My mom explained that Helena was still very scared of meeting new people. I related to her instantly.

I sat down next to my sister, and after a minute or two, Helena crawled onto my lap. I felt all the fear melt away from both of us. I was speechless. I'd never been so physically close to a dog. She curled up in a ball, resembling a small yet scrumptious cinnamon roll, and stayed there for the rest of the evening.

Throughout the week, I found myself making up excuses to go to my mom's house after work. "Did I leave my scarf there?" "Have you seen my softball trophy from high school?" "I just want to make sure your house is level." Once there, I would play innocent. "Oh, wow, I forgot Helena was here. I guess I'll just play with her for a few hours." I felt connected to her in a way I couldn't understand.

Everyone loved Helena, and she loved everyone back, but secretly I knew she loved me the most.

After a couple of weeks, my mom's yoga teacher informed her that if my mom didn't want to keep Helena or couldn't find her a home, Helena would be shipped off to a shelter in Canada, where Chihuahuas were in high demand.

"You're going to keep her, right?" my siblings and I begged my mom, terrified of her answer.

My mom had only been fostering Helena as a favor. Her four kids were finally out of her house, and she quit her nine-to-five job to freelance so she could travel and enjoy her life. She told us she loved Helena but didn't want the responsibility.

We were devastated. Who would take Helena?

My sister's building didn't allow dogs, and my brother had recently moved out and was just getting the hang of being on his own. So what about me? Could I keep Helena? The idea seemed insane. Of course, I loved Helena, but never in my life had I entertained the possibility of having a dog. I mean, up until a few weeks prior, I could barely even pet a dog. Plus, I was so busy. I worked at a clothing store during the day, performed stand-up comedy at night and had to wash my hair twice a week. My plate was full.

But the thought of her being shipped to Canada was simply too much to bear. She was so little she had to wear a sweater on brisk Los Angeles nights. She'd freeze up north.

I resolved to take her only while I tried to find her a home, assuming it would be easy. Who wouldn't want this absolute angel of a dog?

A few weeks went by, and there were no prospects in sight. I was starting to worry. Then one day, my mom called with "great news." She had found someone who wanted Helena. She wanted to know if I could drop off Helena at her house the next day. I burst out crying. No, I couldn't drop off *my* dog so my mom could take her to some stranger's house. In that moment, I realized there was no way I would ever part with Helena. She was mine. All I wanted to do was be near her. She made my worries dissolve. I didn't know how she had found her way to me, but she had. She was, as several people put it, a "once-in-a-lifetime dog."

The next day, I told one of my co-workers that I was going to keep Helena. "Good," she said. "Dogs are good luck." I smiled.

Lo and behold, within one month of having Helena, I landed my first TV writing job. It would take me out of retail forever. Dogs aren't just good luck; they're miracles.

— Chase Bernstein —

Tail of Serendipity

A dog is not a thing. A thing is replaceable.
A dog is not. A thing is disposable. A dog is not.
A thing doesn't have a heart. A dog's heart is bigger
than any "thing" you can ever own.
~Elizabeth Parker, Paw Prints in the Sand

My husband Neal and I always go to the post office a block from our house. But one day, fourteen years ago, we were out running errands that took us right by the post office in the next town, so we stopped and mailed some packages. Heading home, we turned down a street we never go down as a shortcut.

And that's when it happened.

It was early summer — Memorial Day weekend, in fact — and two little kids were standing in front of a house, waving around a big cardboard sign. I expected it to say "Lemonade for Sale" or something similar, but it said, "Free Dog."

Neal looked at me. I looked at him. One of us said, "Uh-oh."

Animal lovers from way back when, we belonged to lots of animal-protection groups and heard all the horror stories related to "Free to a good home" ads.

This dog was in danger.

My mom, animal rescuer extraordinaire, always said, "The first thing you have to do is get the animal somewhere safe. You can worry about everything else later."

Neal turned the car around, and we pulled over to the curb by the kids.

The dog was an adorable, all black, six-month-old female with at least a little Border Collie in her, judging by her face. Her ears seemed too big for her, standing straight up and tipping over at the very top. Her tiny white teeth showed in her open-mouthed smile as she gamboled around in the yard with an older, Boxer-type dog.

The children's mother didn't care when we said we knew people who did rescue work and could find the dog a home. She just wanted the dog to disappear.

Wringing her hands, she said, "My husband wants Princess gone by the time he gets home."

Just then, a pickup truck turned into the driveway.

The woman's eyes grew big. "Here he comes now," she said, with something like fear in her voice.

Neal opened the car door and called the pup, "C'mon, Princess, let's go home."

In the car, she sat bolt upright and motionless in the back seat. The little smile had disappeared, and her mouth was closed tight. Her ears tipped down in concern.

"It's okay," we told her, knowing her life was already better because she was away from a family that didn't want her. Neal and I both knew without saying it that her forever home would be with us.

At our house, she spent some time in the breezeway while we prepared our cats for the new arrival and decided what her new name would be.

The paperwork from the pet store where she had been purchased — on clearance, like last season's shoes — said she'd been born the week of Christmas. We wanted to keep that "s" sound from "Princess" so we named her "Chrissy."

And so, she has been our wonderful girl these past fourteen years. She's turned us from "cat people" to "cat and dog people." She's made certain we get our regular exercise because, even now as a senior, she needs several walks a day. She's made friends with our cats, helped us get to know every other dog in the neighborhood, and is a star at the dog park.

Recently, we brought in another unwanted dog, fifteen-year-old Spike. We knew we could manage the feat because our girl Chrissy has such a loving and generous heart. She has taken Spike under her wing, showing him the ropes around the house and guiding him through our walks around the block. He trails behind her, sometimes so close they bump into each other, which always makes us laugh.

We could learn a lesson in resiliency from these dogs, who both traded the life they knew for a new one with us and never looked back. When life gives us lemons, we make our lemonade. When life sends us dogs in need, we make another space in the house. There's already room in our hearts.

— Kate Fellowes —

A Breath from Bear

*If you want loyalty get a dog. If you want loyalty and
attention, get a smart dog.*
~Grant Fairley

He was a shaggy, little mutt on the day he came to us.
I didn't really want him, I told myself. I already felt
overwhelmed with medical struggles, two kids, two
cats, a hamster and a husband who was often away. I
didn't want another responsibility. Maybe when the kids are older, I
said. My husband wanted a dog, though, so it seemed like fate when
his co-worker had to part with his dog. Thus, Bear fell into our laps.

On the August evening when he came to us, he was skittish,
reserved, and confused. Our sons were excited to see their new fur
ball, but Bear seemed less than thrilled to see them. Anxiously, he
skittered around the house, unsure what to make of his new home. I
tried to be annoyed, but he grew on me almost instantly. I spent his
first week cleaning him up, giving him a new haircut, trimming his
nails, and getting rid of the ticks embedded in his skin. As the weeks
passed, he grew slowly less skittish, although it would take years for
him to come fully out of his shell.

However, it didn't take years for him to make us realize how
much he was meant for our family. It didn't even take months. His
one lopsided ear, generous kisses, and insanely calm nature would
have been enough to win me over. But it was a night, not more than a
month after he came to his new home, when he showed us just how

meant-to-be he truly was.

That September evening wasn't much different from other evenings. The kids and I were on our own while my husband was away, so my mom decided to visit. My younger son had a minor cold, and he and my older son went to bed around eight since my older son had school the next day. My mom and I stayed up way too late, hanging out, and I finally suggested after midnight that we both get some rest.

Having just checked on the boys, I headed to my bedroom. I got ready for bed quickly and lay down, anxious to get to sleep, when Bear came into my room. Still rather timid, he seemed to be acting odd. He started to whine and jump. I tried to ignore him since I had just taken him out and was beyond tired. I knew as soon as my head hit the pillow that I'd be out. He kept persisting, though, finally jumping up on me and biting at my clothing.

This dog was many things, but aggressive was not one of them. I began to wonder if he was hurt or not feeling well. His whines got louder as he continued to pull at me. Finally, I gave in and followed him out the bedroom door. Panicked, he ran, came back to me, and then ran again, urging me along the way. Finally, he stopped outside my kids' door and began scratching.

Something clicked in my head, and I pushed open the door hurriedly. My youngest was sitting upright, staring straight ahead, with pale skin and blue lips. I ran to him and began the struggle to get him to breathe. After the longest few moments of my life, he let out a huge gasp and started crying. He had been unable to get any air into his lungs and had been frozen in panic.

I rushed him out of his room, working continuously to keep him breathing, and called 911. The EMTs arrived within three minutes, and they put him on oxygen. Now relieved I'd found the cause of his panic, Bear sat still and quiet as they entered our home. In the month we had him, and all the years to come, this was the only time he didn't bark when strangers came into his home. Instead, he watched wide-eyed as they continued to work on my four-year-old. I left with my son in an ambulance, and by the time we arrived at the hospital, his color had returned, and he was breathing on his own. Although he was tired, my son was fine and returned home later that morning.

My child was alive and well because Bear, through a closed bedroom door, knew something was terribly wrong with him. He overcame his reticence and persisted to get me out of bed to save my boy. I will never be able to fully express the gratitude I have for Bear.

—Jennifer Oramas—

Chapter 9

Living in the Moment

Flying Blind

Forever is composed of nows.
~Emily Dickinson

I heard the thunk of William's skull on oak when he walked right into the coffee table. I was puzzled. It was an unfamiliar room, and it was midnight, but the hall light was on. Didn't he see the table?

My husband and I and our two dogs were spending the night at my dad's house on a road trip to Nova Scotia for hiking, camping, and birding. William was our five-year-old Italian Greyhound and Pippin was a tan-and-white Terrier mix. We always said our vacations were actually the dogs' vacations; they just needed us to drive.

William blinked and shook his head. I asked if he was okay, and he toddled out after me into the yard to pee. I kept him on the leash coming back in the house so he wouldn't bump into anything else. The next morning, we loaded up and headed east.

At the Canadian crossing, a dour border agent scrutinized our passports and the dogs' vaccine papers and cross-examined us as to the purpose of our visit. Then Pippin stood up in the back seat with a cheerful smile and wagging tail. The corner of the man's mouth tilted up a couple of millimeters. "That," he said, "is a great-looking dog." William growled at him.

We drove, camped, and hiked along the Atlantic shore and through the taiga. There were bald eagles and seals on the beach at Ingonish. The dogs sniffed and explored. A moose wandered into our camp, and William barked at it.

On the way back, we spent a night in a motel in upstate New York. As I brought William in from his pre-dawn business, he blundered straight into the depths of a juniper bush.

Back home in Chicago, I made an appointment with a prominent veterinary ophthalmologist. As she was peering into William's eyes through a lighted ophthalmoscope, I said nervously, "He runs into things when the light is low. I'm worried about progressive retinal atrophy."

"Yep," she said casually. "That's what he's got. He's about 50 percent gone."

Progressive retinal atrophy. It is a genetic disorder to which Italian Greyhounds are prone, especially poorly bred puppy-mill ones. And that's what William, a rescue, was. The cells of the retina in the back of the eye wither away and slough off. It is gradual and painless, but there is no treatment. William would be completely blind before he turned seven. The vet asked if we had another dog, and when I said yes, she said, "Good. That will help him a lot." She sent us home with a book about living with blind dogs. In the car, I took him in my arms and told him, "Don't worry. No matter what, we will take care of you. You will always be safe. No matter what."

William was unconcerned. He had already mapped out our house and yard. He hopped on and off the furniture as he always had, scampered up and down the deck steps, and stole the cats' food. He barked at passersby, especially if they had dogs. At home, you would never have known he was blind. We did put mats at the top and bottom of the stairs so he would know they were there. I taught him cues. "Careful!" meant there was an obstacle in front of him, and he would pause, feel forward with his pointy snout and navigate around it. "Step-step!" meant there was a stair or a curb going down, and "Up-up!" meant a step going up. "Hop!" was a tree limb or something he could jump over.

We still went camping and hiking. He decided for himself that he was just fine following close to our ankles. He became an even better birding companion, happy to wait as I peered at elusive feathered activity in a tree. If something exciting for dogs came up, he simply followed Pippin. Off they would go, investigating, smelling, digging and doing all the things that dogs like to do in meadows, prairies and mountains. He did fall off a rock and bite his lip once, but he shook it off, caught up to Pippin and carried on. Pippin was patient and solicitous. He would stop regularly, look back, and wait for William to catch up. He was William's guide dog.

There is a state park about forty miles from us, with a seven-mile equestrian trail that meanders through acres of lush prairie, filled with wildflowers and birdsong. It's a great place to run dogs, and there are never any horses there. The trail is broad, grassy, and nicely mowed. It is easy walking and comfortable on dog toes. We ambled along one spring morning, and as Pippin ranged farther afield, William joined him. They rooted in the hedges and flopped in some deliciously stinky substance, chasing down noises and smells, both with tails flagged high. I stopped to check out some horned larks in an adjoining field. When I looked up, the dogs were way ahead of us, about to disappear around a bend. I flung out my arms and hollered, "Heeeeey! Yooooooouuu!" They stopped. Pippin must have said something like "Bet I can beat ya back!" and took off.

The two dogs came hurtling toward us — flat out, turbo charged, as fast as they could go. William's ears were flat to his head, his tail low and tight as he rocketed over the ground. He was grinning. He outstripped Pippin (he was a Greyhound, after all) in a few strides. No brake, no restraint, in a thundering sprint in the sun, over the warm grass — a dog who could not see anything at all. Imagine the trust, the bravery, the absolute glee, the unbridled speed — he was joyfully, perfectly free.

For those moments, he wasn't blind.

I was, though. With tears.

— Julie Stielstra —

The Case of the Missing Hot Springs

May your trails be crooked, winding, lonesome,
dangerous, leading to the most amazing view.
May your mountains rise into and above the clouds.
~Edward Abbey

hree strangers in the past month had recommended this
hike to Wally and me, but not one of them had mentioned
that the trail didn't technically exist. The path ducked
in and out of sight among the ponderosa pines. Wally
navigated the underbrush with glee, chasing chipmunks and scoping
new scents, but I kept snagging my backpack on scrub oak branches
and grumbling about losing the way. Yet, two miles into the woods
and nearly a dozen miles from any paved road, my greatest concern
was whether I should have worn my swimsuit.

Like two adventurers on the hunt for the Fountain of Youth, my
dog and I were determined to find the Piedra River's hot springs. We
had no clues to go by other than vague secondhand accounts. I didn't
know what these natural pools looked like, and I had never soaked in
the wild. I wondered if I might get algae in my swim shorts and where
I was supposed to change my clothes.

Wally didn't have to think about such things. He packed only
his blaze-orange bandanna and some well-warranted treats. I did all
the worrying for him. Should a dog even go in the hot springs? What

Living in the Moment | 281

about a dog with cancer? Would drinking sulfurous water react with his medicines? What if he ran off while I was soaking—would I towel off before chasing him?

I stressed about finding our way every time the trail vanished. But we never really got lost. The Piedra River, a clear-water Rocky Mountain stream, streamed by us on the left. The slope cut by that water over thousands of years climbed to our right. By staying between them, Wally and I found our way out of the trees, searching every so often for a clear path down to the water and maybe, if our hunches were accurate, the hot springs.

Our hunches were as accurate as our directions. Not one of the strangers had mentioned hiking so far upriver.

Wally was loving every moment of the search. It was a good day for him. One would never know he was a month into chemotherapy. He trotted with that nonchalant strut that I fell in love with the first time we walked together at the Humane Society. He meandered ahead of me through the forest, his tail swaying, shooting under fallen trees and tuning in to every imagined sound and faded scent. He was on the lookout for something. He didn't know what, but he would sure recognize it when he saw it.

"Five more minutes," I told Wally, getting exasperated with the quest. "If we don't see the springs, we're turning around."

He looked at me the same way he did the other times I had threatened five more minutes. Then he trotted ahead again on the quiet, indistinct trail.

Five minutes later, we stopped. I perched on a log on a slope, and Wally sat with me to eat some treats.

We had failed to find the springs. He didn't appear the least put off by our failure, though. He seemed pleased with himself, content with our walk in the woods. He grinned as handsomely as ever, even with the square IV patch shaved off the fur on his foreleg.

"At least we got a good hike, huh, bud?" I said.

The forest rearranged itself while we lingered there. The homeward trail was clear as a runway. The false clearings and leafy inlets that looked like trails had been swept away to reveal well-trodden dirt.

Yet even with an open trail before us, what was our rush to return? The trail was so steadfast that we decided, at one particularly inviting riverbank, to detour right and visit the waterside. A strand of exotic beach butted up against a still stretch of mountain stream, with a sheer rock face on the other side and a jumble of logs and boulders on the shore that might well have been a nest for ogres.

Wally zeroed in on a screeching sound from the ogres' nest. He tensed; he stared; he bolted. A marmot darted between the rocks. Wally scrambled over stones and across exposed tree roots. He was all over that pile of giant marbles, that impossible game of pick-up sticks. The marmot kept screeching, and Wally kept searching.

Inspired by Wally's enthusiasm, I took off my hiking boots to dip my heels in the still-frigid runoff.

It took me a moment to register the sensations underfoot. The sand underwater was hot! This beach did not look like any hot spring I had imagined. But I had found one anyway, despite my expectations.

I tossed my hiking clothes on a rock and eased myself into the water.

The river was like a two-layer cake, like oil and water. The water above the sand was cold, though without quite the melted-snow chill my skin expected. And the water hovering just above the sand was stove-burner toasty.

I shoveled the sand with my hands to burrow deeper into the flow of water heated by the earth. I felt as relaxed atop this flow of quiet volcanic activity as I remember ever feeling.

Eventually, the marmot made its escape, and Wally missed it entirely. But who was I to interrupt his passionate quest? We had all the time in the world.

Eventually, Wally exhausted his search and returned to the water with a stick. Of course, we played. My dog got as wet as I did — and dirtier, too. He didn't find his marmot, and I didn't find the bubbling, beautiful hot springs I expected, but we enjoyed every moment along the way to not quite getting there.

Wally had the right idea: explore what's present instead of bemoaning what's not.

It turned out the hot springs I was looking for were not ten minutes from where I parked the car. We stumbled upon them on the way back from our long hike. They were just as advertised, but crowded with fishermen and children.

That day, with my dog as my guide, we had found so much more — by losing our way.

— Zach Hively —

Our Corn Dog

If you think dogs can't count,
try putting three dog biscuits in your pocket
and then give him only two of them.
~Phil Pastoret

I jumped at the sound right beside me. My husband Tim had thrown another treat, and it landed on the kitchen floor at my feet. The treat wasn't for me; I'd had enough snacks already that day. The treat was for our overweight Terrier, Walker. In one gulp, he gobbled up the meaty snack from the floor.

Our dog was short, golden brown and round. He had officially become a corn dog.

Tim and I were entering the thirty-sixth day of the COVID-19 crisis with the order to stay at our Indiana home.

Our normal daily schedule included jobs and volunteer work away from the house. Walker was confined to his toddler pen and slept while we were gone. When we returned home, he was free to roam and received his ration of kibble at our shared mealtime.

The new normal was both of us at home 24/7, looking at Walker's sweet face and giving in to the begging and whining for a snack. We confirmed that he slept during the morning. Now he was also sleeping in the afternoon. The begging, whining, and napping were all bad habits he had learned from me.

I said, "We need a weight-loss plan."

Tim agreed that some of us needed it, but not others. I didn't ask for details about his thinking. I had been too privy to them lately. So, I just kept talking.

"Walker needs a limit to his treats and food rations," I said. "If he does have a treat, it needs to be healthy."

On the bright side, there were only two of us at home to feed Walker. If there were any others offering him snacks, Walker would have to be wheeled outdoors for potty breaks. I knew who would do the wheeling.

I had tried hiding the treats, not replenishing the supply, and yelling finally, "No more!" That was the snack advice for me as well.

On top of all that, Walker required medicine in tablet form for his seizures. Tim would push the three tablets into a soft treat in the morning and another dosage in the evening. Those were adding to Walker's weight, too. Tim said, "Let's invent pill pockets for our meds."

I thought we already had. "Those would be called brownies," I said.

I heard Walker scratching at the back door. That was his signal, not for going outdoors, but for a treat, since they were kept in a cabinet near there. I held out my empty hands to him — my signal that the snacks were gone. I found it best not to tell him the truth. Plus, Tim would think the treats were all gone, too.

A dejected Walker went back to his bed to sniff around for one bit of food that might have been left behind. A dejected Tim flipped through the stations looking for the golf channel.

Today, just like the past thirty-six days, I was spending lots of time in the kitchen researching recipes for the available ingredients I had on hand and concocting meals. I had been preparing far too many desserts, too. Cooking and baking were something I didn't normally do. My three favorite words from Tim had always been "let's eat out."

Since Walker was free to roam the house now, he was in the kitchen underfoot constantly — right along with Tim. We needed a bit more physical distancing in our own kitchen.

As I poured the chili ingredients into the slow cooker, I said to Walker, "Why can't you be like those dogs in the exercise videos who help with sit-ups?"

Tim said, "You know I have a bad back." Walker looked up at

me, wondering when the chili would be ready.

On my most recent shopping trip, during the senior shopping hour, I had bought food that was labeled "weight loss for senior dogs." I showed Tim when I got home. He thought that would be a good idea and wished there was a simple food like that for humans.

We ended up feeding Walker larger portions than we intended. Plus, he was still getting the treats.

I tried taking Walker on longer hikes outdoors. We walked our one-acre property several times a day to ramp up our heart rates. Walker was mostly interested in performing a smell inspection for every blade of grass, molehill and tree. After thirty minutes for a one-acre walk, both of us only ramped up an appetite.

Our dog may have looked like a corn dog, but he was a happy corn dog. When we would come back inside from a trip outdoors, Walker would race straight toward Tim like they had been separated for hours. Walker loved to have his ears scratched, probably because he couldn't reach them with his back legs on his own. Walker also loved to race from one side of the house to another, just acting silly.

I suppose all three of us were doing the best we could under the circumstances. A weight-loss plan would just have to go on our to-do list. I gave the chili a stir and put on the lid.

Plop! That was a carrot landing next to me. I guess Tim was trying to get us on the right track. But I wasn't sure if the carrot was for Walker or me.

— Glenda Ferguson —

Everyday Joy

"What day is it?" asked Pooh. "It's today,"
squeaked Piglet. "My favorite day," said Pooh.
~A.A. Milne

To chase a ball across the room
To sleep in sunshine 'til high noon
To lick the face of all my friends
To romp and play 'til daytime ends
To eat the scraps upon the floor
To bark at people at the door
To run as fast as ever I can
To lie beneath a scratching hand
To catch a really scary cat
To sleep 'til morn upon my mat
My joys in life are very few
But, for a dog, a few will do!

— C.H. MacDonald —

The Cycle of Life

Once you have had a wonderful dog,
a life without one is a life diminished.
~Dean Koontz

Baxter was well into his senior years when Dennis and I brought our newborn home from the hospital. He was as set in his ways as any crotchety senior citizen, so we were nervous about it. We stooped to make the introduction, holding our swaddled son out like an offering, and held our breath. Baxter's reaction — a halfhearted sniff and a slow shuffle back to his doggy bed — was anticlimactic.

We'd gotten Baxter, a Pembroke Welsh Corgi, on Valentine's Day the first year we were married. Inside the breeder's heated barn, a stall gate swung open, and a gaggle of puppies bounded out, nipping and tripping over clumps of hay, grain sacks and their own paws.

Baby Corgis are singularly clumsy. Their heads nearly outweigh the rest of their bodies, lending them a center of gravity that makes forward motion pretty tricky. Watching them try (and fail) to run has the same effect as hearing an infant cry — it compels you to scoop them up, nuzzle them under your chin and take care of them forever.

So that's what we did. For the next thirteen years, we arranged our daily lives around Baxter's eating, sleeping and walking schedules. We fussed over his diet and social skills. We taught him all the things a good dog ought to know, like how to shake and not beg. We fretted over trimming his nails and discussed his poop way more than was necessary.

Though we didn't realize it until later, he was excellent practice for the child we weren't sure we'd ever get around to having. He taught us how to function on little to no sleep, use positive reinforcement, get out stubborn stains and remain calm(ish) during trips to the emergency vet. He taught us that a happy house isn't always a clean house, and that the simple joy of cuddles trumps all the hard parts of raising a living thing. Most of all, he taught us patience.

He was an exemplary dog and upstanding family member, and Dennis and I feared that bringing home baby would jinx his easy disposition. When we learned I was pregnant, we started playing recordings of wailing infants to desensitize his adorably disproportionate ears. I kept waiting for him to become protective of me and my life-growing belly, but he remained blissfully unaware that anything was afoot right up to the day we left for the hospital. And despite our lukewarm welcome home, Baxter handled Mac's arrival with more grace than I could muster.

My newborn was like a puzzle I didn't have all the pieces to. When he cried, I ran through my repertoire of remedies — changing, feeding, burping, rocking — and then threw up my hands. I huffed and puffed. I sobbed. And Baxter never left my sleep-deprived, milk-stained side.

I thought of all the books I'd read, classes I'd attended and brains I'd picked to prepare myself for the perfect yet wholly irrational human whose every whim we struggled to satisfy. And how I would've traded it all for five minutes of Baxter's natural ability to just roll with it.

While I tussled with depression, doubt and diapers, Mac and Bax began a May-December romance as unexpected as it was undeniable. They shared all the same interests, chief among them lying around in the air conditioning. They drooled, yawned, whined and hogged the bed with gusto. They reveled in light sleep and short walks. Just when we thought the depths of their love had been reached, Mac graduated to solid foods, ensuring Baxter a steady stream of puffs and blueberries that rained down from on high (chair) like so much mushy manna.

The first time Mac crawled to a napping Baxter and snuggled into his fluffy chest, it stopped me in my tracks. It was part hug, part headlock, all harmony, and they lingered there long enough for me to snap a photo. After returning to work, I'd shut myself in the conference room where I pumped and look at that image whenever stress or exhaustion chased away my letdown reflex. It calmed me. It was how I'd pictured motherhood before I discovered what it really looked like.

One thing about Baxter's easy relationship with the baby bothered me though, and that was the hair. Mac was covered in dog hair. Dennis did his best to convince me it was okay, to stop me from picking constantly at the blankets, the sofa and Mac's snotty nose. "A little dog hair's not going to hurt him," he'd say, and I'd cite the latest horror story I'd read about hair tourniquets, bezoars, asthma or allergies.

But the hair was as inevitable as the passage of time. As Mac sped up, Baxter slowed down, and we knew our time with him was nearing its close. He died on a January morning replete with a pall of low gray clouds. Dennis and I were heartbroken, a fresh wave of sadness washing over us each time we returned to an empty house or muscle memory made us reach for the leash on our way out the door. The sound of Baxter's nails clicking on the hardwood was replaced by Mac's footfalls.

Just as we'd worried Mac's entrance would turn our dog's world upside down, now we feared Baxter's exit would cause our son the same hurt and loneliness we felt. And just as Baxter had been unfazed, so was Mac. He peeked around corners for his canine companion a few times… and that was that.

Without even trying, dogs and kids do something therapists and philosophers tout as the key to a happy life: They live in the moment. Watching Mac and Baxter do that, time and again, together and apart, was the reminder I needed that life goes on through all kinds of changes — even ones as monumental as birth and death.

As if Baxter had passed him a torch, Mac helped me adjust (again) to a strange new routine and a household I didn't quite recognize. He kept me busy and made me laugh. Sadness crept in, but this time when I cried, it was Mac who refused to leave my side.

Last week, I found a fluff of fur on a pair of Mac's pants buried in a drawer since last fall. The white wisp stood out in stark contrast against the dark material. I stared at it for a few seconds, and then refolded the pants and placed them back in the drawer, tiny tuft and all. Dennis was right. A little dog hair's not going to hurt him.

—Tracy Marsh—

Zoey's Simple Blessings

Everything I know, I learned from dogs.
~Nora Roberts

I went over the list of all the things I had to do: laundry, dishes, make beds, run errands, grocery shop, and pick up my boys from school in the afternoon. My heart sped up and I felt anxious thinking about it. I wanted to get most of my work done in the morning before I started a bigger project: cleaning the basement. There just weren't enough hours in the day.

I heard a soft whine and looked down to see Zoey, our Beagle/Collie mix, staring at me. She whined again.

I released a heavy sigh. "Gotta go out, girl?" I asked reluctantly.

She looked at me, tilting her head like she was trying to figure out what I was saying, her floppy ears curling around her sweet, furry face.

Zoey is the latest rescue dog we picked at the Humane Society. We got her as a companion to our other rescue dog, Lilly. We didn't have a fence up yet. In fact, that was on our to-do list. So when our dogs needed to go to the bathroom or on a walk, we took them out on their leashes. We live on a busy road, so I would never risk them going out by themselves.

For a split second, I thought about running upstairs and throwing a load of laundry in before tending to Zoey. But her eyes were fixated on me, and I didn't want to make her wait any longer. I slipped on my junk Crocs and clipped the leash to her harness.

The warm sun beat on our faces, and we heard a hummingbird. Gently, the cool breeze stirred Zoey's hair. I could have stayed outside all day. I pushed away the thought. I had to resist; I had way too much to do.

Zoey sniffed around. She wasn't ready to do her business, and I felt a twinge of irritation. If I hurried her along, I could get my grocery shopping done before the store got crowded.

"Come on, Zoey. Let's get moving." I tugged at her leash gently.

She didn't pay attention and moved on to check out our daisies. They were blooming and inviting. Who could blame her?

"Do you like those?" I asked. She moved on to the garden, checking out our tomato plants.

I bit the bottom of my lip. The list of stuff to do was on my mind like a heavy weight, and I wanted to scream, "Hurry up and go!"

But the neighbors would have thought I was a horrible pet owner, and I couldn't imagine screaming at Zoey. She's the sweetest dog ever. *Oh, for Pete's sake, Zoey, go already,* I thought, playing a gentler version in my mind. I nudged her along, trying not to give in to my irritation.

The smell of lilacs hit us, and the sky was so blue, like an inviting pool on a warm summer day. I just wanted to kick off my Crocs and lie down in the soft grass like when I was a child. Then my inner, more mature voice took over. *Are you crazy? You have a whole lot of stuff to do. Get that dog to pee already and hop to it!*

Zoey led me to a huge patch of shade not too far from the trees, plopped right down in the mud, rolled over and expected a belly scratch.

Ugh, add dog bath to the list now. I nudged at the leash to get her back up, but she wasn't having any of it. She panted and stretched, and I could tell she was really enjoying herself.

I sighed and realized we weren't going anywhere for a while. *Well, if you can't nudge or push them, you might as well join them.* So, I sat down beside her. She was enjoying herself, and I couldn't take this moment away from her, no matter how dirty my clothes would get.

Zoey had come a long way since our first meeting at the Humane

Society. We fell in love with her immediately. I found her online and couldn't wait until my husband came home from work. We all piled into the car with our boys and Lilly to make the trip there and see if she would be a good fit for our family. She was curled up in the back of her cage when we met her. She looked sad and had a bad case of kennel cough. Lilly and Zoey got along well, and we just couldn't stand the thought of leaving Zoey behind, so we adopted her.

The first few days, she lay around, coughed and wouldn't eat. Her checkup had gone well, but I was worried about her lack of appetite. I called the Humane Society, and they told us to keep an eye on her. If things didn't improve, we could bring her back to let the vet look at her. On the third day, I put a little bit of gravy on her dog food. She ate it and then a little more. I was so relieved to see she was eating. After about a week, she seemed a lot more at home, and her kennel cough was going away. She loved fetching her toys, and I could tell she was adjusting well.

Now here she was a well-adjusted dog enjoying herself in the soft grass. Well, I had to admit we both were. I didn't have the heart to move her. I looked around at our yard, the landscaping, the trees and flowers, and our little garden. I felt like I'd hardly noticed them, being so busy working and taking care of my family. Zoey and I watched a woodpecker for a while and took in the scent of honeysuckle. It reminded me of my childhood. A neighborhood friend and I would pull the flower apart gently and enjoy the honey inside. They were great memories of being a kid with little responsibility. I smiled and pulled Zoey close.

She taught me that it was okay to slow down and enjoy the simple pleasures. I don't think dogs understand time like we do, but they sure understand feelings and love. I realized there's always going to be housework and errands to run, but why not take a little time to enjoy life? We sat there in the sunshine, my rescue dog and me, for about a half-hour until Zoey went to the bathroom and trotted toward the back door. Now, it was me who followed reluctantly.

I could probably make it to the grocery store and throw laundry in before I left. Maybe knock something else off my endless to-do list. But Zoey would need to go out again, and I decided to carve out time to sit with her and Lilly in the sunshine, enjoying the day and my blessings. My list could wait a little longer.

— Terri L. Knight —

Off Leash

A dog will teach you unconditional love. If you can
have that in your life, things won't be too bad.
~Robert Wagner

When I first adopted my dog, I was terrified she'd get lost. She's a retired racing Greyhound, bred to run. Most adoption groups recommend keeping Greyhounds leashed, no matter how well they've been trained. It's far too easy for Greyhounds to accelerate to speeds of thirty miles per hour after spotting a small, fluffy creature in the distance.

Hazel, my Greyhound, lacks the predatory drive to truly pursue anything other than (for some reason) chickens — the one thing to which she is allergic. But she doesn't like rules and frequently pretends not to hear me when I call her. I would almost certainly lose her if she was off leash outside our yard.

My fear of Hazel getting lost has morphed over the years into a general fear of losing her for good — which is going to happen one way or another. She's nine years old and grows more luminous by the day. Her red brindle coat has lightened to a lovely gold. Her black snout has become so silvered that I wonder if she will have the pure white face I've seen on other senior Greyhounds.

She's been a steady constant in my life through job losses, career changes, grief and unexpected illness. I comfort her with petting and attention, and she reflects that comfort back to me.

One unseasonably warm fall afternoon, we were walking the neighborhood together as we did nearly every day. Suddenly, I was struck by the golden light of her long body in the sun, her tiger-striped brindle coat, her thin and white-tipped tail, and her dainty steps as she trotted along the cracked asphalt of our suburban streets. I was awed by her beauty and the great fortune I'd had to share my life with her.

It knocked the breath out of me. There she was — my heart outside my body. Her velvet-soft ears twitched, and her deep brown eyes blinked slowly in the sun. There were her paws, which once touched down on racetrack sand, and now settled instead on couches or galloped through grass. There was a depth of love for me in her eyes that I knew I was lucky to see, and might at any moment never see again. And then those eyes and ears pointed forward, on the road ahead.

One day I would lose her, not because I'd let her off leash, but because her time would come. It was a terrifying thought. But in the moment, I was lucky enough to have her here with me. Of all the dogs in all the world, this one — this beautiful, elegant, demanding princess of a dog — came to share my story.

— Meghan Byers —

Learning to Sit

The best therapist has fur and four legs.
~Author Unknown

I taught my Jack Russell Terrier to sit when I was ten years old. Learning that one trick took an entire summer and many boxes of miniature treats. Years later, when my husband and I rescued a black Labrador/Hound mix, our sons Kyle and Tyler trained him. Barkley was so intelligent that he quickly learned lots of commands. In fact, Barkley's cleverness was a blessing and a curse. He was a master escape artist with separation anxiety. He'd bend the metal bars of his crate, pry open the door and destroy shoes, homework packets, library books, packages of toilet paper, dog beds, boxes of printer paper and even a wicker sofa. One day, we returned to find our wooden stairs and a windowsill chewed to shreds.

Strategically placed steel locks secured him — only to have him demolish the floor of his crate. Desperate, we tried to contain him in my office by placing a gate and chairs against the closed French doors. Before we could leave, Barkley stood on his back legs, turned the doorknob with his mouth and bulldozed past the barricade to the family-room sofa.

We learned the crate triggered the anxiety from his shelter days, but the comforts of home controlled bad behavior. When we let him roam the house, he was often in the same spot we left him — snuggled peacefully on the sofa with a fleece blanket.

Barkley was a wonderful companion to our boys. He'd greet them from our low front windows, and I could see their bright smiles through the glass. He loved walks, playing ball in the back yard, and napping in the sunshine. His favorite thing was curling up against them when they read, watched TV or wanted comfort. He knew when Kyle or Tyler needed him.

In March 2020, I suddenly did too. A pandemic of epic proportions had hit our country hard and fast. Schools closed abruptly. Our suburban Philadelphia county was the epicenter of our area. Our favorite place, New York City (where we had enjoyed a carefree visit weeks earlier) was a disaster zone. Life as we knew it was on hold.

I tossed and turned, trying to digest the devastating reality of a worldwide health crisis unfolding. For the first time in my life, I could feel my heart racing as I tried to sleep. When the sun rose, I felt disoriented. It was a school day but I didn't need to rush into the shower to get Kyle to the middle-school bus stop by 7 a.m. I didn't have to make sure Tyler had a big breakfast before heading off to elementary school.

That morning, as Travis set up a home office and the boys slept in, I crept downstairs in my pajamas to turn on the news. I've watched the *Today* show faithfully since college, but always in the background as I prepared for the day.

That day, I didn't need to be in the laundry room washing a jersey for practice — all sports had been canceled. I had no church clothes to iron — services were now online. There were no errands to run for our Florida vacation to Disney World and Phillies Spring Training. For the first time in history, the park had closed indefinitely, and MLB games, along with NBA and NHL games, had been suspended. It was strange for someone who didn't know how to sit still.

As I watched the news in horror, I felt weak in the knees. I was paralyzed with fear for family members at high risk, friends in healthcare, and all the people whose businesses, jobs and financial security were in jeopardy. I tried to absorb the enormity of this crisis and the impact on everyday life. We were at war, and our heroes on the front line were forced into battle without proper ammunition.

Barkley sensed my angst. He jumped up and lay across my thighs.

He did this often with the boys — but not me, because I never sat.

When I tried to get up, I couldn't. He knew by positioning his large body on my small lap that I wouldn't be able to move. It was both hysterically funny and tremendously comforting.

Each morning, I watched the heartbreaking national news and read about the death toll in our own town. Barkley would back himself onto my lap in a sweet and determined way, keeping me glued to that couch.

On the few days I attempted to do something else first, Barkley wouldn't allow it. He followed me around the house, stubbornly gripping my soft pajamas in a tightly locked jaw, and pulling me toward the sofa until he could bury himself in the fleece. He was training me — to sit.

As we adjusted to a new normal, we found we were happiest when we acted like Barkley. The best way to cope with the quarantine was to live like a dog.

We learned to give heartfelt greetings to loved ones through the glass pane of our front window. We found joy in the simplicity of a family walk. We spent hours playing ball in the back yard and developed a renewed appreciation for soaking up sunshine from a comfortable spot. With our busy schedule erased, we had time on the family-room sofa to relax while we read, played games or watched movies, wrapped in fleece blankets.

In a historic period of uncertainty and fear, our smart dog showed us how to face — and embrace — these days. The secret to navigating this anxious situation was to find solace in the comforts of home, take long walks, play in the back yard, soak up sunshine, and make time to relax. And sit.

— Jennifer Kennedy —

91

Happy Tail

Money can buy you a fine dog, but only love
can make him wag his tail.
~Kinky Friedman

I saw Bella's picture on a rescue website. The photo showed her on hind legs in a sweet begging position, but with only a single front paw. Her wiry black coat and her expressive eyes pulled me in. I filled out an adoption application immediately.

Three days later, I learned the word "tri-pawd," and that I had been accepted as Bella's owner! Our new dog would be transported from Hay River, Northwest Territories to us in Calgary, Alberta. My husband joked we couldn't afford a full-sized dog, so we only got a three-quarter one.

Jokes aside, had I thought this through? It had been a while since I'd had a dog. Would having a canine with a missing front leg be much different from one who walked on all fours? Dog walks wouldn't have to be long at least, which suited our busy lifestyle.

Would Bella be okay with our three cats? I needn't have worried. We discovered she was rescued from a hoarding situation and lived with twenty cats!

Our biggest question of all: How did Bella lose her leg? Had she been hit by a vehicle? Life can be harsh in northern Canada. Perhaps Bella had been caught in a trap. Limbs can be lost due to frostbite, a deformity or cancer… But we never learned how Bella became a "tri-pawd."

The scar where her front leg had been revealed a neat incision. Someone had loved Bella enough to have her cared for medically. This dog knew all her commands, so we knew someone had taken the time to train her. My heart ached for Bella. I wondered who she missed back in Hay River, who had given her up, willingly or not.

From the second she burst out of the vet clinic to greet us, she melted our hearts. Her lopsided lope on our first walk together was endearing. When we opened the door to our SUV to take her home, Bella hopped in like it was only natural.

We bonded with Bella that first year. At home, I was often accompanied by the shuffling sound of her off-kilter gait. I couldn't even take a shower without almost stepping on her afterward. We christened her "Bella the Bathmat."

How we laughed hearing Bella's loud snoring. Sometimes, she'd lie quietly on the floor, only to break the silence by passing gas, scaring herself in the process. This resulted in a fearful, three-legged trot away from her rank flatulence.

Whenever Bella wanted her backside scratched, she'd flop down dramatically headfirst. Then, with her wiggly bottom sky high in air, Bella would gleefully await back scratches.

Chasing our local jackrabbit population was part of Bella's outdoor routine. Missing a limb certainly didn't inhibit her primal instincts. Turn on the water hose, too, and our ten-year-old dog went crazy! She was playful as a puppy.

Bella was also a lap dog at heart, albeit a fifty-pound one. There was always a spot on the couch for her to snuggle with us.

She was such a joyful dog that she even developed a problem called happy tail syndrome. We learned about this after finding minute blood spatters on the wall, leading us to notice fresh blood on the tip of her tail as well. Her ecstatic tail wagging was the issue. Some owners get their dog's tail cropped in order to avoid further harm. Instead, we grabbed her "happy tail" whenever she got too excited and this calming tactic worked most of the time.

Sadly, the "kennel cough" Bella had come with got worse. X-rays showed that Bella had a lung tumour. We were utterly devastated. The vet gave her six months to a year to live.

But Bella did not get the memo about her terminal diagnosis. For two more years, she carried on cheerfully. Being down one leg with a lung tumour didn't stop this special dog from relishing life. The radiance of being alive, regardless of obstacles, shone in Bella's demeanour. We gazed upon her in quiet awe, right up to the day we had to say goodbye.

Bella taught us unconditional love. Instead of training her, she trained us to have hope and perseverance despite impediments.

Some days, when I felt like I barely had one leg to stand on, I'd look at Bella, and my faith would be bolstered. Our courageous "tri-pawd" didn't think she was lacking in any way. In Bella's mind, she walked just fine, her damaged tail was meant for wagging, and every remaining day presented a new opportunity for joy.

— Irish Beth Maddock —

92

Thanksgiving Run

Not what we say about our blessings,
but how we use them, is the true measure
of our thanksgiving.
~W.T. Purkiser

On Thanksgiving Day, I find myself going from room to room, looking out the windows, and watching the raw rain. I feel like going for a run despite the cold. I know who will be game to go along — my dog, Josey. And I know just where I feel like going.

We hop in the truck and drive to my old neighborhood, about an hour away. I park and leash him, since it's about five blocks to a place where I can let him loose — old coal lands crisscrossed with dirt paths. The area is pockmarked with old mining equipment, high rusty cranes sticking above the scrubby pines like dinosaurs, and long conveyor belts now leading nowhere.

Although it's been more than four months since we've run this area, I'm hoping to see a couple of the neighborhood dogs, Tippy and Midnight. Tippy is an elderly Collie who spotted us from his porch one day and joined us on the run. A few weeks later, a young black Lab moved into the neighborhood and he started coming with us, too. I made it a point to let the owners know, and they said it was fine. The dogs always peeled off back to their houses when we returned.

Sometimes, I found Midnight and Tippy standing ready at the ends of their driveways, like children waiting for the school bus. Midnight hopped from paw to paw like a dressage horse. On this day, with the near-sleet rain, I don't expect to see the elderly Tippy outside, and I feel certain I hear Midnight's furious barking as we pass his house.

When my dog and I start running and come to the area behind the cemetery, I see the unmistakable silhouette of Bonehead, the auto-repair-shop guard dog. His eyes are squinted against the rain, and his pointed ears loll out to the side. He is staring at the place we appear.

We'd run into him one morning long ago, as he nosed in the brush along the top stone wall of the cemetery on the hill behind the shop. After that first meeting, he rarely missed a morning of running with us. I learned he was always left in the shop overnight as a guard dog. I was disappointed to learn his name. Although he was always dusty, oily and dirty, his eyes were always bright, and he loved the run.

My dog rushes up to Bonehead, and they greet each other happily. Then Bonehead frisks to me, dancing on his hind legs. When I moved, I told all the dogs' owners, but I had no way to explain it to the dogs. Today, the language barrier looms large. I don't know how long he's been waiting in the rain, and it breaks my heart to wonder if he's been sitting by the wall waiting every day for months.

For now, it's enough that we're together again. Although my dog runs in swooping loops through the woods, Bonehead runs right next to me on the path. I let my fingers trail on his head from time to time, and he looks up at me, with his tongue lolling out of one side of his mouth in what looks like a grin.

He makes me realize we're lucky — and what a simple, sweet and happy thing it is to just run.

— Lisa Price —

Chapter 10

Best Friends

The Magic of Bentley

The one absolutely unselfish friend that man can have
in this selfish world, the one that never deserts him,
the one that never proves ungrateful
or treacherous, is his dog.
~George Graham

When I was a kid growing up in Northeast Ohio, my parents had no interest in getting a dog, or any pet. But at least our friends in the neighborhood had dogs, so I was exposed to them throughout my youth. I wasn't afraid of dogs, but I was by no means a dog lover. I was indifferent.

In 2004, my wife and I escaped the cold winters of Ohio by moving to the West Coast with her daughter. We settled in the Coachella Valley of Southern California, where the desert summers are scorching hot but the winters are fantastic.

It didn't take long for my wife and stepdaughter to suggest we get a dog. I wasn't a fan of the idea. I think my mother's mantra about dogs being dirty and hard to take care of had been cemented in my mind, and I remained steadfast against the idea for the first few years in our new location.

But they never relented. Finally, after hearing a story about how a female jogger had been attacked on a trail not far from our home, I began to see things differently. My wife and I are joggers. Well, actually, I'm a jogger, and she's a runner, one who competed in high school and college. I began to see how having a dog for security and peace of mind was worth it. Sometimes, Lori would run on her own, and I felt that having a big dog as her companion made sense.

So, Bentley entered our lives on a bright spring day in 2008. Ben, as we usually call him, came home with Lori and my stepdaughter from a shelter one day, and I must acknowledge that he was pretty damn cute. Rust-colored with crimped ears, he was a Rhodesian Ridgeback mix. Eventually, he would become a seventy-two-pound sleek and athletic animal. We figured he was about three months old when we got him, and we started to train him. As with most dogs, those first few months were tough, but Ben caught on quickly, and it wasn't long before he started to accompany us on our runs and hikes.

I always thought Ben was in the upper echelon of dogs in terms of intelligence. But it wasn't until a trip to St. George, Utah, in 2012 that I determined we truly had a special dog.

On a late spring day, we found a trailhead on the outskirts of a local neighborhood. The trail was in a protected wilderness area and surrounded by beautiful red rocks and an expansive desert valley consisting of cactuses and other native vegetation. As was usually the case, we started to run, and Lori and Ben began to separate themselves from me. After all, she was the runner!

About fifteen minutes into our run, I saw Lori ahead and began to get closer to her. She was walking, and as I approached, I noticed that Ben was nowhere in sight. Once I caught up to her, she told me Ben had taken off when he saw a jackrabbit dart across the trail, which was a regular occurrence. In the past, though, he always gave up the chase and returned to the path. This time, however, he hadn't returned. We continued walking for a while, yelling his name and whistling. But still, there was no sign of him.

Finally, we determined that I would head toward the car, and she would continue her run for another mile or two, both of us hoping we would run into Ben. As I walked and jogged toward the car, I continued to shout his name, hoping to see him running toward me. But time was getting short, and the weather was getting warmer. I was starting to worry that we might never see him again.

Unfortunately, on my way back, I lost my bearings. I made a wrong turn at some point and ended up wasting an additional thirty minutes before I got back on track. By then, I was distraught. It was me, the desert, and no sign of our dog.

Eventually, I saw the trailhead in the distance, and I knew I was getting near our car. As I approached the cul-de-sac where our car was parked, my mood suddenly went from total dread and anguish to jubilation and relief. There he was. Ben was near the car, walking around as if nothing had happened. When he saw me, he cowered as if he knew he had done something terrible. But I couldn't care less. I hugged him tightly and told him how happy I was to see him. I called Lori on her cell phone to tell her the news. She couldn't believe he had found his way back. Neither could I.

We figured we were at least two to three miles from where we had parked when Ben sprinted off. But he had the instinct and intelligence to head to the car, figuring that we would be there eventually. To this day, I think about what happened in St. George. While I had seen signs of his intelligence, as well as his protective loyalty to our family, I knew from that day forward that Ben wasn't an ordinary dog.

So here we are, seven years after that momentous day in St. George. I'm sitting at my computer in our house on the Southwestern Coast of Oregon. We moved here after living in Southern California for twelve years. I retired in 2016 after a twenty-eight-year career in the blue-collar world. Writing is what I do now. It's the middle of the afternoon, and after a nice hike/run, Ben is by my side, only five feet away.

This is how most of my days are spent now. Ben is eleven, and he's slowed a bit. He even has a little gray hair now around his prominent snout. But every day around 9 a.m., he starts to look at me. He knows it's time for our run. It's time for us to head onto one of the many beautiful trails in the area. He still likes to sprint, and I'm amazed at how agile he still is.

He's my companion and pal. I can't think about life without him because it makes me sad when I do. So, I appreciate every day I spend with him. And I'm so thankful he found his way back to our car that day seven years ago. Life would not have been the same if he hadn't.

I can say now, thanks to Ben, I'm officially a dog lover.

—Jeff Marzick—

94

His Inner Clock

The dog lives for the day, the hour, even the moment.
~Robert Falcon Scott

Mack's world got exponentially better on March 24, 2020, when the COVID-19 pandemic hit. Our dog couldn't be more ecstatic that my husband, Don, was now staying home 24/7. Overnight, his most cherished human was available for longer walks, more tugs of war, spontaneous ear scratches, and multiple "Good boy" accolades.

Though I'm retired and home every day, and I know he loves me, Mack is devoted to my husband. Having him around all the time made his little world complete. He reveled in all the extra attention.

Mack hardly left Don's side the first week — following him every-where and leaving a trail of happy doggy drool for me to mop up.

It wasn't until the next Tuesday that we noticed a change in his demeanor. I awoke to hear my husband's muffled words through our closed bedroom door.

"Hey, boy, are you looking for your buddies?" he was saying. I got out of bed and wandered into the living room.

"Is Mack at the window again?" I asked, smiling.

"Yeah, like usual. He must have seen some neighbors walking their dog."

Sure enough, our dog had shoved the blinds aside on our bay window and was staring out toward the road in front of our house. His large head rested on the sill, and a muted whine escaped his throat every few moments as he focused on the scene before him.

It's always been Mack's habit to watch the world go by from the window. His reaction depends on what he sees. Squirrels are the recipients of short yips. Certain dogs he considers enemies or threats have him emitting low, rumbling growls. Others who he determines may be potential playmates are met with excited yelps and whines.

We opened the blinds to let in the morning sun. Mack seemed disinterested in abandoning his vigil, so we left him to go have our morning coffee, confident that he'd join us in the dining room shortly.

That day, the road was empty, but Mack maintained his vigil. He did leave his post at the window eventually, but not for long. For days, he continued to whine sadly, the sounds getting more distressed and frequent. He would stop his mysterious surveillance only to go out and relieve himself, devour his food quickly, and nap sporadically, but he always returned to that window.

He still went for walks, but grudgingly. Don claimed he always seemed in a hurry to get back home. At night, instead of his habitual "security rounds," he paced frantically and non-stop. His bizarre behavior began to concern us.

"He must be sensing the tension around him with this COVID-19 outbreak," I theorized worriedly. "I've read dogs do that."

"Possibly," Don responded. "I hope he's not sick."

Mack is twelve years old and a large breed. His white muzzle and slowed movements of late are clear reminders of his advanced age. "Maybe we should have him checked," I suggested that Saturday morning. "He's been like this four days. I know our vet is open during this virus, but not on weekends."

Though we were urged to stay home, we could still go out for walks, groceries, or emergencies as long as we maintained social distancing. I was sure we'd be allowed access beyond the regional barriers that were set up between our town and the next where Mack's vet was located.

"If he's not better on Monday, I think I'll do that," Don agreed.

That same afternoon, while we watched a movie, Mack left the window long enough to walk over to his water bowl. As he slurped halfheartedly, the phone rang, and I answered. It was my son, David.

We talked for a few minutes, and then I asked to speak to my four-year-old granddaughter.

"Hi, Kara!" I greeted her in that loud, high-pitched, semi-condescending voice that I could never seem to repress with her—a tone exclusive to adults addressing young children.

The moment I said her name, Mack whipped his head around with a loud yelp and ran toward the window. He skidded to a halt, jumped up, and planted both front paws on the sill. He looked out expectantly and began a series of enthusiastic barks.

I ended my call quickly, promising to call Kara back in a few minutes, and stared at my husband. His expression of incredulous shock and realization mirrored mine.

My son has joint custody of his daughter and gets her every other week. On Tuesdays of those weeks, like clockwork, he brings her to visit. Though we see her on other days while he has her too, we can always count on her punctual arrival at the same time every second week. Evidently, so can Mack!

Mack and Kara are inseparable when she's here. When they're not playing together, he will lie at her feet no matter where she is—watching television, sitting at the table drawing, or reading. He even waits for her outside the bathroom door. During sleepovers, he can be found curled up beside her bed all night.

We'd both forgotten that Mack always seems to know when she's coming and waits at the window for the car to pull up. Because we were self-isolating, Kara and David were unable to make their usual visit that week. We never realized that Mack couldn't understand why his little girl wasn't coming.

We watched as his tail slowly halted its happy wag. His ears and shoulders drooped, and he resumed his woebegone expression, laying his chin on the sill in sad, listless dejection.

I called my son back and explained the situation. Then I ran to get Mack's dry shampoo, which I applied quickly, followed by a safe pet-sanitizing spray for everyone's protection. Then I led him outside into the back yard.

We didn't have to wait long. My son lives fifteen minutes away from us, and he was there in record time with his daughter in tow. Mack's joyous, welcoming barks were all we needed to convince us we'd stumbled on the correct reason for his strange depression.

We kept our distance, watching from the patio, while the two played outside together for almost an hour. Both Kara and Mack were a mess from the melting snow and mud, but their happy faces were well worth the ruined clothes and matted fur.

Kara understands that she needs to avoid her grandma and grandpa for a little while longer, so she blew kisses our way as she and her daddy got back into the car. My son wrapped her in an old blanket until he could get her home and cleaned up. We led Mack directly to our tub where he patiently tolerated a thorough bath. Later, he curled up on his blanket with a happy sigh, dozing off into the first peaceful sleep he'd had in days.

During this terrible pandemic, we came to realize that Mack's inner clock ticks in unison with his heartbeat — and that both will remain finely tuned as long as all his beloved humans are nearby.

— Marya Morin —

95

A New Snoopy for Grandma Agnes

*You know, a dog can snap you out of any kind of bad
mood that you're in faster than you can think of.*
~Jill Abramson

Grandma Agnes is ninety-nine years old and still lives in
the same house she's lived in for more than sixty years.
She was one of thirteen children raised on a farm. And
now, she is rather set in her ways.

For twelve years, Grandma Agnes enjoyed the company of her dog,
Snoopy. The black-and-white spotted mutt was a constant presence in
her home and her yard. During the time that she had Snoopy, Grandma
Agnes started showing signs of dementia. My family worked together
to keep her living independently but safe. It was difficult for my dad
the day he pulled the battery from her car to keep her from using her
still-valid driver's license. Every visit after that day, Grandma Agnes
would insist that he buy her a new car battery because hers was dead
again. Dad nodded and agreed to do it, knowing that the conversation
would soon be forgotten.

Three years ago, Snoopy passed away. My dad, Aunt Carol and
Uncle Ed thought of ways to ensure that Grandma Agnes would know
that Snoopy was gone. They had a burial service in the back yard with
Grandma. Uncle Ed printed a picture of Snoopy with "Rest in Peace"
written across the bottom and stuck it to the refrigerator. But on the

daily visits, Grandma Agnes still asked about Snoopy. She accused the neighbors of taking her dog because she was sure that she heard him barking from their yard.

Having a family member with dementia is heartbreaking and trying. For every visit I've made in the past five years, my dad has made a point to tell me that she probably won't remember who I am nor that my kids are her great-grandchildren. I've sat through conversations where we patiently repeated answers to questions that were answered a few moments before. Grandma Agnes is still there, and she's still her stubborn self, but she doesn't grasp the world around her. And yet she insists on living independently.

Since her house is less than a mile away, Aunt Carol has spent years making daily visits, cooking countless meals, and caring for Grandma Agnes. Being a tech genius, Uncle Ed put security cameras in her home. He and my cousin can check in on Grandma throughout the day and overnight when she's prone to wander. On those cameras, they regularly saw Grandma searching for Snoopy.

A few months ago, Uncle Ed came up with a brilliant idea. He purchased a robotic dog for Grandma Agnes. It has soft fur and barks when it senses motion nearby. When you pet its back, you can feel a heartbeat. Grandma quickly adopted the dog as her new Snoopy.

While dementia is terrible in that it robs you of your mental capabilities, Grandma's dementia has turned into something that is beautifully childlike. My other grandmother battled dementia at the end of her life, but her mind often slipped away to terrible memories that haunted her and left her feeling like she was living in a nightmare. Grandma Agnes's dementia has led her to cling to her new "dog" with fervor, believing that he is an animal and not a robot.

As with any new pet, there was a period of adjustment for Grandma Agnes. She grew accustomed to Snoopy's barks and interpreted them as requests for food or a nap. Kibble and water dishes were set up outside on the covered patio and refilled daily. The food disappearing every night helped convince Grandma that Snoopy was a real dog. Aunt Carol and Uncle Ed were puzzled, wondering what was eating Snoopy's food. But Uncle Ed solved it by putting up a camera focused on the patio. Any motion would trigger the camera to start recording. Recordings started most nights around 7 p.m. when the neighbor cat would climb over the fence and slink into the yard to eat all the dog food.

Grandma Agnes takes excellent care of Snoopy. She always shares Aunt Carol's ham with him. Often, my dad or Aunt Carol have to clean ham fragments out of the robotic dog's mouth from Grandma trying to force-feed it. If Snoopy is "sleeping" in the living room, Grandma won't allow anyone in who might disturb him. And throughout the day and often late at night, Snoopy is placed gently in a patch of grass in the back yard so he can do his business.

Life with Snoopy has been good for Grandma Agnes. She still deals with the challenges of dementia, but having the "dog" helps her focus her attention and nurture someone.

As a family, everyone is pleased that Grandma Agnes has taken so well to Snoopy. The only major hiccup came when she called Aunt Carol in a panic because the dog was sick. He wouldn't move, eat or bark. Uncle Ed hurried to Grandma's house and inspected Snoopy. After a sly and quick battery change, Snoopy was back to his normal self.

Dementia and Alzheimer's can be devastating. It's a challenge for anyone to watch a loved one slip away. But our family is grateful that a robotic dog has brought Grandma Agnes companionship and someone to love. It's beautiful that her love of dogs can continue through this time in her life. We just worry about the day she tries to give Snoopy a bath.

— Annie Lisenby —

96

First Comes Love

*Each day of our lives, we make deposits in the memory
banks of our children.*
~Charles R. Swindoll

t all started so innocently. During a conversation with Kim, our school principal, she told me about her dog Chibi, a sleek black-and-tan Shih Tzu that played well with her twins. We bonded as I told her stories about our own AJ, a fluffy black-and-white Shih Tzu.

"Why don't we trade dog care?" I suggested. We both liked the idea of our dogs being in a home with children they could play with.

"Do you think the two dogs will get along?" asked Kim. "They might not even like each other."

"There's only one way to find out. Let's get together tomorrow at my house."

Little did we know that when we set up a blind play date, it would be a match made in heaven.

A casual rendezvous here and there turned quickly into weekends. When Kim's family went on vacation, the "love pups" cuddled on the couch, nudged each other's noses, shared meals, and romped playfully about the house. Love at first sight swiftly grew into a whirlwind romance.

Daily, AJ kept his post diligently, pacing the couch and peering out the windows with a forlorn hope that his dearest would return.

The phone would ring. "Of course, Kim, bring her over," I'd say.

Hanging up the phone, I would shout from the kitchen, "AJ, Chibi's coming!"

Leaping to his paws, his square little body on high alert, he would begin his frenzied search throughout the house. Finally poking his nose through the curtains, he would anticipate her arrival. His reward would come an hour later with the thump of a car door. AJ would fly to the entryway, whining as he sniffed and scratched the threshold, his tail wagging as fast as it could. His beloved had returned!

Chibi would enter, straining on her leash, which was quickly unclipped. No prim and proper courting for this princess. She would plunge into her true love's paws, wrestling and racing, cavorting and caressing.

With such love in the air, friends and family began to ask, "When will there be puppies?" Puppies. Our hearts melted. Kim and I knew they were a perfect combination.

"I told the kids that pretty soon AJ will be the father to Chibi's puppies," said Kim. "They jumped up and down." She paused and then continued with an amused twinkle in her eyes, "But they want to know, if AJ and Chibi are going to have puppies together, shouldn't they get married first?"

Laughing, I sang the playground taunt kids know. "'AJ and Chibi, sitting in a tree, K-I-S-S-I-N-G! First comes love. Then comes marriage. Then come puppies in the baby carriage.' You know, the kids have a point. Let's plan a wedding!"

She didn't need to convince me. As a United Methodist pastor, I'd performed hundreds of weddings in church sanctuaries, but also on beaches and boats, in gardens, living rooms and back yards, and even at Disney World.

"I've never performed a 'Puptials Ceremony,' but I'm sure we can figure it out. This is going to be fun. Got your calendar? Let's set the date."

The wedding was an intimate ceremony in Kim's living room with only one outside guest, our favorite school counselor, accompanied by the "Best Dog."

The reception table looked festive, with lemonade, cupcakes, nuts and mints. I set down a special platter of dog biscuits that looked like mini-hamburgers and hot dogs. "Don't eat those," I warned the children.

Chibi's gown-like coat was brushed to a smooth, lustrous shine, the white highlighting the black-and-caramel swirl of hair. Her dark eyes sparkled. With no tiaras or pearls, her only accessory was a simple pink bow that pulled her hair up into an adorable tuft.

AJ looked very dapper with his freshly trimmed moustache. He stood tall, a full ten inches. With his black-and-white coat, he was the epitome of a tuxedoed groom.

I stood ready at the fireplace, adjusting my suit and holding a small black book of ceremonies. I turned the gold-gilded pages as my daughters sang "Here Comes the Bride."

Chibi and AJ wriggled on their leashes as the twins, their faces wide with smiles, pulled the couple forward, tails wagging.

"Dearly beloved, we are gathered here to join Chibi and AJ in holy puptials. If anyone can show just cause why these two should not be wedded, let him speak now or forever hold his peace."

At the word "speak," the Best Dog let out a series of loud, deep barks.

"Thank you for your approval," I said, trying to retain a bit of dignity in the wake of giggles.

"Who gives Chibi to be married to AJ?"

"We do." The twins' voices quivered with mirth as they tried to be serious.

"Who gives AJ to be married to Chibi?"

"My sister and I do." My girls smirked, one holding flowers, the other a small pillow with dog tags.

"AJ and Chibi, do you vow to love each other?" The twins moved the dogs' heads up and down in agreement. AJ looked up at me as if to say, "What's going on here?"

"May I have the tags, please?" I lifted them up. "These red metal hearts are engraved with the name of his/her beloved, symbolizing the love they share.

"Let us pray: Dear God, we thank you for the love you have for all your creatures, human and animal. We thank you for friends and for family. On this special day, we thank you for our dogs, who are not just pets but precious members of our families. Help us to give them the affection and care they deserve every day. We ask you to bless the union of AJ and Chibi, and to bless their future puppies with health and happiness. Amen."

Beaming, my daughters fastened the tags to their collars.

"Now that Chibi and AJ have given themselves to each other with loving vows, with the joining of paws and the giving of tags, I announce to you that they are married in the love of God."

Cheers went up, with thunderous barking by the Best Dog.

"AJ, you may kiss the bride." Miraculously, he obeyed, licking Chibi's nose.

"They're married, and now they can have puppies," proclaimed the twins.

Three months later, we sat on the kitchen floor watching Chibi and AJ romp and play with five little bundles of fluffy Shih Tzu joy.

— Rev. VickiJolene Lindley Reece —

Fate Brought Me Dylan

*Fall in love with a dog, and in many ways you enter
a new orbit, a universe that features not just
new colors but new rituals, new rules,
a new way of experiencing attachment.*
~Caroline Knapp

In 2013, I'd beaten breast cancer, dealt with financial challenges and solved them, and moved into my Las Vegas home full-time. I yearned for a dog who would love me unconditionally, no questions asked, and be there for me if I needed a hug or a look of encouragement and trust. So, I began to scan photos on local shelter websites.

I'd had Aussies several years before and loved their intelligence and loyalty. The local Humane Society brought adoption dogs to a pet store in my area on Saturdays and Sundays, and I'd learned they were bringing a black-and-white female Australian Shepherd that fateful Saturday. Just looking at her photo reminded me so much of Travis, one of my previous dogs. I was sure she would be the one. Visions of taking her for walks and snuggling with her danced in my head as I drove to the shopping center, only to find that a man had just signed adoption papers for her. She was no longer available. My spirits crashed.

The woman in charge said, "We do get Australian Shepherds. Do you want to put your name and phone number on a waiting list?"

Before I could answer, she added, "By the way, have you seen Dylan? He's not an Aussie but might turn out to be just the dog you are looking for. He's adorable. One of my favorites."

She led me over to the temporary enclosure filled with adoptable dogs waiting for a forever home. A light tan, medium-sized dog that looked like a Golden Retriever puppy came bounding over. Tail wagging, he stood up on his hind legs and rested his front paws on the grid. One look into his big brown eyes melted my heart. His foster mother told me he was part Golden and part Cocker Spaniel, and he was as big as he would get. They thought he was about two years old and had a hard history.

When his owner moved, Dylan had been abandoned in the back yard with no food or water. Neighbors heard him crying and called the Humane Society.

"I have to be honest with you," Amy said. "He has been adopted twice and brought back. The people didn't like that he barked at strangers, but he's my first foster and I love him so much. I want him to find a good home."

She smiled. "Let me take him out for you. You'll see what I mean."

Dylan bounded out of the enclosure and came right up to me. He looked from Amy to me and back to Amy. His eyes and expression seemed to say to Amy, "Can't I stay with you?"

Knowing his history, I could understand, but looking at that sweet dog I could not understand how anyone could have been cruel enough to abandon him in a back yard. Silently, I thanked those neighbors for looking out for him. So what if he barked at strangers? I'd fallen in love with him the minute I saw that wagging tail and those huge brown eyes.

Amy kept him over the weekend so I could get a dog bed, food and other things for him. She brought him to me on Monday and stayed for a while so he could get used to my house. I hadn't anticipated what happened next. He was clearly heartbroken when Amy left; he sat by my front door and wouldn't move. He wouldn't eat dinner until I coaxed him with pieces of chicken. That night, he ignored the new dog bed and slept by my front door, waiting for Amy to come back. My heart went out to him, and I sat on the floor next to him giving him hugs.

By the following day, he had warmed up to me and ate some of his breakfast. He began to stick to me like glue, following me everywhere. I guess in his sweet dog mind, he thought I was going to leave, too. If I sat on the sofa, he wanted to cuddle with me. At night, he wanted to sleep on the bed.

Shortly after I adopted him, I had to be gone for most of the day. While I was gone, he chewed the Levolors covering four windows, obviously trying to get out. Maybe he was hoping to find his way back to Amy. When I came home and saw what he'd done, I couldn't get mad at him. He was scared and trying to be a survivor, like me. The minute I walked in the door, he went crazy, running around me in circles, grabbing one of his toys and looking at me with loving eyes. I had come back. He wasn't abandoned again.

That was in October 2013. To this day, he still has separation anxiety. I helped Dylan, but I think he helped me even more. People talk about emotional support dogs. Well, Dylan is that to me without knowing it. From the day Amy brought him to me, my life has continued on a positive path. Dylan is always there offering huge doses of unconditional love and affection, and I give it back gladly.

As it turned out, his veterinarian estimated his age to be more like four or five, so as closely as we can tell, he's about eleven now. Through the years, Dylan has had health challenges, including three surgeries, a staph infection and diabetes. He is the perfect patient, the most loving companion, and turned out to be exactly the best friend I'd hoped for the day I thought I was going to adopt an Australian Shepherd.

— Morgan St. James —

98

Smooth Talker

No one appreciates the very special genius
of your conversation as the dog does.
~Christopher Morley

One of the best things about having a dog is that you always have someone to talk to. I'm not a crazy, old lady talking to herself. I'm a crazy, old lady talking to a Yorkipoo!

What do I tell Captain? Everything!

"I came very close to slapping an annoying library patron today."

"I can't wait to see my grandson again!"

"Why on earth do otherwise intelligent women wear stilettos?"

According to an article in *Reader's Digest*, Captain has the intellect of a human two-year-old and only a sixty-five-word vocabulary, mostly focused on Captain-related things like "walk," "dog" and "treat."

"Stiletto" and "grandson" are probably not part of my dog's vocabulary.

And yet, when I start blathering away about my day, he never walks away. Instead, he listens attentively. Of course, he could just be listening carefully in the hope that he'll hear me say "walk" or "treat." Either that, or he just thinks that listening to me is part of his job as a dog.

It's a job he does very well.

Recently, I asked my dog-owning friends if they talk to their dogs. Of course, every single one of them does. When I asked them what they talked about, here's what they told me:

"I speak to my dog just like I would any other friend. She always listens."

"I narrate the whole day to her, and I think she appreciates it."

"I tell her what a good dog she is. Or what a bad dog she is. Often in baby talk."

"I've been known to throw open my front door and yell, 'What's shaking, baby cakes?' at my dog."

"I'm forever apologizing to Cejas for various infractions, including serving a dinner that isn't to his liking or providing an insufficient number of treats."

"I talk to Butch about everything, including my deepest, darkest secrets. Dogs never tell."

"Of course, I talk to my dog! And then I pretend to be my dog and answer back in a squeaky voice."

"I have better conversations with my dog than I do with most people."

"Who's a pretty girl? Are you a pretty girl?"

"I ask her what she thinks she's doing when she's chewing up a shoe or engaging in other destructive behavior."

"I sing to my dog. I also rewrite show tunes so they're all about her."

"I always talk to Ringo the Wonder Retriever. The fact that he's now deaf doesn't stop me."

"When my chubby dog begs for food before it's dinnertime, I give her diet tips like, 'Drink some water!'"

"I often ask my dog for his advice. For example, 'Cooper, what am I going to do about this situation at work?'"

"Hey, baby puppy! It's my baby puppy. You're the cutest little doggy in the whoooooole world. You're my little poopy face."

"While I'm rubbing his tummy, I tell him that he needs to start pulling his weight and contributing to the finances, housework, and general life upkeep because he's a fuzzy-bottomed, freeloading, little bozo."

"Stop going barky-bark. No one wants to hear that."

"I tell my dogs to stop fighting, to get their faces out of one another's behinds, and to stop trying to trip me. Sometimes, they do as I ask. Sometimes, they talk back to me."

"Buddy passed away four months ago, but I still talk to him. I say good night. I tell him how good he is. I remind him that he was a handsome boy and how much I love him."

"When I leave for work, I tell Kreplach that I love him."

"When I leave the house, I always say, 'You're in charge!'"

"When I come home, I always ask my dog how his day was."

Is the fact that I talk to the dog a problem? Does it make me anti-social? Does having a Yorkipoo to confide in stop me from putting my profile on a dating website and finding somebody to talk with who actually understands the words "grandson" and "stiletto"?

Perhaps. Still, I don't think talking to Captain is a problem.

If he ever starts to answer me… That's when I'll worry.

— Roz Warren —

99

The Crayons and the Bone

Animals are such agreeable friends.
They ask no questions; they pass no criticisms.
~George Eliot

I watched her play on her pallet of precisely folded Minnie Mouse blankets on the dark blue floor. There was so much innocence within the boundaries of those pink blankets and the clear-cut lines they provided for Savannah during floor time. Those clear pink lines defined Savannah's space from the blue expanse around her. Savannah's space was where she organized her toys, processed information and discovered the world around her. Even though she was almost eighteen, floor time was just as important to her development as it had been when she was two.

Finn knew there was something special about Savannah. Instinctively, he knew the first time he met her, as he watched her hesitant gait carry her to him. He knew from the way she pressed her arms against the sides of her head, hiding most of her face and stifling unfamiliar sounds. He knew by the heavy weight of her fingers pushing on him when she tried to pet him, despite my constant reminders of "gentle touches" and hand-over-hand demonstrations.

"Stroke his fur."

Finn knew Savannah was special from the way she never spoke. She laughed and giggled, a contagious laughter with squeals and bounces that bubbled through the air, infecting everyone around. But except for the occasional "Mom" and "no," Savannah didn't talk. Only those who loved her best could decipher her few words. Finn was one of those who loved her best, even when she petted him too hard or wouldn't share her crayons.

Savannah lined up her crayons in perfect rows. Red, blue, orange. Green, purple, yellow. She arranged them by color and then rearranged them again. Ensuring the lines were straight. Trying to get the colors just right. Concentrating with the utmost perfection with occasional glances at the cartoon on TV. Mickey Mouse and friends were still her favorite.

Blue, green, red.

Finn walked slowly over to her, in his coyote way of slinking, and sniffed the waxy sticks. Savannah's brow furrowed. She placed her hand on the white patch of his chest and pushed him back until only one large paw remained on her pallet. His brow matched her creasing wrinkle, but his was pleading. He took another step back, standing solely in the dark blue expanse. He was so curious about her crayons. She lowered her head to make sure her eyes were matching his, her hand firm on his chest. Their eyes stayed locked.

No words were exchanged. No words were needed.

When she was sure Finn understood, her hand left his furry chest, and her eyes left his. She returned to the work of arranging her crayons. Orange, yellow, purple. Finn stood for a moment in hesitation before leaving the room. He knew what had to be done. But where had he put it? He found it in the back bedroom: the biggest and best bone he had. He lifted it in his massive jaws. His sharp teeth penetrated the tough hide. It banged into the doorway as he maneuvered it into the hallway. It wobbled and clanked into the hall walls, but finally Finn made it into the living room. He brought it to the pink Minnie Mouse pallet and laid it next to the crayons. He looked up at Savannah.

"Share," his eyes pleaded.

She looked up at him. Her sweet blue eyes were quite stern. It was not the right color. He nudged the bone closer. Her brow furrowed once more. He sniffed his bone to show her what a fine bone he had brought her, but she returned her attention to her crayons. Purple, green, blue. She was still not interested in sharing. Her lines were perfectly straight. Finn began to paw his bone, pulling it away from the crayons, turning it until he could lie down next to his girl on her bright pink pallet. Then he began to chew on his mighty fine bone, with only the occasional glance toward the coveted crayons.

And Savannah let him.

I wondered at Finn's secret. Sixteen years of multiple therapies, and he had successfully touched on them all. Communication, socialization, sensory and more, all in a matter of minutes. I marveled at how this wild-looking dog had entered her world so naturally. Was it his patience, flexibility or determination? Was it his acceptance of Savannah? All the differences and disabilities that kept her trapped within the lines of her flesh were normal to him. Finn had no expectations of Savannah. Finn just wanted to be with her. There was so much to learn from the big dog we had found lying behind cold bars at the shelter.

All Finn wanted and all he gave was love.

They stayed side by side on that Minnie Mouse blanket, with Savannah playing with her crayons and Finn chewing on his bone, watching Mickey and Pluto on TV. Savannah didn't share her crayons that day, but she did share her space. As I sat there with my coffee watching them, and they sat there watching Mickey scratch Pluto's ears, I heard Mickey say, "Who's my pal? Who's my pal?" And Savannah's lips curled into a smile.

— sarah elizabeth —

Fuzzer

Happiness is a warm puppy.
~Charles M. Schulz

We found him on our front porch one summer morning, curled up and shaking. We had no idea where he came from or how he got there, so we took him in and fed him puppy chow. My mom said we'd take care of him until we found out who'd lost him. Then we would return him to his rightful owners.

Mom was a teacher at the local school in our Wisconsin town. She knew everyone, so I figured she'd find his people right away.

I'd always wanted a dog, but we couldn't have one because my sister was allergic. When I was four years old, I wanted a dog so badly that I walked a neighbor girl on her hands and knees with a jump rope looped around her neck. She barked and carried on just like a real dog, playing her role perfectly. She enjoyed being a dog, and I enjoyed having a dog. When I learned to write, the first story I wrote told of a dog who needed a voice: "The Dog Who Couldn't Say Roof!"

Now at twelve years old, I still longed for a dog. But so far, my pleas had been fruitless. I had to be satisfied with caring for the neighbors' dog when they went out of town. Now, the little red-and-white puppy who appeared on our doorstep gave me the chance to play with and feed and care for a dog.

We didn't give the pup a name since we didn't expect to have him for long. I didn't dare think of him as my own, but when a whole day went by with nobody claiming him, I began to hope. That night, he slept next to my bed. I hung my hand over the side, touching him all night, dreaming that I was his very own girl.

Another day went by. The pup and I were becoming inseparable, playing together all day in the shade in the back yard. I had to remind myself that somebody would claim him sooner or later. Yet I loved the way he followed me around the yard, stumbling over his big clumsy feet, red ears flopping up and down, his chubby belly barely clearing the ground. I even adored the way he mouthed me with his sharp puppy teeth.

In the evening on the second day, the phone rang. When Mom answered, my heart sank. Somebody was asking about the puppy. I lurked around the corner to eavesdrop on the conversation, cradling the puppy and holding my breath. The other person was doing most of the talking, so I couldn't tell where the conversation was headed. But it sounded like this pup was a match, and our time together was about to end.

When she hung up the phone, my mom went into the other room to have a private conversation with my dad. What was going on?

A few minutes later, Mom came out. She told us that the puppy, called "Fuzzer," belonged to some kids who'd taken him to the tennis court across the street. When it was time for them to go home, Fuzzer had wandered off, and they couldn't find him. When word got out that we'd found a lost puppy, their mother called my mom. My stomach dropped. This was it. We'd have to give the puppy back.

But then Mom continued, saying that the kids had won Fuzzer at the county fair. They already had an older dog at home that didn't get along with the puppy. Their mom had never consented to keeping Fuzzer and wanted to find him another home!

My parents saw how well I'd bonded with and cared for Fuzzer, and they knew I had always wanted a dog. Amazingly, my sister had not had an allergic reaction to him. Mom told us that Fuzzer now belonged to us. We got to keep him!

The name "Fuzzer" stuck. The vet told us he was probably a Brittany Spaniel/Border Collie mix. Fuzz and I were inseparable as we grew up together. He was my true companion throughout my teenage years, when having a canine companion was indeed a blessing.

Fuzzer taught me many things over the years. But, best of all, he taught me that it's okay to hope, it's okay to love, and that sometimes, even against seemingly insurmountable odds, a young girl's prayers can be answered.

— Jenny Pavlovic —

The Houdinis and Me

Without wearing any mask we are conscious of,
we have a special face for each friend.
~Oliver Wendell Holmes

I had just set up my mat and blanket for a yoga class on Zoom when my cat alerted me to the two barking dogs outside my window. It was the big black-and-white Border Collie and the little white part-Maltese who live down the block. I never knew their names. I've always called them Big Houdini and Little Houdini because they are escape artists.

Their owner insisted his yard was securely fenced in, but they managed to escape every couple of months.

The first time I ran into the Houdinis, I was a little leery, not knowing if they were friendly or not. I approached them carefully. There was some trepidation on their part, too. Eventually, they got to know me, and they would run up to me with delight. If I had to drive to catch them a couple of blocks away, they would gladly jump in the car, one in the front seat and one in the back, as if going for a joyride with their Auntie Eva. I always returned them to their own yard.

After several escapes, the Houdinis didn't even try to go far — only as far as my kitchen window. Once they got to know me, they would plant themselves on our lawn and bark, as if calling me to come out and play. Off I'd go to reel them in with treats. When they trusted me, no treats were necessary.

But this day as I watched through the window, I could see them running through the street haphazardly. My heart skipped a beat as a car travelling down our street barely missed Little Houdini.

A large house across the street was being repaired from recent storm damage and several construction workers were outside bustling about — social distancing as best they could during the COVID-19 pandemic. About five heavy-duty trucks were parked in front of the house, but other vehicles were travelling up and down the ordinarily quiet street. The traffic was too busy for two dogs to be running through it wildly. They were dodging the workers and vehicles. It was a disaster waiting to happen.

That was it for yoga. I had to save the Houdinis.

Quickly, I threw on a jacket over my yoga clothes and grabbed my car keys, just in case. I put on my plastic gloves and my facemask, and dashed out the door to save the pups!

I don't know how many years I've been catching them and bringing them back to their owner, but I think these Houdinis got to like me so much that they would escape so they could visit me. Why else would they always end up four houses away in *our* yard outside *my* kitchen window?

But this time, as I ventured out my front door, the Houdinis were out of sight. I called out, "Houdini! Here, Big! Here, Little!"

I must have been a sight running around and yelling frantically in my plastic gloves and mask. I ran up and down the block and between houses calling for the dogs. "Here, boy! Here, girl!"

The construction workers stopped what they were doing and pointed down the block. Suddenly, I saw the two rascals in an alley. I called out to them again. Usually, they run out and bark with glee when they hear my voice, but this time they stopped dead in their tracks. What were they doing? Social distancing? Their stares frightened me. Suddenly, their barks turned menacing, and they began to growl.

Big Houdini: "GRRRRRRRR!"

Little Houdini: "Grrrr."

How could they growl at me? I had saved them from traffic and worse. I had known them for years. I had always rescued them, taken them home safely, given them treats — albeit cat treats — but still.

Their demeanor frightened me. "Houdinis," I tried. "It's me."

The snarling became more intense. Their lips curled back, revealing threatening teeth. Big H lunged toward me, and Little H followed.

I froze. I was afraid to move forward or back. I tried retreating a few steps. They were charging toward me and barking furiously between growls.

I tried my soothing voice. "Houdini, baby. Good boy. Good girl." (I still didn't know if they were boys or girls.) When they were about a foot away, it appeared that they were ready to pounce. I could barely breathe with fear. I realized my mask wasn't helping with my breathing. In a panic, I pulled off my plastic gloves and the mask and flung them away.

A two-second silence ensued. We stared at each other. Then the expressions on the dogs' faces shifted to surprise. Big Houdini approached me first, slowly sniffing my feet, hands and body. Little H followed in his footsteps.

Suddenly, I could almost read their canine minds: "Is this that nice Auntie who saves us every time we get lost?"

In no time at all, the pups were leaping at me with their tails wagging furiously and licking my hands and face enthusiastically.

They had been afraid of my mask. They had not recognized me. As soon as I discarded the mask, things returned to normal. Well, at least "normal" for the Houdinis and me.

I am still waiting for things to get back to normal with the rest of the world.

After the dogs were safe at home, I rushed back to my virtual yoga. The class was almost over. After the Houdini shenanigans, I was too pooped for yoga anyway.

— Eva Carter —

Meet Our Contributors

Janette Aldridge received her Master of Education from Old Dominion University in 2014. She has a beautiful daughter who is closely guarded by her Labradoodles, and she enjoys teaching first grade. She loves swimming and hiking, and is currently working on illustrating a children's book about, what else, dogs!

Elizabeth Atwater lives with her husband, Joe, in a small town in North Carolina. They raise standard bred racehorses. Elizabeth enjoys reading, working in her rose garden, and of course, writing. In her spare time, she volunteers with senior services and hospice.

Katie Avagliano teaches writing at Rutgers University in her home state of New Jersey. Katie has been a puppy raiser for The Seeing Eye for fifteen years and volunteers at hospital therapy programs with her German Shepherd, Wolcott. Follow their adventures on Instagram @ sheriff_wolcott.

David-Matthew Barnes is an author, playwright, poet, and screenwriter. He writes in multiple genres, primarily young adult. He earned an MFA in Creative Writing at Queens University of Charlotte in North Carolina. He loves tacos, Disney villains, Nancy Drew, and everything written by Judy Blume.

Tracy Beckerman writes the syndicated humor column "Lost in Suburbia" which is carried weekly by Gannett newspapers. She is the author of the books *Lost in Suburbia: A Memoir* (2013) and *Rebel without a Minivan* (2008). She is also a contributor to *Chicken Soup for the Soul: Laughter Is the Best Medicine*.

Lesley Belcourt taught in London, emigrated to Canada (1969), taught in the Dene Tha community of N. Alberta, earned her BEd in 1972 and her MA in English in 2001 at University of Alberta and Speech/Drama Licentiate in 1991 from Trinity College London. Lesley loves her animals!

Chase Bernstein is a stand-up comedian and writer residing in Los Angeles, CA. She has appeared on Comedy Central as well as NBC and has written for shows on Netflix, truTV, and VH1. She could go on but you're probably too impressed to keep reading.

Cheri Bunch grew up on a farm in rural Elma, WA. After traveling some and rushing through life, she moved to Salem, OR and received her Associate of Science in 1990. She loves gardening, arts and crafts, and animals. She has written a couple of children's books and hopes to publish them in the near future.

Jill Burns lives in the mountains of West Virginia with her wonderful family. She's a retired piano teacher and performer. She enjoys writing, music, gardening, nature, and spending time with her grandchildren.

Meghan Byers is a freelance writer in New Jersey and holds a bachelor's degree in creative writing from Fairleigh Dickinson University. She has spent her life in a constant state of enthusiasm for dogs.

Jack Byron received his degree in illustration and has published art criticism in addition to writing for the *Chicken Soup for the Soul* series. Always encouraging others to write, he believes that the best stories are written first in our daily lives before ever being committed to paper. Follow him on Twitter @jackbyron13.

Thomas Canfield aspires to worry less, for which purpose he has taken up the study of children, and to laugh more, for which purpose he has taken up the study of politicians. He lives in North Carolina.

Eva Carter is a freelance writer and amateur photographer whose background is in telecommunications. She was born in Czechoslovakia, grew up in New York and now lives with her husband in Dallas, TX.

Capi Cloud Cohen loves making quilts, baby clothes, and more recently, masks for nurses and family members. She and her husband wish their children and grandchildren lived closer but are thankful for FaceTime. They sadly said goodbye to Shaggy this past February. They hope to find the next perfect dog very soon.

Mary Cook is a UK-based freelance writer whose articles, poems and short stories have appeared in numerous publications, both in print and online. She lives in England in the small town of Gainsborough with her husband Nigel and rescue dog Kamu.

Eilley Cooke is a Vermont resident who spends her time writing, painting, and playing music. She has two kids, ages seven and eight, who inspire her every day, and a pet turtle, Shelley. Her dog, Mojo, passed away in early 2020.

Gwen Cooper received her B.A. in English and Secondary Education in 2007 and completed the Publishing Institute at Denver University in 2009. In her free time, she enjoys krav maga, traveling, and backpacking with her husband and Bloodhounds in the beautiful Rocky Mountains. Follow her on Twitter @Gwen_Cooper10.

Kat Crawford is the author of *Dew Drops of Hope*, and *Buckets of Hope* as well as a contributor to many titles in the *Chicken Soup for the Soul* series. E-mail her at katcrawford927@gmail.com.

Married with dogs, **Amanda Sue Creasey** writes and teaches outside of Richmond, VA. Her favorite hobbies include hiking with her dogs, reading, and (surprise!) writing. Visit her online at AmandaSueCreasey. com, where she maintains Mind the Dog Writing Blog, or find her dogs on Instagram @Mind_the_Dog_Writing_Blog.

Sergio Del Bianco has a background in fine arts and psychology. He is an artist and writer, interested in the intersection of art, psychology and the humanities. He resides in Europe with his spouse and growing family of rescue animals. E-mail him at sergiodelbianco@yahoo.com or through Twitter @DelBianco97.

Rose Eaton currently lives in Cincinnati pursuing a graduate degree in computational biology. She enjoys traveling, doing crafts, and baking in her spare time. She does not currently live with a dog but hopes to adopt a puppy soon.

Rebecca Edmisten is a veteran classroom teacher of English and Theatre who lives in northeast Tennessee. Becky says that writing about dogs allows her to combine two of her greatest passions — the written word and all things canine! "Quarantine Tank" is her fifth publication in the *Chicken Soup for the Soul* series.

sarah elizabeth is an emerging writer in the East Tennessee mountains and is a contributing author to the *Storytime Radio* show on the NPR station WETS. She enjoys spending time with God, her children and their rescue dog, Finn, and can be followed on both Instagram and Twitter @s_elizabeth_31.

Scott Elliff received his B.S. in Psychology from Southern Illinois University Edwardsville in 1986. He is the program coordinator at the Madison County Juvenile Detention Center in Edwardsville, IL. He lives with his two loves: his wife Carla and their adorable companion Gypsy. He enjoys writing when inspired.

Jeanne Felfe is primarily a women's fiction author. Her first novel is titled *Bridge to Us*. She serves on the board of Saturday Writers in St. Peters, MO. Jeanne enjoys reading, gardening, playing with two tiny dogs who think they are human, and hanging out with her wine-making hubby.

Kate Fellowes writes mystery novels, romantic short stories, personal experience essays, and poetry. She loves animals and books and the feel of a pen scratching over paper. She blogs about work and life at katefellowes.wordpress.com.

Glenda Ferguson received her education degrees from College of the Ozarks and Indiana University. Since retiring from a forty-year teaching career, she has been volunteering as a tour guide at two historical hotels. Glenda enjoys writing devotionals about her dog Walker and Speckles the cat.

Candy Fox is a writer, educator, and crazy dog lover who has fostered, adopted, and otherwise shared canine space with dozens of dogs over the years. However, her time fostering guide dog puppies for the blind transformed her understanding of the human-canine connection.

Betsy S. Franz is an award-winning freelance writer and photographer specializing in nature, wildlife and both humorous and inspirational human-interest stories. She is dedicated to encouraging others to see, appreciate, and protect the wonders of nature around them.

Peggy Frezon is the contributing editor of *All Creatures* magazine, and a regular contributor to *Guideposts*. She is the author of *The Dog* in the Dentist Chair: And other true stories of animals who help, comfort, and love kids (Paraclete Press, 2018) and dog mom to Pete and Ernest Look for her new book about miniature therapy horses (Revell, 2021).

Elizabeth Gardner has a passion for teaching and helping people. After a career in accounting and homeschooling her children, she is pursuing a lifelong love of writing. Life is busy with her husband of thirty-five years, two grown children (one with disabilities), and a furry beast (a.k.a. Labradoodle). She lives in Waynesboro, PA.

Anita Lear Gonzales is thrilled to be part of this *Chicken Soup for the Soul* book. Each dog is a special member of her family and she delights in sharing stories about them. Anita resides in Long Beach, CA, where the ocean provides her inspiration for anecdotes and poetry, touching others with her lifelong love for writing.

Carol Graham received the Woman of Impact Award and Author of the Year for her memoir, *Battered Hope*, and the global award for One Woman Fearless given to women who have faced their fears and made the world a better place for women to thrive. She hosts a talk show "Never Ever Give Up Hope" and has rescued more than thirty dogs.

Holly Green is a wife, mother, besotted grandmother, novice gardener and retired nurse as well as an author. She has written non-fiction for years, plus one book on domestic violence and numerous articles for women and family magazines. Her dream has always been to write novels — she's working on that now.

Sheryl Green is a speaker, author, and passionate animal advocate. She lives in Las Vegas, NV with her two dogs, Akasha and Bodhi, and a startling number of houseplants.

Anne Gruner served in the American Embassy in Paris from 1989-1992. Her work has appeared in *The Avalon Literary Review*, *Hippocampus Magazine*, *The Intelligencer*, *War-on-the-Rocks*, and *Stories from Langley*. She and her husband live in McLean, VA with their two Golden Retrievers. Learn more at www.annegruner.com.

Kelly Frances Hanes is the author of *Random God Sightings*, and *The Other Sermon*. She received her Bachelor of Arts in English, with honors, from the University of Houston in 2012. Born and raised in Ohio, she now lives in Houston, TX. She is a wife, human mother to four and dog mother to two. She enjoys running, reading and writing.

Marisa Hanna is a wife and a mother to two children. She currently works in nutrition services for a local elementary school in Washington State. She has plans to pursue more book writing opportunities. Marisa's hobbies include riding her horse, training her dogs, and enjoying everything the Pacific Northwest has to offer.

Zach Hively writes poetry, nonfiction, alt-folk music, and the award-winning "Fools Gold" humor column. He plays guitar and harmonica in the duo Oxygen on Embers, and his poetry is proudly displayed at the Magdalena Lily McCarson gallery in Santa Fe, NM. He dances Argentine tango and lives near Abiquiu, NM with his dog.

Jeanie Jacobson is on the Wordsowers Christian Writers leadership team. She is published in venues such as *Focus on the Family* and *Live* magazines, *Chicken Soup for the Soul* books, and other anthologies. Jeanie loves visiting family, reading, hiking, and dancing. Grab her book, *Fast Fixes for the Christian Pack-Rat* online. Learn more at JeanieJacobson.com.

Deborah Kellogg lives with her family, cats, and other wildlife in Eagan, MN. She's head of the German Department at Normandale Community College in Bloomington, MN. When not teaching, she enjoys traveling, writing (in both German and English), biking, cooking, photography, reading, and spending time with her grandchildren.

Jennifer Kennedy is a Susquehanna University graduate and freelance writer. Her stories have appeared in *Chicken Soup for the Soul: The Wonder of Christmas* and *Chicken Soup for the Soul: Think Positive, Live Happy*. She lives in the Philadelphia suburbs with her family, who share her lifelong love of rescue dogs. E-mail her at jenniferkennedypr@gmail.com.

Linda Kinnamon is the author of *Alchemy of the Afterlife*, an award-winning memoir about her life after death experiences as a hospice nurse. Her newest writing partner and fetch enthusiast is Hazel, a Lab/Boxer mix. Photos of her dogs can be found at lindakinnamon.com.

Alice Klies is president of Northern Arizona Word Weavers. Her novel, *Pebbles in My Way* was released in September 2017. Alice is an eight-time contributor to the *Chicken Soup for the Soul* series. She lives in Arizona with her hubby and two Golden Retrievers. Learn more at aliceklies.com.

Terri L. Knight has a degree in psychology, teaches elementary school students, and writes. She has several pieces published in literary magazines, books, and newspapers and she has won several writing contests. When she is not writing or working, she takes care of her family and three rescue animals.

Cathi LaMarche has contributed to more than thirty anthologies. As the director of operations of a financial planning firm, she surrounds herself with numbers during the day and prefers to immerse herself in the written word each evening. Cathi and her husband reside in Missouri with their two faithful Collies.

Janet Lane is a seventy-one-year-old retired schoolteacher. She is married to a retired Southern Baptist pastor. They have four married children and ten grandchildren. Janet is a die-hard country gal and is blessed to be living on her family's farm. She loves traveling, writing, reading, and horses.

Tim Law is a practicing lawyer in Philadelphia, PA. He represents businesses, charities, and universities in disputes with their insurance companies. He volunteers with organizations that advocate for consumers and victims of human trafficking.

Kathie Leier, her husband Ivan, and Keiko, their beloved senior Shih Tzu, moved from Regina, SK in 2016 to retire to the beauty and solitude of Riding Mountain National Park, MB. In November 2017, after being a most loving companion for ten years, Keiko went to doggie heaven at the age of fourteen. He is dearly missed.

Annie Lisenby, a native of the Missouri Ozarks, has an MFA in theatre. She teaches at the local community college, writes for the local newspaper, and recently completed her second young-adult novel. Having lived overseas and worked in the film industry, she enjoys sharing her experiences with others through her writing.

Ilana Long is a writer, actress, stand-up comic, English teacher, and mom of twins. She is the author of *Ziggy's Big Idea* (Kar-Ben 2014) and a recently completed science fiction novel.

L.M. Lush received her Bachelor of Arts from the State University of New York in 1990. She then enjoyed a twenty-five-year career in IT. Now an adjunct college professor and professional writer, she teaches Creative Writing, Music Appreciation, piano and cello. She and her dog, Sadie, live in New York's Lower Hudson Valley.

C.H. MacDonald lives with a giant (who's also one-part ogre) and is the mother of one plus a few strays. Her love of animals, especially the canine, chicken or fish variety, has led to many stories and poems being written for the young and young-at-heart. Several have been published, including in the *Chicken Soup for the Soul* series.

Pet lover extraordinaire, **Irish Beth Maddock** is the award-winning children's author of *The Great Carp Escape*. Irish lives in Calgary and would like to dedicate her story about Bella to Albert and Pauline Fountain, formerly of Hatfield, UK. For more information please check out her Facebook profile "Write MEOW! Ink." or e-mail her at info@irishbethmaddock.com.

Keith Manos was named Ohio's English Teacher of the Year by OCTELA in 2000 and inducted into the National Honor Roll of Outstanding American Teachers in 2006. Keith has a master's degree in English (Creative Writing) from Cleveland State University. Learn more at www.keithmanos.com.

Joshua J. Mark is an editor/director and writer for the online history site "Ancient History Encyclopedia." His nonfiction stories have also appeared in *Timeless Travels* and *History Ireland* magazines. His wife Betsy passed on recently from cancer and he lives with his daughter Emily and their dogs in upstate New York.

Tracy Marsh is a Nashville-based mom and writer who could cave into her son's relentless pleas for a dog any minute. Her work has appeared in *Southwest: The Magazine*, *Nashville Arts & Entertainment*, *Military Officer*, and more.

Jeff Marzick is a freelance writer/blogger living in Brookings, OR. He received his Bachelor of Specialized Studies degree from Ohio University in 2013. He is an avid sports fan who loves to golf, fish, hike, and play tennis.

Courtney McKinney-Whitaker is an award-winning author of fiction, essays, and poetry. She lives with her family, including a Sheltie mix, in Pennsylvania. Learn more at courtneymck.com or connect on Twitter @courtneymckwhit.

Marya Morin is a freelance writer. Her stories and poems have appeared in publications such as *Woman's World* and Hallmark. Marya also penned a weekly humorous column for an online newsletter and writes custom poetry on request. She lives in the country with her husband. E-mail her at Akushla514@hotmail.com.

AJ (Cross) Nunes lives in East Selkirk, Manitoba with her husband Dillon, their dog Bella, her cat Lacey and five chickens. AJ and Dillon are high school sweethearts and new entrepreneurs planning to open a wedding and event venue in 2021. They love their friends, family, and the outdoors.

Joan Oen, her husband Shawn and son Erik live in Minnesota with their beloved Goldendoodle Ole. Ole provided great comfort during the trials of COVID-19. Joan loves to read and believes in the power of stories to teach, heal, and inspire. She makes a memorable living as a seventh grade English teacher. Follow her on Twitter @ms_oen.

Jennifer Oramas was born in New York City and majored in creative writing. She later moved to North Carolina, where she is currently pursuing her writing career. She is the author of the *Peter the Porcupine* children's book series. E-mail her at peterqporcupine@gmail.com or connect with her at www.facebook.com/jennifer.oramas.

Andrea Arthur Owan is an award-winning writer, fitness pro, and chaplain. She and her husband enjoy life in Tucson, AZ, with Hami and their feisty Sheltie, Dolly. Connect with her at andreaarthurowan.com, where she helps you live your best life physically, emotionally and spiritually. Follow her on Twitter @AndreaOwan.

Jenny Pavlovic, Ph.D. is the author of *8 State Hurricane Kate*, *The Not Without My Dog Resource & Record Book*, and many published stories. She lives in Wisconsin with dogs Cayenne, Herbie and Audrey and cat Junipurr. She loves everyday miracles, walking dogs, gardening, swimming and kayaking. Learn more at 8statekate.net.

Ruth Penderghast lives with her family and pets in Utah. A veteran people-watcher, she has always enjoyed collecting true stories, sharing them with family and friends. Recently, she began writing them down to share with a larger audience. It is her goal to become a published author of a book — this is the first step.

Lee E. Pollock has had many different careers during his short seventy years of life. He has been a salesman, owned a hardware store for twenty-three years and been a pastor for twelve years, to name a few. He is now retired and spends his time writing and ministering in prisons. Follow him at www.facebook.com/Author-Lee-E-Pollock.

Lisa Price is a freelance writer from Pennsylvania. She was glad to learn that her first words were Bow Wow. She enjoys traveling with her five dogs. She is a columnist for the *Ruffed Grouse Society* magazine, where she writes a column called "Purely Dogs."

Connie Kaseweter Pullen lives in rural Sandy, OR, near her five children and several grandchildren. She earned a B.A. degree, with honors, at the University of Portland in 2006, with a double major in Psychology and Sociology. Connie enjoys writing, photography and exploring nature. E-mail her at MyGrandmaPullen@aol.com.

Judy Quan has advocated for homeless animals in various capacities for many years. She served on a local animal shelter advisory committee and, with her husband, has incorporated two nonprofit animal advocate organizations. Together, with a dog rescue friend, they have rescued more than 1,000 dogs from kill shelters.

VickiJolene Lindley Reece empowers people to embrace the power of vulnerability and ride through their fears into a life of courage at www.secretsofladygodiva.com. She is a United Methodist pastor, international motivational speaker, television producer/writer, former Chicago fashion model, and avid dog lover.

Melissa Richards lives in Scotland after taking the scenic route through life. She writes mostly for relaxation.

Donna L. Roberts is a native upstate New Yorker who lives and works in Europe. She is an Associate Professor and holds a Ph.D. in Psychology. Donna is an animal and human rights advocate and when she is researching or writing she can be found at her computer buried in rescue cats.

Patricia Ann Rossi is an outdoor enthusiast. She enjoys gardening, bicycling and running. She has a passion for reading and writing.

Patricia volunteers as a facilitator for "writing to heal" workshops for cancer survivors. She is an active member in her community. She also serves on her college alumni board.

Judy Salcewicz lives and writes in New Jersey where dog walks inspire her essays, poetry, and historic fiction. She is a cancer survivor who embraces each day with gratitude. E-mail her at penwit@aol.com.

Leslie C. Schneider grew up in Montana, married her husband Bill fifty years ago, and together, they raised two sons. She has three granddaughters and one grandson. Self-taught, she's had a love of the written word since childhood. She writes part-time and is currently planning a novel. E-mail her at Leslie@airpost.net.

Julie A. Sellers is a Spanish professor, court interpreter, and author living in Kansas. In addition to writing prose and poetry, Julie enjoys traveling, reading, and walks with her husband, PJ, and dog, Mozzie.

Ashley Simpson has been a freelance writer for more than eight years. When she is not busy typing away, she enjoys spending time on her front porch with her husband and two pups, Cricket and Harper. She also enjoys spending time with family, reading, and crocheting. She hopes to publish her own collection of short stories.

Tanya Sousa has written and published short fiction, nonfiction, magazine articles, three children's books, a novel, and a novella. Most of her work connects in some way to animals and nature overall. She lives in Vermont with the love of her life and a small menagerie of "cuddle beasts."

Former interior designer **Morgan St. James** lives in Las Vegas, NV with her rescue dog Dylan. She is on the board of Writers of Southern Nevada, has eighteen books in publication and has published over 600 articles on diverse subjects. She gives workshops and talks at writers' conferences, writers' panels and for groups and organizations.

Diane Stark is a wife and mother of five human kids and two canine kids. She is a frequent contributor to the *Chicken Soup for the Soul* series. She loves to write about the important things in life: her family and her faith.

Marla Sterling is a poet, a third passion in her life following careers as actor and teacher. She has degrees from NYU in Education and from Manhattanville College in Creative Writing. She lives in Connecticut, gardening and walking her dog, where contact with the garden, woods, and beach invigorate and inspire her daily.

Julie Stielstra lives with her husband, two dogs, and four cats, sometimes in Chicago and sometimes in rural Kansas. She has published over a dozen short stories, and the historical novella *Pilgrim*. Her youth novel, *Opulence, Kansas*, is forthcoming in 2020. Learn more at juliestielstra.com.

Julie Theel lives in sunny Rancho Mirage, CA with her husband, two teenage daughters, three furry dogs and two fluffy cats. When not busy shuttling her daughters to their many activities, Julie spends her time rescuing animals and running her business selling the Rippys — her patented rip-apart toys for dogs.

Delores E. Topliff has a C.Ed.D. and writes and teaches college classes. She divides her year between Minnesota and Mississippi and loves world travel, especially mission trips. Her grandchildren love her children's books. She has written historic novels and now contemporary, and an Israel travelogue. Learn more at dtopliff@yahoo.com.

Michele Pullia Turk is a Connecticut-based writer, editor and writing instructor. She has published articles and essays on a wide range of topics, including health, education, parenting, and business. Learn more at MicheleTurk.com.

Pat Wahler is a Missouri native and proud contributor to seventeen previous *Chicken Soup for the Soul* books. Pat is the author of three novels and is currently at work on her next book under the supervision of two rescues: one bossy cat and a spoiled Pekingese/Poodle mix pup. Learn more at PatWahler.com.

Roz Warren writes for everyone from the *Funny Times* to *The New York Times* and is happy to have been included in thirteen *Chicken Soup for the Soul* books. You can read more of her work at muckrack.com/roz-warren. E-mail her at roswarren@gmail.com.

Jennifer Watts is a writer living in New Zealand. She is a former journalist who has travelled and lived in several countries. She enjoys tennis and volunteer work and is always looking to get lost in a binge-worthy book, movie or podcast. Jennifer is a mother to two, wife and friend to anyone who buys her coffee.

Ray Weaver is in his eighties and has been married to his wife, Ellie for sixty-one years. They have six grandchildren. He has been writing for the past sixteen years and is currently working on his eleventh novel. Ray and Ellie are proud of the fact that they have been Suncoast Hospice volunteers for more than fifteen years.

After he obtained a B.A. degree, **Mr. Weiskircher** gathered his wife and sailed into life. Breast cancer had other plans. When his wife died, he was thrown into a torrential storm, but he had a unique group of dogs by his side — herding dogs. They not only helped him endure it, they showed him where the sun was.

History buff and tropical island votary, **PeggySue Wells** parasails, skydives, snorkels, scuba dives, and has taken (but not passed) pilot training. Writing from the 100-acre woods in Indiana, she is the best-selling author of twenty-nine books, translated into eight languages.

Leslie Wibberley lives in a suburb of Vancouver, Canada with her amazing family and an overly enthusiastic Cocker Spaniel. She writes across a wide range of genres, age groups, and narrative styles. Her award-winning work is published in multiple literary journals and anthologies. E-mail her at lawibberley@gmail.com.

Lisa Workman lives on a farm in the Blue Ridge Mountains of Virginia with her husband, three boys, three cats, two horses, a dog, and four chickens. She teaches psychology at a local college and enjoys writing, running, and gardening in her free time. Her writing has appeared previously in *Horse Talk Magazine*.

Jerry Zezima writes a syndicated humor column for Hearst Connecticut Media Group and is the author of four books, *Leave It to Boomer*, *The Empty Nest Chronicles*, *Grandfather Knows Best* and *Nini and Poppie's Excellent Adventures*. E-mail him at JerryZ111@optonline. net or read his blog at www.jerryzezima.blogspot.com.

Meet Amy Newmark

Amy Newmark is the bestselling author, editor-in-chief, and publisher of the Chicken Soup for the Soul book series. Since 2008, she has published 168 new books, most of them national bestsellers in the U.S. and Canada, more than doubling the number of Chicken Soup for the Soul titles in print today. She is also the author of Simply Happy, a crash course in Chicken Soup for the Soul advice and wisdom that is filled with easy-to-implement, practical tips for enjoying a better life.

Amy is credited with revitalizing the Chicken Soup for the Soul brand, which has been a publishing industry phenomenon since the first book came out in 1993. By compiling inspirational and aspirational true stories curated from ordinary people who have had extraordinary experiences, Amy has kept the twenty-seven-year-old Chicken Soup for the Soul brand fresh and relevant.

Amy graduated magna cum laude from Harvard University where she majored in Portuguese and minored in French. She then embarked on a three-decade career as a Wall Street analyst, a hedge fund manager, and a corporate executive in the technology field. She is a Chartered Financial Analyst.

Her return to literary pursuits was inevitable, as her honors thesis in college involved traveling throughout Brazil's impoverished northeast region, collecting stories from regular people. She is delighted to have come full circle in her writing career — from collecting stories "from the people" in Brazil as a twenty-year-old to, three decades later, collecting stories "from the people" for Chicken Soup for the Soul.

When Amy and her husband Bill, the CEO of Chicken Soup for the Soul, are not working, they are visiting their four grown children and their grandchildren.

Follow Amy on Twitter @amynewmark. Listen to her free podcast — "Chicken Soup for the Soul with Amy Newmark" — on Apple Podcasts, Google Play, the Podcasts app on iPhone, or by using your favorite podcast app on other devices.

Thank You

We owe huge thanks to all of our contributors and fans. We received thousands of submissions for this popular topic, and we spent months reading all of them. Our Senior Editor, Barbara LoMonaco, and our editors Elaine Kimbler, Crescent LoMonaco, Laura Dean and Susan Heim read all of them and narrowed down the selection for Associate Publisher D'ette Corona and Publisher and Editor-in-Chief Amy Newmark.

Susan Heim did the first round of editing, D'ette chose the perfect quotations to put at the beginning of each story, and Amy edited the stories and shaped the final manuscript.

As we finished our work, D'ette Corona continued to be Amy's right-hand woman in working with all our wonderful writers. Barbara LoMonaco and Mary Fisher, along with Elaine Kimbler, jumped in at the end to proof, proof, proof. And yes, there will always be typos anyway, so feel free to let us know about them at webmaster@chickensoupforthesoul.com, and we will correct them in future printings.

The whole publishing team deserves a hand, including our Senior Director of Marketing Maureen Peltier, our Vice President of Production Victor Cataldo, and our graphic designer Daniel Zaccari, who turned our manuscript into this beautiful, entertaining book.

About
American Humane

American Humane is the country's first national humane organization, founded in 1877 and committed to ensuring the safety, welfare, and wellbeing of all animals. For more than 140 years, American Humane has been first to serve in promoting the welfare and safety of animals and strengthening the bond between animals and people. American Humane's initiatives are designed to help whenever and wherever animals are in need of rescue, shelter, protection, or security.

With remarkably effective programs and the highest efficiency ratio of any national humane group for the stewardship of donor dollars, the nonprofit has earned Charity Navigator's top "4-Star" rating, has been named a "Top-Rated Charity" by CharityWatch and a "Best Charity" by Consumer Reports, and achieved the prestigious "Gold Level" charity designation from GuideStar.

American Humane is first to serve animals around the world, striving to ensure their safety, welfare and humane treatment—from rescuing animals in disasters to ensuring that animals are humanely treated. One of its best-known programs is the "No Animals Were Harmed®" animals-in-entertainment certification, which appears during the end credits of films and TV shows, and today monitors some 1,000 productions yearly with an outstanding safety record.

American Humane's farm animal welfare program helps ensure the humane treatment of nearly a billion farm animals, the largest animal welfare program of its kind. And recently, the historic nonprofit launched the American Humane Conservation program, an innovative initiative helping ensure the humane treatment of animals around the globe in zoos and aquariums.

Continuing its longstanding efforts to strengthen the healing power of the human-animal bond, American Humane pairs veterans struggling to cope with the invisible wounds of war with highly-trained service dogs, and spearheaded a groundbreaking clinical trial that provided for the first time scientific substantiation for the effectiveness of animal-assisted therapy (AAT) for children with cancer and their families.

To learn more about American Humane, visit americanhumane. org and follow them on Facebook, Instagram, and Twitter.

AMERICAN★HUMANE
FIRST TO SERVE*

Editor's Note: Chicken Soup for the Soul and American Humane have created *Humane Heroes*, a FREE new series of e-books and companion curricula for elementary, middle and high schoolers. Through 36 inspirational stories of animal rescue, rehabilitation, and humane conservation being performed at the world's leading zoological institutions, and 18 easy-to-follow lesson plans, *Humane Heroes* provides highly engaging free reading materials that also encourage young people to appreciate and protect Earth's disappearing species. To download the free e-books and learn about the program, please visit www.chickensoup.com/ah.

Changing the world one story at a time®
www.chickensoup.com